CONTEMPORARY'S

PRE-GED

SOCIAL STUDIES

CB

CONTEMPORARY BOOKS

a division of NTC/CONTEMPORARY PUBLISHING GROUP
Lincolnwood, Illinois USA

1,399a

Acknowledgments

Cartoon on page 6 by Dick Locher. Copyright © Dick Locher. Reprinted by permission of Tribune Media Services.

Graphic on page 7 from the *Chicago Tribune*, March 21, 1993. Reprinted by permission of the *Chicago Tribune*.

Cartoon on page 77 by David Hardin Cox. Reprinted by permission of Hardin, *Northwest Arkansas Morning News*.

Cartoons on pages 78 and 79 by Jerry Barnett. Reprinted by permission of the *Indianapolis News*.

Excerpt on page 107 from *In Their Own Words—A History of the American Negro*, edited by Milton Meltzer.
     Copyright © 1964 by Milton Meltzer. Reprinted by permission of HarperCollins Publishers.

Excerpt on page 132 from *Hard Times: An Oral History of the Great Depression* by Studs Terkel.
     Copyright © 1970 by Studs Terkel. Reprinted by permission of Random House, Inc.

Cartoon on page 139 by Denny Pritchard. Copyright © 1993 by Denny Pritchard. Reprinted by permission of the artist.

Cartoon on page 144 by Gary Varvel. Copyright © 1993 by Gary Varvel. Reprinted by permission of the *Indianapolis News*.

Excerpt on page 147 from "Restoration: New Ideas, New Understanding, New Hope" by Michael Parfit, *National
     Geographic* magazine, November 1993. Reprinted by permission of the National Geographic Society.

Graphic on page 230 from the *Chicago Tribune*, July 24, 1994. Reprinted by permission of the *Chicago Tribune*.

Cartoon on page 269 by Ed Stein. Copyright © 1993 by Ed Stein. Reprinted by permission of the *Rocky Mountain News*.

Graph on page 275 from the *Chicago Tribune*, October 25, 1994. Reprinted by permission of the *Chicago Tribune*.

Cartoon on page 280 by Mike Smith. Copyright © 1994 by Mike Smith. Reprinted by permission of *USA Today*.

Map on page 288 from the *Chicago Tribune*, April 18, 1993. Reprinted by permission of the *Chicago Tribune*.

Photo Credits

Cover photos: Lincoln Memorial, © Allen Russell/ProFiles West; Earth, © Yutaka Kawatchi/Nonstock Inc.; Cloudscape, © Picture Perfect USA. Interior photos: David Stoecklen/The Stock Market, 18; Ron Chapple/FPG, 36; Picture Perfect, 52, 70, 208; Tribune File Photos, 82, 148.

Project Editor
Cathy Niemet

Series Developer
The Wheetley Company, Inc.

ISBN: 0-8092-3493-9

Published by Contemporary Books,
a division of NTC/Contemporary Publishing Group, Inc.,
4255 West Touhy Avenue,
Lincolnwood (Chicago), Illinois 60646-1975 U.S.A.
© 1995 by NTC/Contemporary Publishing Group, Inc.
8 9 0 CU 11 10 9 8 7 6 5

Editorial Director Mark Boone	*Editorial Production Manager* Norma Underwood	*Cover Design* Michael Kelly
Editorial Sharon Weissbeck Lisa Black Leah Mays Sandra Hazel	*Production Editor* Thomas D. Scharf *Electronic Composition* Victoria A. Randall	*Interior Design* Lucy Lesiak *Illustrations* The Wheetley Company, Inc.

Contents

To the Student

Congratulations on your decision to use *Pre-GED Social Studies* to strengthen your critical-thinking skills in comprehending, applying, analyzing, and evaluating social studies materials. You will also learn how to read and understand passages, graphs, charts, and maps in the content areas of U.S. history, political science, behavioral sciences, geography, and economics.

Here is an overview of what you will find in this book, along with some tips on using the book.

Social Studies Pre-Test   The Pre-Test, found on pages 1–15, will help you decide which skills you need to work on the most. It will direct you to the parts of the book you may want to spend the most time with.

Chapter 1: Comprehending Social Studies Materials   By working through Chapter 1, you will review how to find the main idea of passages and pictographs, find details in passages and circle graphs, recognize an unstated main idea, and look for context clues.

Chapter 2: Applying Social Studies Ideas   In this chapter you will learn how to apply what you read in passages, maps, and bar graphs to new situations.

Chapter 3: Analyzing Social Studies Materials   This chapter teaches you how to recognize the patterns in which information is presented, such as comparison and contrast, cause and effect, and sequence of events. You will also learn how to interpret ideas in line graphs, how to make inferences, and how to draw conclusions.

Chapter 4: Evaluating Social Studies Materials   In this chapter you will learn how to recognize the difference between fact and opinion, evaluate a writer's logic, infer tone, and analyze editorial cartoons.

Chapter 5: U.S. History   This chapter presents a brief survey of important events in America from the 1400s through the present. You will learn about foreign and domestic policy, important eras, major trends, and movements for social change.

Chapter 6: Political Science   This chapter presents an overview of various types of government, the American political process, interest groups and political parties, the U.S. Constitution, branches and duties of federal, state, and local government, and international relations.

Chapter 7: Behavioral Sciences   This chapter teaches you the practical uses of the behavioral sciences, which include the areas of psychology, sociology, and anthropology. You will also learn about culture and values in society.

Chapter 8: Geography   In this chapter you will learn about the elements of geography, various land regions, population and migration, urban growth, and how to read different types of maps.

Chapter 9: Economics   This chapter introduces you to the topics that economists study, early economic systems, how the economy works, how businesses behave, financial institutions, the federal reserve system, the stock market, and the government's role and consumers' role in the economy.

Writing Activities   Every chapter allows you an opportunity to write about various social studies topics and, in this way, improve your writing skills.

Pre-GED Practice   At the end of every chapter, and sometimes more frequently throughout the book, you will answer items that are formatted with five-item multiple-choice questions to help you prepare for GED-level study. The Pre-GED Practice at the end of each chapter serves as a review of the skills you have learned in the chapter.

Social Studies Post-Test   The Post-Test, found on pages 267–295, will help you to see how well you have learned the critical-thinking and reading skills presented in this book. The Post-Test consists of 64 multiple-choice questions.

Answer Key   This feature gives answers and explanations for all the questions in this book. Use the Answer Key only after you have attempted to answer a set of questions in an exercise.

Glossary   Throughout the book, key terms that are important for you to know are printed in boldface and italic type and are defined either in keyword boxes or in the glossary at the back of the book.

Good luck with your studies! Keep in mind that knowing how to read and analyze social studies materials is worth learning for many reasons.

The Social Studies Pre-Test that follows is a guide to using this book. You should take the Pre-Test before you begin working on any of the chapters. The test consists of 32 multiple-choice questions that test the social studies reading and reasoning skills covered in this book. All of the questions are based on charts, graphs, diagrams, and reading passages.

Answer each question as carefully as possible. Choose the best of five answer choices by filling in the corresponding circle on the answer grid. If a question is too difficult, go ahead one and come back to that question later. When you have completed the test, check your answers on pages 13–14.

Using the Evaluation Chart on page 15, circle the number of each question that you missed. If you missed many of the questions that correspond to a certain reading skill, you will want to pay special attention to that skill as you work through this book.

1 ① ② ③ ④ ⑤	9 ① ② ③ ④ ⑤	17 ① ② ③ ④ ⑤	25 ① ② ③ ④ ⑤
2 ① ② ③ ④ ⑤	10 ① ② ③ ④ ⑤	18 ① ② ③ ④ ⑤	26 ① ② ③ ④ ⑤
3 ① ② ③ ④ ⑤	11 ① ② ③ ④ ⑤	19 ① ② ③ ④ ⑤	27 ① ② ③ ④ ⑤
4 ① ② ③ ④ ⑤	12 ① ② ③ ④ ⑤	20 ① ② ③ ④ ⑤	28 ① ② ③ ④ ⑤
5 ① ② ③ ④ ⑤	13 ① ② ③ ④ ⑤	21 ① ② ③ ④ ⑤	29 ① ② ③ ④ ⑤
6 ① ② ③ ④ ⑤	14 ① ② ③ ④ ⑤	22 ① ② ③ ④ ⑤	30 ① ② ③ ④ ⑤
7 ① ② ③ ④ ⑤	15 ① ② ③ ④ ⑤	23 ① ② ③ ④ ⑤	31 ① ② ③ ④ ⑤
8 ① ② ③ ④ ⑤	16 ① ② ③ ④ ⑤	24 ① ② ③ ④ ⑤	32 ① ② ③ ④ ⑤

Question 1 refers to the following passage.

1. In 1968, Congress passed the Truth in Lending Act. This act requires that lenders tell people buying on credit the annual percentage rates for interest and the total interest charges over the life of the loan. This act is an example of

   (1) consumer protection laws
   (2) Congress following a policy of economic protectionism
   (3) Congress making laws that control profit
   (4) the Federal Reserve trying to control credit
   (5) a government policy that lets lenders do as they please

Question 2 refers to the following passage.

The National Weather Service still uses outdated equipment such as large computers with less power than a desktop computer and old-fashioned radar equipment. An ambitious modernization program is over budget and behind schedule.

2. Based on this information, which of the following can you conclude about the National Weather Service?

   (1) It should be shut down.
   (2) It can no longer make accurate predictions of any kind.
   (3) It might not be able to predict the approach of dangerous storms.
   (4) What worked in the past should work well today.
   (5) Americans should not spend money on new equipment with no proven value.

Questions 3 and 4 refer to the following passage.

The Fall Line is the boundary between the eastern coastal plain and the foothills of the Piedmont. The Fall Line had a great influence on early settlement patterns in the eastern United States. Barge traffic from the coast had to stop at the Fall Line because of steep waterfalls and rapids in the rivers. This forced traders to move larger bulk cargo from riverboats into smaller batches that could be carried overland. Towns grew where such changes were made.

In addition, the water power provided by the falls and rapids along the Fall Line was put to industrial use. As a result, textile and shoe manufacturing plants, lumber mills, and other industries grew. This allowed for further growth of towns and cities.

3. The Fall Line was important to early towns in the eastern United States because it

   (1) provided water for drinking
   (2) protected towns from flooding
   (3) helped river navigation
   (4) provided water power for industry
   (5) prohibited all land travel

4. Based on this passage, you can conclude that

   (1) climate determines city location
   (2) geographic factors that aid economic activity can influence a town's location
   (3) geographic factors do not affect a city's location
   (4) westward expansion was blocked by the Fall Line
   (5) the Fall Line was responsible for new methods of transportation

Questions 5 and 6 refer to the following passage.

The Articles of Confederation were passed by the Continental Congress in 1781 as the constitutional framework for the new United States. The articles gave a great deal of power to the states and relatively little power to the central, or federal, government. Later developments proved that the new federal government was too weak to deal with securing the country's frontiers, creating a strong military defense, protecting trade, and handling unrest during the troubled 1780s.

Most of the leaders of the revolution were worried about the ineffective federal government. They called for a Constitutional Convention to develop a constitutional framework with a stronger federal government. They hoped to keep the United States from breaking up into separate countries. The convention was held in 1787. A new constitution was then written that established a strong federal government.

5. The Articles of Confederation were replaced because they
   (1) gave too much power to the president
   (2) gave too much power to the federal government
   (3) displeased the states
   (4) created an all-powerful national government
   (5) created a weak and ineffective federal government

6. You could infer from this passage that the leaders of the revolution supported a more centralized system because they wanted to
   (1) protect the nation's survival
   (2) have political power for themselves
   (3) establish the president with power like a king's
   (4) have the United States become a world power
   (5) protect their own wealth and investments

Question 7 is based on the following passage.

The American political system is often described as pluralist. A pluralistic system gets its strength from the large number of interest groups that take part in politics. These groups must share power and make compromises to get things done.

7. Which of the following would be characteristic of decision making in such a system?
   (1) Political decisions are always made very quickly.
   (2) One group always tends to dominate the process.
   (3) No single group wins all the time.
   (4) There is very little political conflict and argument.
   (5) Political parties play a very small role.

Questions 8 and 9 refer to the following chart.

FEDERAL GOVERNMENT EXPENDITURES

defense	19.6%
Medicare	9.0%
health care services and research	7.1%
Social Security	20.7%
income security*	14.1%
veterans benefits	2.4%
education, training, and employment	3.5%
transportation	2.4%
science, space, and technology	1.2%
interest on public debt	20.1%

Source: *American Almanac: Statistical Abstract of the United States, for 1993*

*Includes housing assistance, food and nutrition assistance, unemployment compensation, and federal employees' retirement

8. Many social scientists agree that one important way to determine the real priorities of a society is to examine how it spends its money. Based on the chart, the federal government places the highest priority on

    (1) national defense
    (2) Social Security
    (3) Medicare
    (4) education, training, and employment
    (5) paying interest on the national debt

9. Based on the chart, you can infer that

    (1) more Americans are living longer and require old-age benefits
    (2) paying off the national debt is the country's top priority
    (3) the nation's concern for education is reflected in the federal budget
    (4) a large number of Americans move or travel to different locations
    (5) the expenditure for the space program has expanded over the past twenty years

Questions 10 and 11 refer to the following passage.

Today, almost all U.S. citizens over the age of eighteen have the legal right to vote. However, this was not always the case. The Constitution originally let the states determine qualifications for voting. The right to vote was at first limited to white male property owners.

Property qualifications were gradually eliminated. By 1830 most white males over the age of twenty-one could vote. African Americans gained the legal right to vote from the Fifteenth Amendment in 1870. Women gained the right to vote with the Nineteenth Amendment in 1919.

Some states still tried to deny African Americans the right to vote. Poll taxes, literacy tests, and sometimes scare tactics were used to keep African Americans from voting.

The poll tax on voting in federal elections was finally erased by the Twenty-fourth Amendment in 1962. The Voting Rights Act of 1965 guaranteed the right to vote to all citizens, regardless of race or sex.

10. What provision did the Constitution first make for voter qualifications?

    (1) It gave all white adult males the right to vote.
    (2) It gave all citizens the right to vote.
    (3) It left it up to the Supreme Court to decide.
    (4) It left it to the states to set qualifications.
    (5) It gave all property owners the right to vote.

11. The main idea of this passage is that

(1) equality in voting rights has always been a principle of American democracy

(2) voting rights have been granted to all groups without struggle

(3) the right to vote was not won by all citizens at the same time, but over time and with much social conflict

(4) the Voting Rights Act was the most important legislation of the 1960s

(5) without the Fifteenth Amendment, women and African Americans would still not have the right to vote

Questions 12 and 13 refer to the following passage.

Many social scientists have linked the changing nature of the American family to the growth of the women's liberation movement. The rights and freedoms won by women have increased their participation in the work force. This has changed child-rearing patterns, as more children attend day-care centers while their mothers work. The increased number of working women has also changed the division of labor between husbands and wives in the home. Many experts link the increased divorce rate to increased job opportunities for women. Jobs allow women to feel more economically secure on their own. Increased job opportunities for women also have caused a decrease in the population growth rate because more women are delaying childbirth or not having children at all.

12. The main idea of this passage is that

(1) women's liberation has destroyed the American family

(2) the women's liberation movement has brought about many changes in the American family

(3) men now take most of the responsibility for child rearing

(4) women's liberation has had little effect on anyone except children

(5) the nature of the American family has changed due to the high divorce rate

13. Based on this passage, what principle of social change can you conclude?

(1) Change is bad for the family unit.

(2) Change in one aspect of society is unlikely to affect other aspects of society.

(3) Too much freedom will ruin a society.

(4) Change in one aspect of society usually brings about changes in other aspects.

(5) Social changes have little effect on people's daily lives.

Question 14 refers to the following passage.

One of the most important factors affecting home purchases is the interest rate on mortgages. Some economists say that each 1 percent increase in mortgage interest rates makes homes unaffordable to more than 1 million families. The effects of this were clearly seen in 1983. Declining mortgage rates in early 1983 increased home sales very rapidly. The rates dropped in May to around 12 1/2 percent. By August they had climbed to almost 14 percent. Economists said that 2.4 million families could no longer afford to buy homes. This slowed home sales by 35 percent.

14. Based on the details in this passage, you can conclude that a continuing rise in mortgage interest rates would

(1) increase home sales

(2) not affect home sales

(3) not affect the price of homes

(4) cause more homes to be built

(5) decrease home sales

15. The main idea of the cartoon is that

(1) the economy needs tinkering with

(2) taxes will stay where they are until the economy catches up

(3) taxes will get a faster start than the economy

(4) the economy is large while taxes are small

(5) the tax-collecting machinery is always ready to work

16. How would you describe the condition of the U.S. economy as represented by the truck?

(1) large and operating efficiently

(2) small and probably not working well

(3) shrinking in size but working well

(4) large but not working as well as it should

(5) in complete disrepair

Questions 15 and 16 refer to the following cartoon.

Questions 17 and 18 are based on the passage and graphs below.

The typical U.S. family of 50 years ago was made up of children and both a mother and father. Now only half of American children under age 18 live in this traditional nuclear family. The Census Bureau gives three reasons for the rise in the number of nontraditional families: economic difficulties, rising divorce rates, and a rising number of illegitimate births.

**CHILDREN LIVING IN
TRADITIONAL NUCLEAR FAMILIES**

(with both parents and only full siblings, if any)

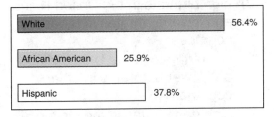

**CHILDREN LIVING
WITH ONE PARENT ONLY**

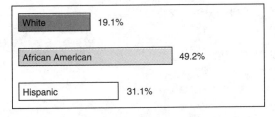

**CHILDREN LIVING
IN BLENDED FAMILIES**

(at least one stepparent, stepsibling,
or half-sibling)

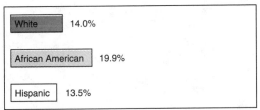

Source: *U.S. Census Bureau*

17. What is the total percentage for the group that includes a Hispanic child living with her mother, a stepfather, and a half-brother?

(1) 37.8 percent
(2) 49.2 percent
(3) 31.1 percent
(4) 14.0 percent
(5) 13.5 percent

18. Based on the graphs, which of the following statements is true?

(1) More than 50 percent of white children live in traditional nuclear families.
(2) More than 50 percent of white children live with one parent only.
(3) More than 50 percent of African American children live with one parent only.
(4) Less than 15 percent of Hispanic children live with one parent only.
(5) Less than 15 percent of African American children live in blended families.

Question 19 is based on the passage below.

Many influential Americans during the late nineteenth and early twentieth centuries believed in the philosophy of Social Darwinism. It stressed that society was based on the survival of the fittest. Government aid to the needy was wrong because it tampered with nature.

19. Social Darwinists would believe that a government food stamp program should be

(1) expanded to include more people
(2) maintained with the present level of spending
(3) run by the state governments
(4) sure that the unemployed received the aid
(5) cut completely

Questions 20 and 21 refer to the following chart.

20. Comparing the two lists, which country will no longer be among the top ten most populous countries in the year 2025?

(1) China
(2) United States
(3) Japan
(4) Nigeria
(5) Brazil

21. Which of the following might be a logical explanation for the United Kingdom dropping from the list by the year 2025?

(1) low birthrate in the United Kingdom and higher birthrates in other countries
(2) high birthrate in the United Kingdom and lower birthrates in other countries
(3) low birthrate in the United Kingdom and lower birthrates in other countries
(4) high death rates in the United Kingdom caused by bubonic plague
(5) strict government birth control measures

WORLD'S 20 MOST POPULOUS COUNTRIES: 1993 AND 2025

	1993			2025	
Rank	Country	Population	Rank	Country	Population
1.	China	1,178,500,000	1.	China	1,546,300,000
2.	India	897,400,000	2.	India	1,379,600,000
3.	United States	258,300,000	3.	United States	334,700,000
4.	Indonesia	187,600,000	4.	Indonesia	278,200,000
5.	Brazil	152,000,000	5.	Pakistan	275,100,000
6.	Russia	149,000,000	6.	Nigeria	246,000,000
7.	Japan	124,800,000	7.	Bangladesh	211,200,000
8.	Pakistan	122,400,000	8.	Brazil	205,300,000
9.	Bangladesh	113,900,000	9.	Iran	161,900,000
10.	Nigeria	95,100,000	10.	Russia	152,300,000
11.	Mexico	90,000,000	11.	Ethiopia*	140,800,000
12.	Germany	81,100,000	12.	Mexico	137,500,000
13.	Vietnam	71,800,000	13.	Japan	125,800,000
14.	Philippines	64,600,000	14.	Vietnam	107,200,000
15.	Iran	62,800,000	15.	Egypt	104,600,000
16.	Turkey	60,700,000	16.	Zaire	104,500,000
17.	Egypt	58,300,000	17.	Philippines	100,800,000
18.	United Kingdom	58,000,000	18.	Turkey	98,700,000
19.	Italy	57,800,000	19.	Tanzania	73,000,000
20.	France	57,700,000	20.	South Africa	70,000,000

Source: *1993 World Population Data Sheet of the Population Reference Bureau, Inc.*
*includes Eritrea

Questions 22 and 23 refer to the following graph.

POVERTY RATES IN THE U.S.

	1972	*1982*	*1991*
White	9.0	12.0	11.3
African American	33.3	35.6	32.7
Hispanic	22.8	29.9	28.7
Total	**11.9**	**15.0**	**14.2**

Source: *American Almanac: Statistical Abstract of the United States* (113th ed.)

22. Based on the graph, you can conclude that between 1972 and 1991, the percentage of people living below poverty level

    (1) increased among African Americans and Hispanics but decreased in the total population
    (2) decreased among whites and Hispanics and increased among African Americans
    (3) increased for all categories
    (4) decreased for all categories
    (5) decreased among African Americans and increased among Hispanics and whites

23. Which of the following groups had the highest percentage of people living below poverty level?

    (1) African Americans in 1982
    (2) Hispanics in 1982
    (3) whites in 1991
    (4) whites in 1982
    (5) Hispanics in 1972

Question 24 is based on the following passage.

During the 1970s and 1980s, there were several federal court decisions concerning the powers of the president and Congress. In the Watergate affair, the courts ruled that the president could not claim executive privilege as a reason to keep certain information from Congress. In 1983, the Supreme Court halted the use of the so-called legislative veto, which had been used by Congress to control and limit many actions of the executive branch.

24. The series of events described in the passage demonstrates that the separation of powers provided for under the Constitution is actually

    (1) very dictatorial
    (2) too rigid
    (3) not guiding the government efficiently
    (4) flexible and open to interpretation and change
    (5) the weakest part of the Constitution

Question 25 refers to the following graph.

WHO PAYS FOR HEALTH CARE?

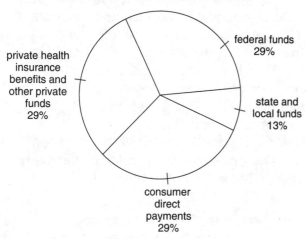

private health insurance benefits and other private funds 29%

federal funds 29%

state and local funds 13%

consumer direct payments 29%

25. Based on the graph, which of the following statements is true?

    (1) Private health insurance and other private funds pay most of the cost of health care.

    (2) State and local funds should pay more for health care.

    (3) The high cost of health care is hardest on the consumer.

    (4) Consumer payments, private health insurance benefits, and state and local funds pay equal portions of the total cost of health care.

    (5) Private health insurance benefits, federal funds, and consumer direct payments cover 87 percent of the total cost of health care.

Questions 26 and 27 refer to the following passage.

"... the peculiarity of American institutions is the fact that they have been compelled to adapt themselves to the changes of an expanding people—to the changes involved in crossing a continent, in winning a wilderness, and in developing each area of progress out of the primitive economic and political conditions of the frontier. ..."

    —Frederick Jackson Turner

26. The main idea of this passage is that

    (1) the rise in cities was a major influence in economic and political development

    (2) American character has been dominated by its European origins

    (3) settlement of the frontier has been the chief force in the development of the American character

    (4) industrialization has been the chief force in creating American institutions

    (5) the primitive economic conditions of the frontier have created American institutions that resist change

27. To Turner, what event would mark an end to the American ability to make changes?

    (1) the end of exploring new frontiers

    (2) the development of the wilderness into a place of economic and political power

    (3) the rise of large cities in the East

    (4) the end of our close ties to Europe

    (5) the crossing of the continent

Question 28 refers to the following passage.

In the 1880s and 1890s, many American small farmers were driven off the land or forced to become tenants by changing economic conditions. They formed protest organizations and demanded government reforms. They thought reforms would save the small farmers and their way of life, but their efforts were unsuccessful. The small farmers continued to decline in number as agriculture became more mechanized, and larger farms took over the small ones.

28. The American small farmer of the late nineteenth century was a member of a(n)

(1) upwardly mobile social class
(2) rich elite
(3) powerful majority
(4) social class in decline
(5) revolutionary social class

Questions 29 and 30 refer to the map below.

29. This map shows

(1) branches of the Mississippi River
(2) state boundaries in 1860
(3) the first telegraph lines
(4) U.S. railroads in the East in 1860
(5) major highways in 1860

30. You can infer from this map that

(1) the Northeast had more commerce and industry than the Southeast
(2) river travel was more extensive in the Northeast
(3) communication among cities in the Northeast was not well developed by 1860
(4) few highways had been built in the Southeast
(5) Texas was not yet a state in 1860

RAILROADS IN THE EASTERN UNITED STATES, 1860

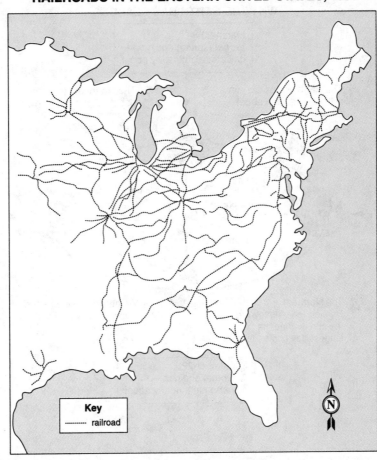

Key
-------- railroad

Questions 31 and 32 are based on the passage and diagram below.

Most parts of the world experience four seasons—spring, summer, fall, and winter. The seasons are divided by equinoxes and solstices. (Find these on the diagram below.)

All four seasons are the opposite in the Southern Hemisphere. When we experience summer in the United States, people in South America are having winter.

31. The Northern Hemisphere has its shortest day of the year about December 21 because the

(1) Northern Hemisphere is tilted at its greatest point toward the sun
(2) Northern Hemisphere is tilted at its greatest point away from the sun
(3) equinox marks the beginning of winter
(4) solstice marks the beginning of summer
(5) sun's rays are directly over the equator at that time

32. If you were an avid skier, on which date would you find the most snow-covered ski slopes in the Southern Hemisphere?

(1) December 21
(2) January 21
(3) March 20
(4) June 21
(5) September 22

WHY THE EARTH HAS SEASONS

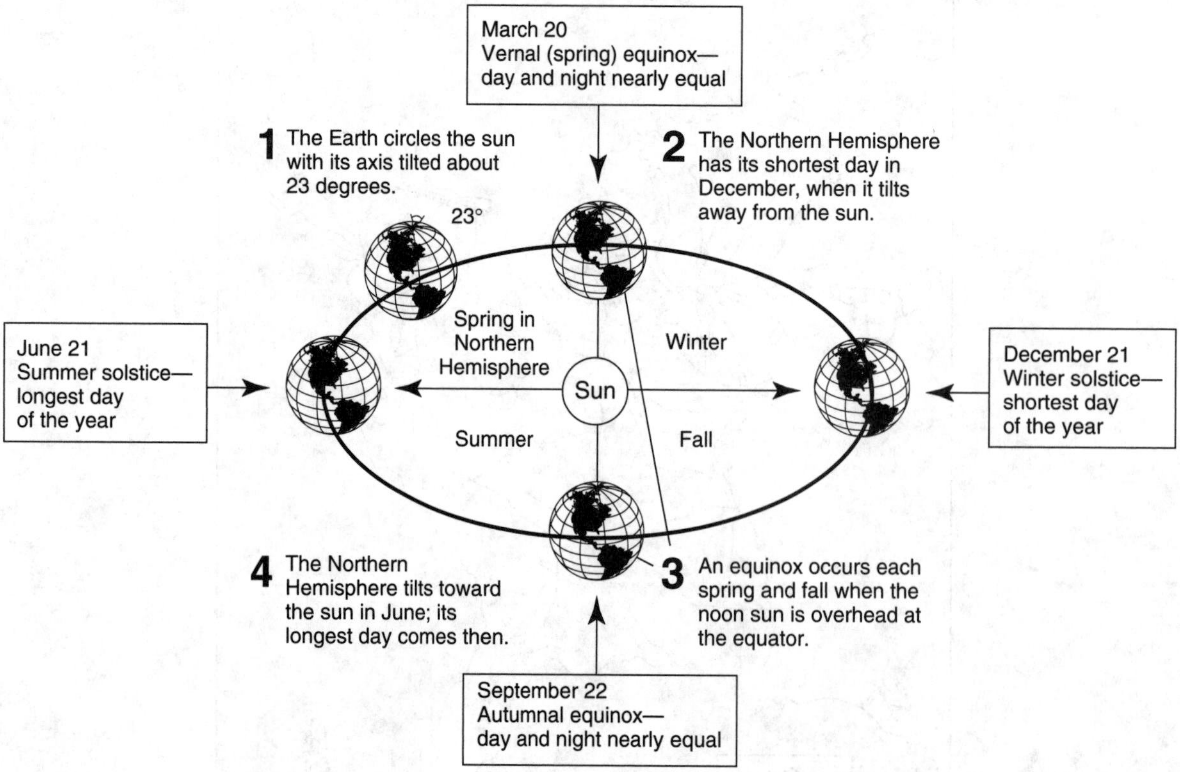

March 20
Vernal (spring) equinox—
day and night nearly equal

1 The Earth circles the sun with its axis tilted about 23 degrees.

2 The Northern Hemisphere has its shortest day in December, when it tilts away from the sun.

23°

June 21
Summer solstice—
longest day of the year

Spring in Northern Hemisphere

Winter

Sun

December 21
Winter solstice—
shortest day of the year

Summer

Fall

4 The Northern Hemisphere tilts toward the sun in June; its longest day comes then.

3 An equinox occurs each spring and fall when the noon sun is overhead at the equator.

September 22
Autumnal equinox—
day and night nearly equal

1. **(1)** People who buy things are consumers. The question tells you that the Truth in Lending Act requires that lenders tell the truth to buyers. Therefore, the people protected by this legislation are consumers.

2. **(3)** The passage indicates that outdated equipment is used. The logical conclusion is that it might not be able to predict storms very well.

3. **(4)** The second paragraph of the passage says that water power along the Fall Line was put to work for industry.

4. **(2)** The passage shows that towns grew up along the Fall Line because of industry's need for power.

5. **(5)** The passage refers to the federal government as having "little power" and as being "too weak" and "ineffective."

6. **(1)** The third sentence lists the problems faced by the new nation. These problems suggest that survival was at stake. There is no evidence in the passage for the other choices.

7. **(3)** The last sentence says that "These groups must share power and make compromises to get things done." This sentence suggests that all groups get some of what they want but that no single group dominates.

8. **(2)** The most money is spent on Social Security, so choice (2) is the best answer. The other choices relate to categories with lower percentages of federal spending.

9. **(1)** With Social Security representing nearly 20.7 percent of the budget, you can infer choice (1).

10. **(4)** The third sentence says that it left it to the states to decide voting qualifications.

11. **(3)** The passage tells you how several different groups gained the right to vote, all at different times. It also describes the obstacles that African Americans faced in exercising this right.

12. **(2)** The first sentence of the passage gives you the main idea. None of the other choices are stated in the passage.

13. **(4)** The passage shows that changes in American women's employment patterns have affected child-rearing patterns, division of labor, and divorce rates.

14. **(5)** When mortgage interest rates rise, fewer families can afford to buy homes, and sales fall.

15. **(3)** The race car symbol shows that taxes are ready to go—very likely upward—while the economy lags behind.

16. **(4)** The driver looking under the hood of the truck shows that the economy may need some work. The large truck, however, is still in one piece and none of its tires is flat.

17. **(5)** The Hispanic child lives in what the graph labels a "blended" family. The percentage of Hispanics in that category is 13.5 percent.

18. **(1)** Analysis of the graph shows that only choice (1) is correct.

19. **(5)** A Social Darwinist would believe giving out food stamps was wrong. It would artificially assist those who are not capable of taking care of themselves.

20. (3) Japan dropped from a rank of 7 in 1993 to 13 in 2025. The other countries remained in the top ten.

21. (1) Only a low birth rate in the United Kingdom and a higher birth rate in other countries (most of which had larger populations) explain the dropping of the United Kingdom from the list. Choices (4) and (5) cannot be predicted.

22. (5) The graph shows that poverty decreased among African Americans between 1972 and 1991, but increased among Hispanics and whites during that period.

23. (1) The graph shows that 35.6 percent of African Americans lived below poverty level in 1982.

24. (4) The paragraph describes how the courts reinterpret the constitutional balance of power. The other choices are not supported by the information given.

25. (5) Adding up the percents in the graph, choice (5) is the correct answer.

26. (3) Choice (3), that American institutions have had to change to meet the challenges of an expanding and pioneering nation, best restates the main idea of the passage.

27. (1) From Turner's remarks, you can infer that without new frontiers (areas of challenge) to explore, America's ability to make changes would come to an end.

28. (4) The passage describes American small farmers as being part of a declining social class. American small farmers were forced to change their way of life due to massive economic and technological changes.

29. (4) The title of the map shows that choice (4) is correct.

30. (1) The map shows a greater concentration of railroads in the Northeast than in the Southeast. Railroads made the movement of goods and raw materials in the Northeast easy and enabled this region to develop much faster economically than the Southeast.

31. (2) The diagram shows that the shortest day of the year takes place on December 21 because the Northern Hemisphere is tilted at its greatest point away from the sun.

32. (4) The passage says that winter takes place in the Southern Hemisphere while the Northern Hemisphere has its summer, so choice (4), June 21, is correct.

Pre-Test Evaluation Chart

Use the Answer Key on pages 13–14 to check your answers to the Pre-Test. Then, on the chart below, circle the numbers of the questions you missed. If you missed many of the questions that correspond to a particular reading skill, you will want to pay special attention to that skill as you work through this book. The numbers in darker type are based on graphics.

Skill Area/ Content Area	Comprehension	Application	Analysis	Evaluation
U.S. History (pages 83–147)	10, 11, 26, **29**	27	19	**30**
Political Science (pages 149–183)	5	7	24	6
Behavioral Sciences (pages 185–207)	12, **17**	**23**	**18**	13, **22**, 28
Geography (pages 209–233)	3, **20, 31**	2	**32**	4, **21**
Economics (pages 235–265)	**15**	**8**	**25**	1, **9**, 14, **16**

CRITICAL THINKING SKILLS
IN SOCIAL STUDIES

- ■ Comprehending Social Studies Materials
- ■ Applying Social Studies Ideas
- ■ Analyzing Social Studies Materials
- ■ Evaluating Social Studies Materials

1 Comprehending Social Studies Materials

When you ***comprehend*** social studies materials, you understand what they mean. Social studies writers always have a purpose in mind. They present an idea to give you information or to convince you of a certain point of view. First, they communicate their ***main idea***. Then, they use details to support and defend this main idea.

MAIN IDEA OF PASSAGES

The main idea of a passage or paragraph is usually found in the first sentence. Sometimes it appears elsewhere. In a longer passage, the main idea usually can be found in an introductory or concluding paragraph.

Follow the steps below to identify the main idea.

- Read the entire passage.

- Find out what the passage is about.

- Look for the main idea in the first or last sentence of a paragraph or a passage.

As you read the following passage, look for the main idea.

Direct Military Action

American military leaders did not want to get involved in direct action in Bosnia-Herzegovina during the early 1990s. They knew the American public would not support direct military action. High-level U.S. Defense Department sources reported that military leaders were well aware of the unpopularity of the Vietnam War. In that war, 58,000 Americans were killed and 153,000 were wounded. The war cost more than $140 billion. Because of the lack of public support for the Vietnam War, U.S. military leadership urged the administration to be cautious about direct military involvement in Bosnia-Herzegovina.

The main idea of the passage is that military leaders

_____ **1.** did not want American soldiers to be killed in Bosnia-Herzegovina

_____ **2.** were worried about the high cost of military action

_____ **3.** wanted to begin direct military action in Bosnia-Herzegovina

_____ **4.** were reluctant to urge military action in Bosnia-Herzegovina

_____ **5.** believed that public support justified direct military action in Bosnia-Herzegovina

You were correct if you chose (4), that military leaders *were reluctant to urge military action in Bosnia-Herzegovina.* The last sentence states the main idea of the passage. The rest of the passage supports this central idea. Details are given about the high cost of the war and the great number of Americans killed or wounded in the Vietnam War. These details tell why the Vietnam War became so unpopular in America.

EXERCISE 1

Directions: Read the passage below and then put a check in front of the correct answer to each question.

Teen Suicide

Suicide is now the third highest cause of death among youths 15 to 19 years old. It ranks just behind accidents and homicide. Youth suicide increased nearly 200 percent between 1970 and 1990. One in every 8,000 adolescents commits suicide. From 1 in 7 to 1 in 15 attempt suicide at least once. While public attention has focused on teenage drug abuse and pregnancy, teenage suicide has been increasing at an alarming rate.

1. What is the main idea of the passage?

_____ **(1)** The increase in teenage suicide is a disturbing new trend.

_____ **(2)** Drug abuse is the main problem facing American youth.

_____ **(3)** Pregnancy is a growing problem among teenagers.

_____ **(4)** Youth problems are on the decline.

2. The most logical follow-up story would answer the question of why more American teenagers are

_____ **(1)** on drugs

_____ **(2)** getting pregnant

_____ **(3)** committing homicides

_____ **(4)** committing suicide

ANSWERS ARE ON PAGE 297.

MAIN IDEA OF PICTOGRAPHS

Graphs simplify information. Long passages can be confusing and hard to understand, so graphs are used to show information visually.

When you read a graph, look first at all the important features: the title, how the graph is organized, and the key that shows the meaning of the figures, bars, or lines.

PICTOGRAPHS

One of the easiest graphs to read is a ***pictograph***. It uses a series of symbols to show an amount or a quantity. The graph below shows you what to look for in a pictograph.

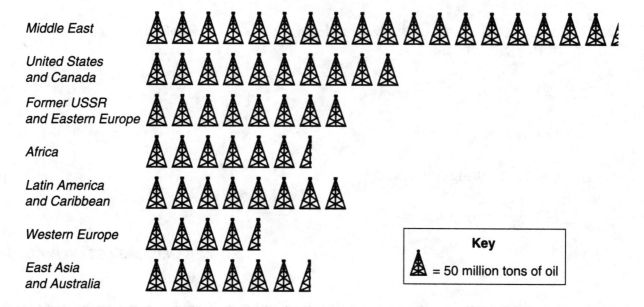

YEARLY WORLD OIL PRODUCTION BY REGION
(in millions of tons)

To understand the main idea of a graph, ask yourself:

- What is the topic (title) of the graph?
  (yearly world oil production by region)

- What does each symbol represent?
  (50 million tons of oil—shown in the key)

- What does the graph compare?
  (oil production in different regions)

To read the graph, multiply the value that you are given for a symbol by the number of times it appears on the line. In this graph, you multiply 50 times the number of symbols given after each region. This will show how many million tons of oil each region produces yearly. Note that the last symbol on the line after "Africa" stands for 1/2 (25 million tons of oil).

Based on the graph, fill in the answers to the questions that follow.

1. How much oil was produced by the nations of Africa?

_____ tons

2. How much oil was produced by the United States and Canada?

_____ tons

3. Which region produced more oil—the Middle East or the former Soviet Union and Eastern Europe combined? _____

4. Which region produced the least amount of oil?

_____

5. Which two pairs of regions each produce 400 million tons of oil?

_____

_____

To answer the first question, you count the number of oil wells in Africa (6 1/2) and multiply the amount times 50. The correct answer is *325 million tons.* For the second question, you count the number of oil wells in the United States and Canada and multiply times 50. The correct answer is *500 million tons.* For the third question, compare the amount of oil produced by each region. The Middle East produced about 900 million tons of oil (18 1/4 x 50); the former Soviet Union and Eastern Europe produced 400 million tons (8 x 50). So *the Middle East* is the correct answer. For the fourth question, you can see that *Western Europe* has fewer oil wells than any other region, and thus has produced the least amount of oil. For the fifth question, both *the former USSR and Eastern Europe combined* and *Latin America and the Caribbean combined* produce 400 million tons of oil each (8 x 50).

EXERCISE 2

Directions: Study the pictograph below and then answer the questions that follow.

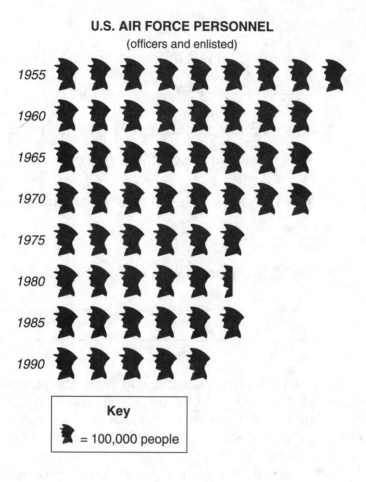

U.S. AIR FORCE PERSONNEL
(officers and enlisted)

Key

= 100,000 people

1. How many military personnel were in the U.S. Air Force in 1980?

   _____

2. Which year had the highest number of Air Force personnel?

   _____

3. Which three years showed the number of U.S. Air Force personnel as 800,000?

   _____

4. Which year had the fewest number of U.S. Air Force personnel?

   _____

ANSWERS ARE ON PAGE 297.

DETAILS

Social studies writers support their main idea with **_supporting details_**. These supporting details expand on the main idea or make it clearer.

For example, if important wars are being presented, the writer might include such details as the dates of each war, the countries involved, the number of casualties suffered, and the causes and outcomes of each war.

Scanning is an important skill to learn. It will help you save time when you are looking for details. **_Scanning_** is looking over a passage to find a specific detail. Suppose you are reading an article on the history of immigration to the United States. You want to find out quickly from which countries the immigrants came. As you read the following article, focus on the word _immigrant,_ and look for references to the countries from which immigrants came to the United States.

A Nation of Immigrants

Scholars believe that the very earliest settlers in what is now the United States crossed over from Asia more than 25,000 years ago. While we think of Native Americans as always having been in the United States, they, too, were immigrants.

The earliest European immigrants came from Spain. They settled in the Southwest and in Florida. In the 1600s, permanent settlers came from northern European countries such as England, the Netherlands, and Germany. Some sought political and religious freedom. Others wanted the opportunity to make a better living for themselves. At the same time, Africans were forcibly carried off from their homeland to work as slaves on large plantations.

After the United States became an independent nation, waves of immigrants came from many different countries. The Chinese and Irish came for political and economic reasons. In the early twentieth century, many more immigrants came from Italy, Greece, Russia, and other European countries. Recent immigrants have come to the United States from Mexico, Central America, and the countries of Asia looking for better jobs and political freedom.

EXERCISE 3

Directions: Scan the passage on page 25. Circle *T* for each true statement, or *F* for each false statement.

T F 1. The earliest immigrants probably came from Asia.

T F 2. The first Spanish immigrants settled in California.

T F 3. Early immigrants from northern Europe sought political and religious freedom and to make a better living.

T F 4. African immigrants were brought to the United States by force to work as slaves.

T F 5. In the early twentieth century, large numbers of immigrants came from France and Spain seeking religious freedom.

T F 6. The largest number of recent immigrants have come from countries outside of Europe.

T F 7. Native Americans were immigrants to the United States.

T F 8. Chinese and Irish people came to the United States before it became an independent country.

T F 9. Recent immigrants from Asia, Mexico, and Central America hope for better employment opportunities in the United States.

T F 10. Many German, English, and Dutch settlers came to live in the United States in the 1600s.

ANSWERS ARE ON PAGE 297.

EXERCISE 4

Directions: Scan the following passage for important details. Then fill in the blanks with the correct answers from the passage.

The Spread of Slavery in the United States

The Southern slaveowners won many victories from 1820 to the beginning of the Civil War in 1861. In 1820, the Missouri Compromise opened new areas of the country to slavery. The Kansas-Nebraska Act of 1854 cleared more areas for the potential growth of slavery. The greatest victory for the supporters of slavery came in 1857 with the *Dred Scott* decision. In this case, the Court declared that no slave or free black person could claim U.S. citizenship. Thus, it opened almost all the territories to slavery.

1. The Civil War began in _____.

2. During the 1800s, Southern slaveowners won many _____.

3. The first event to open new areas of the United States to slavery was

the _____ in 1820.

4. The _____ Act also opened up new areas for the growth of slavery.

5. The _____ decision was the greatest victory for the supporters of slavery.

6. The *Dred Scott* decision opened almost all the _____ to slavery.

ANSWERS ARE ON PAGE 297.

WRITING ACTIVITY 1

Write a paragraph convincing someone that a person should be eighteen to get a driver's license. Use several supporting details to expand on your main idea.

ANSWERS WILL VARY.

MAIN IDEA AND DETAILS IN CIRCLE GRAPHS

Circle graphs are sometimes called pie graphs because of their shape. Circle graphs show how a total amount of something is divided into parts. The parts of the circle must add up to a whole, or 100 percent. These graphs can be used to show the percentage of groups of people that make up a country. Another use for circle graphs is to show how a budget is divided into different categories. Use the graphs below to practice reading circle graphs.

PERCENTAGE OF PEOPLE BELOW THE POVERTY LEVEL, 1991

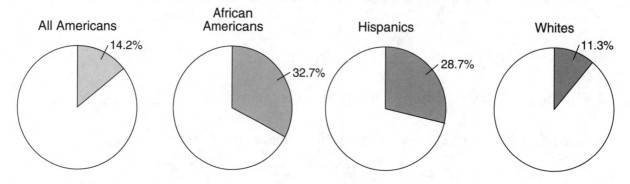

The four circle graphs compare different amounts. You must be able to read each graph by itself. In three of the circle graphs, each whole circle represents 100 percent of a particular group of people—African Americans, Hispanics, or Whites. The first graph represents all the people in the United States. The segments, or parts, of the circle in each graph represent the percent of the whole who fell below the poverty level for 1991.

What is the average number of people in the United States who fell below the poverty level? Look at the graph labeled "All Americans." You can see that category was 14.2 percent. In the graph labeled "Hispanics," you can see that slightly more than one-quarter of the whole is below the poverty level (28.7 percent).

Do the circle graphs show how many people have incomes below the poverty level? No, you would need to have the total population of the United States to find out how many people make up 14.2 percent. You would also need the total number of African Americans, Hispanics, and Whites to find out the number of people for the other graphs.

≡ PRE-GED Practice ≡
EXERCISE 5

Questions 1–4 are based on the graphs below.

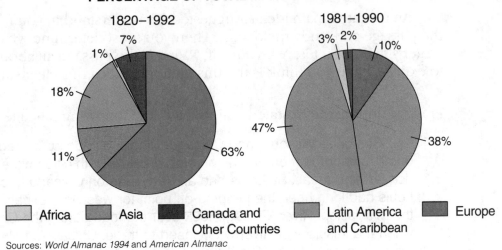

PERCENTAGE OF TOTAL IMMIGRATION TO REGION

1820–1992

7%
1%
18%
11%
63%

1981–1990

3% 2%
10%
47%
38%

☐ Africa   ☐ Asia   ☐ Canada and Other Countries   ☐ Latin America and Caribbean   ☐ Europe

Sources: *World Almanac 1994* and *American Almanac*

1. Between 1820 and 1992, the largest group of immigrants to the United States came from

   (1) Europe
   (2) Asia
   (3) Latin America and the Caribbean
   (4) Africa
   (5) Canada and other countries

2. From 1981 to 1990, the largest group of immigrants came from

   (1) Europe
   (2) Asia
   (3) Latin America and the Caribbean
   (4) Africa
   (5) Canada and other countries

3. Based on the graphs, which region made the greatest percentage gain in 1981–1990 compared to the period from 1820–1992?

   (1) Europe
   (2) Asia
   (3) Latin America and the Caribbean
   (4) Africa
   (5) Canada and other countries

4. Between 1820 and 1992, what percentage of immigrants to the United States were from Africa?

   (1) 1%
   (2) 7%
   (3) 11%
   (4) 18%
   (5) 63%

ANSWERS ARE ON PAGE 297.

UNSTATED MAIN IDEA

A key inference skill is understanding an implied or **unstated main idea**. You have already learned how to locate a main idea when it is stated directly. How would you identify a main idea when it is not stated directly?

An unstated main idea is suggested. To understand it, you must read the passage and study the details. Then you must determine what the writer's main point is. Ask yourself, "What is the passage all about?" Try to express what you think is the unstated main idea in a clear statement.

Practice finding the unstated main idea in the following passage.

St. Louis, Missouri, and Chicago, Illinois, competed for regional domination throughout the nineteenth century. Both cities were close to rich farming areas. St. Louis had an early lead on Chicago because St. Louis had long been the jumping-off point for westward expansion up the Mississippi River. Chicago took over the lead during the Civil War when the Mississippi River was closed to trade. Chicago's railroads still ran, and access to the Great Lakes remained open. As a result, Chicago flourished as a grain and meat-packing center.

Put a check in front of the unstated main idea of the passage.

_____ **1.** The Civil War caused Chicago and St. Louis to grow rapidly.

_____ **2.** During the Civil War, St. Louis dominated trade because of its better location.

_____ **3.** Chicago became the leading regional city because of its access to trade routes during the Civil War.

_____ **4.** The Civil War caused both St. Louis and Chicago to decline.

_____ **5.** Chicago pushed ahead of St. Louis because it was a more modern city.

The correct answer is choice (3). The third sentence says that "Chicago took over the lead during the Civil War when the Mississippi River was closed to trade." The fourth sentence mentions that "Chicago's railroads still ran, and access to the Great Lakes remained open."

≡ PRE-GED Practice ≡
EXERCISE 6

Questions 1–3 are based on the passage below.

Identifying with a Political Party

Political analysts have predicted from time to time that one or both of the major political parties will break up. Increasing numbers of people are calling themselves independents. During the 1970s, the number of people describing themselves as strong Democrats fell from 20 percent to 15 percent. By 1990, the figure was back up to 20 percent. The number of people defining themselves as strong Republicans climbed slowly from 9 percent in the 1970s to a high of 14 percent in 1988. By 1990, the number had dropped to 10 percent. Independents shrank from 15 percent in 1976 to 11 percent in 1990.

1. According to the passage, the number of people describing themselves as strong Democrats from the 1970s to 1990

   (1) remained at 9 percent
   (2) dropped to 10 percent
   (3) remained at 14 percent
   (4) dropped to 15 percent
   (5) rose again to 20 percent

2. According to the passage, the number of people defining themselves as strong Republicans in 1990

   (1) fell from 20 percent to 15 percent
   (2) climbed to 9 percent
   (3) dropped to 10 percent
   (4) shrank to 11 percent
   (5) went back up to 20 percent

3. Which of the following statements best summarizes the main idea of the passage?

   (1) The two-party system appears unlikely to change in the near future.
   (2) The Republicans and Democrats are losing hard-core support.
   (3) More and more people are leaving the Republican party to become Democrats.
   (4) The Democrats can no longer assume the support of union members.
   (5) The growing number of independents will cause the two-party system to break up.

ANSWERS ARE ON PAGE 297.

CONTEXT CLUES

While working in this book, you may encounter words you have not seen before. Don't let this stop you from reading the passage. You can get the general meaning of a passage even if you don't know a particular word.

Rebel city council members held a conclave last month. At the secret meeting, they discussed ways to embarrass the mayor.

If you did not know the meaning of *conclave,* you could guess from the words following it. A conclave is a secret meeting. Here you have used a word's **context**–the words surrounding the unknown word–for clues to its meaning. Sometimes you can get the meaning of a word you don't know by looking at its opposite meaning. Consider the sentence below.

Unlike the United States, with its official policy of racial integration, South Africa practiced apartheid until the early 1990s.

If you did not know what *apartheid* meant, you could guess that it means "the official policy of racial segregation"–the opposite of a policy of integration. The word *unlike* is a clue to look for an opposite meaning.

Finally, the meaning of a word may not be stated directly. You will have to infer it from the supporting details. This skill is like that of inferring the meaning of an unstated main idea. See if you can determine the meaning of **Gross National Product** from the following passage.

The U.S. Gross National Product (GNP) doubled from 1980 to 1990, from $2.7 trillion to $5.5 trillion. The rapid growth was determined by adding together the total value of goods and services bought by both consumers and businesses.

From the passage, you can infer that GNP is the total value of

_____ **1.** consumer goods

_____ **2.** consumer and business goods and services

_____ **3.** business goods and services

_____ **4.** consumer goods and services

The meaning of *Gross National Product* is choice (2), *the goods and services bought by both consumers and businesses.* These are added together to make up the GNP.

EXERCISE 7

Directions: Read the passages below. Then put a check in front of the correct answer to the questions that follow.

Many supporters of school prayer would like to see all schoolchildren recite a standard prayer. They argue that everyone would accept a nondenominational prayer. The prayer would refer to God only in a nonspecific way. It would make no mention of Jesus Christ, the Holy Trinity, Mohammed, or any other religious figure central to the beliefs of a particular religious group.

1. You can infer that *nondenominational* means

____ **(1)** standardized

____ **(2)** not dominant

____ **(3)** not connected with any particular religious group

____ **(4)** connected with a particular religious group

Historically, Manchuria in China has been the setting for different nomadic peoples who migrated back and forth from Central Asia to the Pacific. It has long been a meeting ground for different peoples and a point of conflict for different national interests.

2. You can infer that *nomadic* refers to peoples who

____ **(1)** settle in one region for a long period of time

____ **(2)** have many different interests

____ **(3)** move from one place to another

____ **(4)** thrive on conflict

ANSWERS ARE ON PAGE 297.

≡ PRE-GED Practice ≡
EXERCISE 8

Questions 1 and 2 refer to the following pictograph.

CITY TAXES PER PERSON

Key $=$100

New York ——— $ $ $ $ $ $ $ $

San Antonio ——— $

San Francisco —— $ $ $ $

Washington, D.C. – $ $ $ $ $ $ $ $ $ $
                   $ $ $

New Orleans ——— $ $

Source: *U.S.: A Statistical Portrait of the American People*

1. Which statement can be supported by the graph?

   (1) San Antonio has the lowest city taxes of all the cities in the United States.

   (2) New York and San Francisco have higher taxes than Washington, D.C.

   (3) San Antonio and San Francisco have lower taxes than New Orleans.

   (4) Of the cities on the graph, Washington, D.C., New York, and San Francisco have the highest city taxes per person.

   (5) Of the cities on the graph, New Orleans and San Francisco have the lowest city taxes per person.

2. What is the main idea of the graph?

   (1) Washington, D.C. is one of the most expensive cities in the country in which to live.

   (2) Washington, D.C. has more public services than New York has.

   (3) San Antonio and New Orleans have very low city taxes.

   (4) City taxes in the United States can range from as little as $100 to as much as $1,300 per person.

   (5) City taxes in San Francisco are reasonable, so most people could afford to live there.

Questions 3 and 4 are based on the graph below.

MONTHLY BUDGET

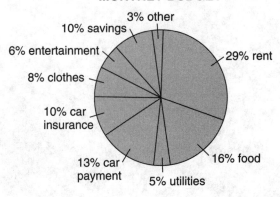

3. Which statement is best supported by the graph?

 (1) This person's biggest expense is food.
 (2) This person spends most of her money on necessities.
 (3) More than half of this person's income goes to food and utilities.
 (4) This person saves more of her income than she spends on food.
 (5) This person probably goes to many movies.

4. Which two categories combined account for 18 percent of this person's expenses?

 (1) car insurance and entertainment
 (2) food and car payment
 (3) clothes and rent
 (4) car payment and utilities
 (5) entertainment and other

Questions 5 and 6 are based on the following passage.

 The great American megalopolis stretches over four hundred miles from Boston to Washington, D.C. Including such cities as New York, Philadelphia, Newark, and Baltimore, it is the largest urban area in the world.

5. A megalopolis is a

 (1) large city and its suburbs
 (2) state government
 (3) group of connected cities and suburbs
 (4) large lottery
 (5) group of cities in the eastern part of the United States

6. An urban area refers to a

 (1) state
 (2) nation
 (3) city
 (4) suburb
 (5) local government

ANSWERS ARE ON PAGE 298.

2 Applying Social Studies Ideas

Have you ever had to read a map to plan a vacation you were taking, to give a friend directions to your home, or to read a chart or graph to find out specific information? If so, you were applying social studies ideas to your everyday life. One of the most important ends of learning is an ability to apply what you have learned.

In this chapter, you will apply ideas you learn in these ways:

- using information

- reading maps

- understanding ideas in bar graphs

APPLICATION OF IDEAS

When you *apply* an idea, you use information from one situation to explain or understand another. For example, if an airplane flies on a straight course for a long time, you can determine that it will eventually return close to the point where it started. How do you figure this out? Use the idea that Earth is round. Then apply this knowledge to the flight of the airplane.

Practice applying ideas by answering a question about the following passage.

Monroe Doctrine

By 1823, Spain had lost most of its colonies in the Western Hemisphere. Many Americans feared that other European countries might take over these colonies. President James Monroe announced the Monroe Doctrine in a speech to Congress. The Monroe Doctrine warned that any European interference with an independent state in this hemisphere would be regarded by the United States as an unfriendly act.

The Monroe Doctrine would be violated if a European country sent troops to intervene in the affairs of

____ **1.** Libya

____ **2.** New Zealand

____ **3.** Mexico

____ **4.** Vietnam

____ **5.** Turkey

The best choice is (3), *Mexico.* You need to understand the basic principle of the Monroe Doctrine—that the United States will not tolerate European interference in the Western Hemisphere. You then must remember your geography and apply this intervention to a country in this hemisphere—Mexico.

EXERCISE 1

Directions: Read the passage below and then put a check in front of the correct answer to the questions that follow.

At the heart of economic growth is the growth in labor productivity. One way to measure productivity is by the output of each worker per hour of labor. The more that can be produced per hour, the more productive the economy. The more productive the economy, the faster the economy can grow.

There are several ways to improve productivity. The most important method has been the introduction of modern technology. In the past, the introduction of technology to agriculture produced the greatest surge in farm productivity in European and American history. Today, the introduction of modern technology, such as computers, is leading to increased manufacturing productivity. Other means of increasing productivity include improving management, increasing worker morale, and identifying more efficient ways to speed up the work process.

1. Suppose that Japan had a large lead on the United States in the successful use of modern technology, such as the use of robots in automobile production. As a result, the growth of Japan's economy would

_____ **(1)** be slower than in the U.S. because of lower productivity

_____ **(2)** decline because robots cannot buy anything

_____ **(3)** be about the same as the United States

_____ **(4)** grow faster than the U.S. economy

2. A company wishing to increase productivity should focus its efforts on

_____ **(1)** better marketing

_____ **(2)** better supervision of workers

_____ **(3)** introducing new technology

_____ **(4)** reducing its prices

3. All of the following factors are mentioned as increasing productivity EXCEPT

_____ **(1)** improving employees' morale

_____ **(2)** measuring workers' output

_____ **(3)** improving management

_____ **(4)** increasing speed and efficiency

ANSWERS ARE ON PAGE 298.

APPLYING INFORMATION IN MAPS

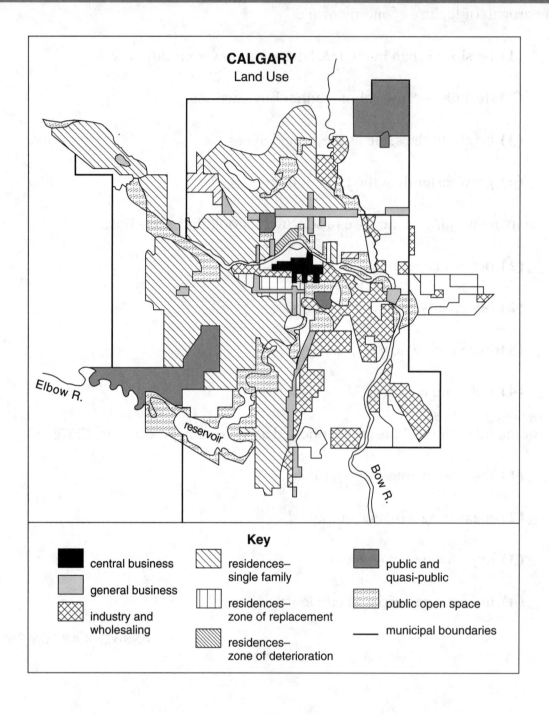

CALGARY
Land Use

Elbow R.

reservoir

Bow R.

Key

■ central business

▨ residences—
single family

▧ public and
quasi-public

▦ general business

▥ residences—
zone of replacement

▨ public open space

▨ industry and
wholesaling

▨ residences—
zone of deterioration

— municipal boundaries

Maps come in an almost endless variety. Physical maps show different geographic features such as mountains, deserts, lakes, and rivers. Special-purpose maps use different colors, patterns, and symbols to give information.

Most maps also include a key. The ***key*** (sometimes called a legend) explains the symbols used on the map. Symbols can be route arrows, dots and stars for cities, and different lines for roads, railroads, and canals. Sometimes the key features boxes that explain the colors or patterns used on the map.

Practice using the key on the Calgary map by putting a check in front of the correct answer to the questions that follow.

1. This map shows Calgary's

_____**(1)** voting districts

_____**(2)** water system

_____**(3)** land uses

_____**(4)** high and low points

2. According to the map, public open spaces are

_____**(1)** surrounded by the central business district

_____**(2)** near the reservoir and outlying areas

_____**(3)** beyond the city limits of Calgary

_____**(4)** next to the Elbow River

The answer to the first question is (3), *land uses.* The title of the map also helps you answer this question. The answer to the second question is (2), *near the reservoir and outlying areas.* The key shows markings for "public open space." On the map, you find these dots near the reservoir and the outlying areas.

EXERCISE 2

Directions: Based on the map, circle *T* for each true statement, or *F* for each false statement.

NATURAL RESOURCES OF AUSTRALIA

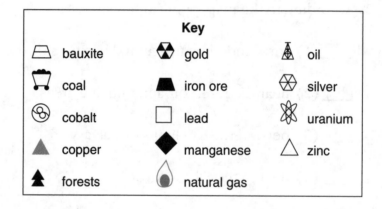

T F **1.** Australia's most abundant natural resource is gold.

T F **2.** Wherever gold mines are located there are also coal mines.

T F **3.** Most of Australia's natural resources are found in the interior of the country.

T F **4.** This map shows that natural gas is a renewable natural resource.

T F **5.** Zinc mines are located only at the southern tip of Australia.

T F **6.** Australia produces more bauxite than uranium.

T F **7.** Cobalt is Australia's chief export.

T F **8.** Australia's coal mines are located in the country's eastern border.

T F **9.** Most of Australia's forests are located in the country's interior.

T F **10.** Australia produces more gold than silver.

T F **11.** Australia imports a large amount of manganese.

T F **12.** Australia has more natural resources than most other countries.

ANSWERS ARE ON PAGE 298.

WRITING ACTIVITY 2

Think about a time when you referred to a map to find a place you had never visited before. Write two paragraphs describing the route you took and the scenery you saw during the trip.

ANSWERS WILL VARY.

APPLYING IDEAS IN BAR GRAPHS

Bar graphs make it easy to compare quantities. The longer the bar, the greater the quantity being measured. Bar graphs have two axes: the horizontal axis across the bottom and the vertical axis along the side. Generally, each axis is labeled and has a certain value.

To read a bar graph, you have to be able to tell the value at the top of the vertical bar. Read across from the top of the bar to the axis at its side. Sometimes the line across from the top of a vertical bar does not meet an exact value. You must then estimate your answer.

Use the graph below to practice reading bar graphs. Put a check in front of the correct answer to the questions that follow.

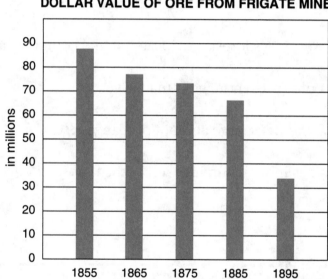

DOLLAR VALUE OF ORE FROM FRIGATE MINE

1. In which year was the dollar value of ore taken from the mine at the lowest point?

_____ **(1)** 1865

_____ **(2)** 1875

_____ **(3)** 1885

_____ **(4)** 1895

2. What was the approximate dollar value of ore taken from the mine in 1865?

____ **(1)** $80 thousand

____ **(2)** $70 thousand

____ **(3)** $78 million

____ **(4)** $80 million

3. The greatest decline in the value of ore taken from the mine took place between

____ **(1)** 1855 and 1865

____ **(2)** 1865 and 1875

____ **(3)** 1875 and 1885

____ **(4)** 1885 and 1895

4. In which year was the dollar value of ore taken from the mine about $67 million?

____ **(1)** 1855

____ **(2)** 1865

____ **(3)** 1875

____ **(4)** 1885

To answer the first question, the shortest bar is above the year *1895,* choice (4), indicating the smallest dollar value for that year.

To answer the second question, find the bar labeled "1865" across the horizontal axis. Then read across from the top of the bar at 1865 to the points on the vertical axis. The top of the bar falls between "70" and "80," more than halfway up. Choice (3), *$78 million,* is correct.

The third question asks you to compare the dollar value of ore in two different years. The greatest decline occurs between *1885 and 1895,* choice (4).

For the fourth question, the bar for *1885,* choice (4), reached to about the $67 million mark.

EXERCISE 3

Directions: Study the bar graph shown below. Then fill in the blanks with the correct answers.

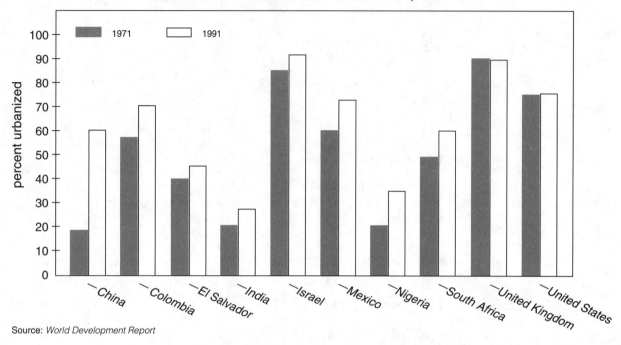

URBANIZATION IN SELECTED COUNTRIES, 1971–1991

Source: *World Development Report*

1. China and India are the countries with the greatest number of people. Which of the two had the greatest increase of urbanizaton from 1971 to 1991?

_____

2. Which two countries experienced the least change in urbanization during this period?

_____

3. Which country had the highest level of urbanization in 1991?

_____

4. Which two countries were slightly less than 20 percent urbanized in 1971?

_____

5. Which two countries had about the same percent of urbanization as the United States in 1991?

_____

6. About how much did South Africa's urbanization rate increase from 1971 to 1991?

_____

7. Which country had a higher percentage of urbanization in 1991—the United Kingdom or the United States?

_____

8. Which country was the most urbanized in 1971—Nigeria or El Salvador?

_____

9. In which year was Colombia's urbanization rate at about 70 percent?

_____

10. What can you infer from the figures for all countries during the years of 1971 to 1991?

_____

_____

ANSWERS ARE ON PAGE 298.

Questions 1–7 are based on the graphs below and the information given about them.

Notice that the graph on the left is labeled "millions" on the vertical axis. The graph on the right is labeled "thousands." In order to find the number of casualties, you need to multiply each number by 1,000. For example, in World War I there were 320,000 casualties.

CASUALTIES IN PRINCIPAL U.S. WARS

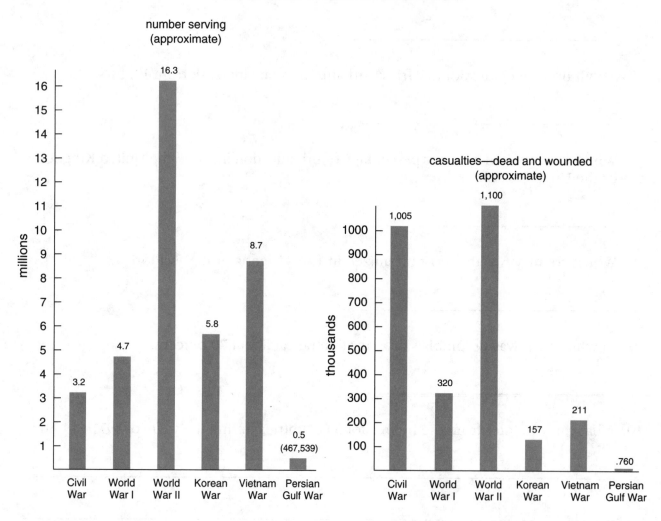

1. The fewest number of casualties occurred in which two wars?

   (1) Korean War and Vietnam War
   (2) Korean War and Persian Gulf War
   (3) World War I and World War II
   (4) World War I and Persian Gulf War
   (5) World War II and Korean War

2. Which war had the greatest number of casualties compared with the number of soldiers serving?

   (1) Civil War
   (2) World War I
   (3) World War II
   (4) Korean War
   (5) Persian Gulf War

3. In which war did the fewest number of soldiers serve?

   (1) Civil War
   (2) World War I
   (3) Korean War
   (4) Vietnam War
   (5) Persian Gulf War

4. In which two wars did the greatest number of casualties occur?

   (1) World War I and Persian Gulf War
   (2) World War II and Korean War
   (3) Civil War and World War II
   (4) World War I and Vietnam War
   (5) World War II and Persian Gulf War

5. About how many persons served in the Vietnam War?

   (1) 468 thousand
   (2) 3 million
   (3) 4.5 million
   (4) 6 million
   (5) 8.7 million

6. About how many casualties occurred during World War I?

   (1) 157 thousand
   (2) 211 thousand
   (3) 320 thousand
   (4) 1 million, 5 thousand
   (5) 1 million, 100 thousand

7. The data on the graphs support which of the following conclusions?

   (1) Modern weapon systems have accounted for a great increase in casualties.
   (2) The greatest number of American casualties took place during the Civil War and World War II.
   (3) Modern medical techniques have failed to save lives on the battlefield.
   (4) American war casualties have increased steadily during the twentieth century.
   (5) Modern military technology has resulted in a decline in casualties.

Questions 8–11 are based on the following map.

NATIVE AMERICANS OF NORTH AMERICA

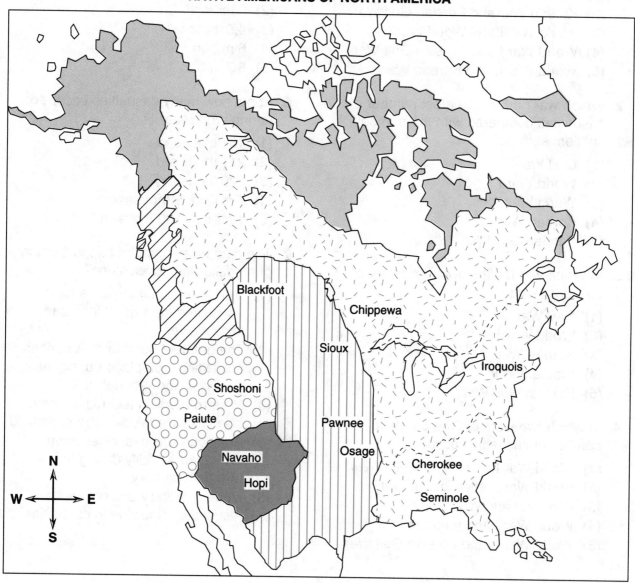

8. The Pawnee were part of the

(1) Eskimo and Aleut
(2) Eastern Forest Indians
(3) Plains Indians
(4) Northwest Coast Indians
(5) Southwest Indians

9. The far north of the continent was inhabited by which group or groups?

(1) Eskimo and Aleut
(2) Eastern Forest Indians
(3) Plains Indians
(4) Northwest Coast Indians
(5) Southwest Indians

10. Which of the following tribes was Southwest Indians?

(1) Cree
(2) Paiute
(3) Cherokee
(4) Sioux
(5) Hopi

11. The Cherokee were part of the

(1) Eastern Forest Indians
(2) Plains Indians
(3) Northwest Coast Indians
(4) California–Intermountain Indians
(5) Southwest Indians

Questions 12 and 13 are based on the following graph.

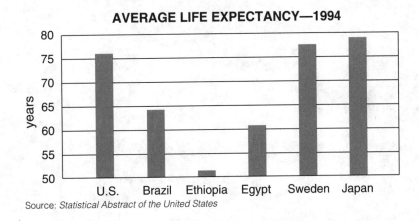

AVERAGE LIFE EXPECTANCY—1994

Source: *Statistical Abstract of the United States*

12. Which statement is best supported by the graph?

(1) All the people in the nations shown have a shorter life expectancy than people in the United States.
(2) The average person in Japan lives about ten years longer than the average person in Ethiopia.
(3) People in the Western Hemisphere live longer than people in the Eastern Hemisphere.
(4) The nation with a life expectancy most similar to the United States is Sweden.
(5) People lived longer in 1994 than they did in 1900.

13. Which nations have the longest life expectancy?

(1) United States, Egypt, and Sweden
(2) United States, Japan, and Brazil
(3) Japan, Sweden, and United States
(4) Sweden, United States, and Brazil
(5) Sweden, Japan, and Brazil

ANSWERS ARE ON PAGE 298.

3 Analyzing Social Studies Materials

When you *analyze* something, you break it down into its basic parts. In social studies, you look at how material is organized to better understand the meaning of the whole passage or graphic. In this chapter, you will learn how to analyze social studies materials in these ways:

- comparing and contrasting ideas

- identifying cause-and-effect relationships

- finding out the sequence of events

- making inferences

- drawing conclusions

COMPARISON AND CONTRAST

Writers use *comparison* when they want to examine similarities, or how things are alike, and *contrast* to look at differences between people, things, or ideas. For example, a social studies passage might compare and contrast various countries.

To show how countries are alike or different, such things as land use, number of cities, rivers, and lakes, natural resources, climate and vegetation, languages, peoples, cultural customs, art, music, architecture, economic systems, types of industry, population patterns, religions, places of interest, educational systems, imports and exports, and types of government might be compared and contrasted.

EXERCISE 1

Directions: Use the information in the passage below to fill in the chart that follows.

Rich and Poor in the Cities

American cities are returning to a pattern similar to that of European cities during the Middle Ages. At that time, the rich and their servants lived in the inner city. The working classes and the poor lived on the city's outer edge.

In the United States for much of the twentieth century, wealthy people have lived in the suburbs and the poor have lived in the inner cities. However, in recent years, wealthy people have begun to move back to the central part of cities like New York and Chicago. Run-down living units are gradually being rehabbed for people with higher income levels. This move is called *gentrification*. The process of gentrification has restored parts of the downtown areas and the inner cities. At the same time, it has pushed the poor to live in the outer edges of the city or in the older suburbs.

CHANGES IN LIVING PATTERNS OVER TIME

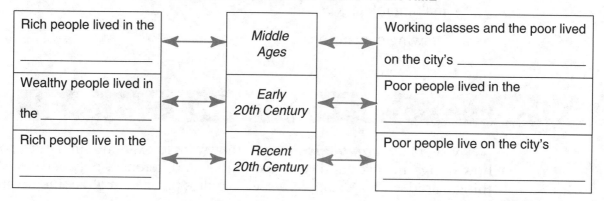

ANSWERS ARE ON PAGE 299.

INFORMATION IN TABLES

A **table** is a list of numbers placed in columns and rows to make it easier to make comparisons. A table has a title at the top. The separate columns and rows within the table are also labeled. This way you will know what information they contain.

Look at the table on the next page. What does the table title tell you? The title tells you that the table has information on the amount of money the winners in Senate elections spent on their election campaigns.

The column headings at the top tell you that these figures cover the elections of 1976, 1984, and 1990. The row headings on the left tell you how much money was raised and how much money was spent.

**FINANCIAL ACTIVITY OF WINNING
SENATE CANDIDATES**
(in millions of dollars)

	1976	1984	1990
raised	$21.0	$100.9	$121.5
spent	$20.1	$97.5	$115.4

See how well you do in reading this table by answering the questions below.

1. How much more money was raised in 1990 than in 1976?

_____

2. Did the winning candidates in the years shown spend more money or less money than they raised?

_____

3. What kind of trend for senatorial election campaigns do the figures indicate?

_____

4. What other figures would you need to determine whether this increased spending pays off for the winning candidates?

_____

The answer to the first question is *$100.5 million.* Look at the columns with the headings "1976" and "1990." Then read across the left-hand row labeled "raised" to the two columns. The difference between the $121.5 million raised in 1990 and $21.0 million raised in 1976 is $100.5 million.

The answer to question 2 is *less money than they raised.* If you compare the "raised" and "spent" columns for all three election years, you will see that the winning candidates raised more money than they spent. The year 1976 was close, however, with a $900,000 difference.

The answer to the third question is that *candidates have been raising greater sums of money to win the election from 1976 to 1990.* To answer question 4, you would need to know *how much the losing candidates spent.*

EXERCISE 2

Directions: Study the table below and then put a check in front of the correct answer to the questions that follow.

**CONSUMPTION OF MAJOR FOOD COMMODITIES
IN THE UNITED STATES PER PERSON PER YEAR**
(in pounds)

	1970	1980	1990
red meat	132.0	126.4	112.4
fish	11.7	12.4	15.0
poultry products	33.8	40.6	55.9
eggs (number per year)	309.0	271.0	233.0
fats and oils	52.6	57.2	62.7
fresh fruit	79.4	87.0	92.6
selected fresh vegetables	88.8	92.7	110.9

1. The food category in which consumption rose by more than 50 percent from 1970 to 1990 was

   _____ **(1)** red meat

   _____ **(2)** fish

   _____ **(3)** poultry products

   _____ **(4)** fresh fruit

2. The information in the table supports which of the following conclusions?

   _____ **(1)** Most Americans are becoming vegetarians.

   _____ **(2)** Americans are consuming less meat and more fruits and vegetables.

   _____ **(3)** Americans consume too much sugar and salt.

   _____ **(4)** The price of fresh vegetables has risen by 50 percent.

3. From 1980 to 1990, Americans ate

_____ **(1)** fewer eggs and less chicken

_____ **(2)** fewer eggs and more red meat

_____ **(3)** more eggs and less chicken

_____ **(4)** more fresh fruit and more fish

4. Americans decreased the consumption of which of the following foods between 1970 and 1990?

_____ **(1)** poultry products

_____ **(2)** fresh fruit

_____ **(3)** red meat

_____ **(4)** selected fresh vegetables

ANSWERS ARE ON PAGE 299.

CAUSE AND EFFECT

Writers frequently use a ***cause-and-effect*** pattern to organize social studies passages. They show how one event causes another event to happen. For example, the introduction of new technology has led to greater productivity for some companies. So a positive outcome has resulted. On the other hand, because the new technology allows machines to do much of the work that people had done in the past, workers in many industries are now out of work (a negative effect).

CAUSES		**EFFECTS**
development of new technology	→	more productivity
machines replace people	→	increased unemployment

How do you identify a cause-and-effect relationship? A good way to do so is to look for key words and phrases such as *because, since, therefore, as a result, consequently, if . . . then, the reason was, led to, the outcome was, the result was, brought about, was responsible for,* and *accordingly.*

☰ PRE-GED Practice ☰
EXERCISE 3

Questions 1 and 2 are based on the passage below.

Population Growth in the Third World

The term *Third World* refers to the developing nations. These are the poorest countries in the world. Unlike the United States, they do not have large industries. These countries remain largely agricultural, depending on farmland for survival.

In recent years, public health measures have greatly influenced the rapid growth of Third World populations. United Nations health efforts have had a big impact on controlling malaria, yellow fever, and other diseases. One result has been a great drop in infant mortality (the death rate of babies in the first year of life). In some countries, the infant mortality rate has dropped from 200 to 50 deaths per 1,000 births. This rapid decline in infant mortality is the main reason for increased population growth. Even further growth is expected because more young women will reach child-bearing age.

1. What has been a major cause of the reduction in infant mortality?

   (1) more young women now at child-bearing age
   (2) public health measures that help control diseases
   (3) increased population growth
   (4) better food and housing conditions
   (5) malaria, yellow fever, and other diseases

2. What effect will increased survival of infants have on future population growth?

   (1) reduce it by increasing the demand for effective family planning
   (2) increase it because more young women will reach child-bearing age
   (3) decrease the number of child-bearing women
   (4) reduce population growth because it causes food shortages
   (5) reduce the need for public health measures

ANSWERS ARE ON PAGE 299.

SEQUENCE OF EVENTS

Many social studies writers use a ***sequence-of-events*** approach to organize information. Presenting events in the order in which they happened is especially common in history passages or time lines. As you read these materials, you need to keep in mind the series of events that the writer describes. Writers often use key words such as *first, second, third, before, after, next, then,* and *finally.*

PRE-GED Practice
EXERCISE 4

Questions 1 and 2 are based on the passage below.

The Cuban Missile Crisis

In October 1962, an American spy plane—the U-2—found signs of Soviet nuclear missile bases in Cuba. President Kennedy began a U.S. naval blockade of Cuba. He also threatened to invade Cuba and strike back at the Soviet Union, as Russia was known then, if the Soviets began an attack on the United States from the Cuban bases.

When the Soviets were shown photographs of the bases, they agreed to negotiate with the United States. First, the Soviets offered to remove their bases from Cuba if the United States removed its missiles from Turkey. But the United States refused to do so. Then, the Soviet Union agreed to withdraw the missiles and tear down its bases in Cuba. In turn, the United States ended its blockade and agreed not to invade Cuba.

1. When did the United States blockade Cuba?

    (1) when the Soviets asked the United States to remove its missiles from Turkey
    (2) when the Soviet Union first set up missile bases
    (3) when U.S.–Soviet negotiations broke down
    (4) when the United States discovered signs of Soviet nuclear missile bases in Cuba
    (5) when Cuba launched an attack from its bases

2. When did the United States end the blockade?

    (1) after the missile bases were dismantled
    (2) when the Soviet Union agreed to negotiate
    (3) before the Soviet Union agreed to dismantle its bases
    (4) when the Soviet Union removed the missiles from the bases
    (5) when the Soviet Union threatened to attack the United States

ANSWERS ARE ON PAGE 299.

WRITING ACTIVITY 3

Think about two countries that are currently at war or have fought with each other in the past. Write one paragraph explaining the causes of the war. Write a second paragraph describing the effects of the war on the countries' people, lands, and culture.

ANSWERS WILL VARY.

IDEAS IN LINE GRAPHS

Line graphs show how one or more items of information have changed over time. A line graph has a series of connected points. Each point represents a value at a particular point in time. The points are then connected by a line. The line's movement up or down on the graph shows a trend. Like a bar graph, a line graph is plotted on a pair of axes. You can read down to find a value on the bottom (horizontal) axis. You can read across to find a value on the side (vertical) axis.

The following graph shows the growth of world trade and world output, or production. Circle *T* if the statement is true, or *F* if it is false.

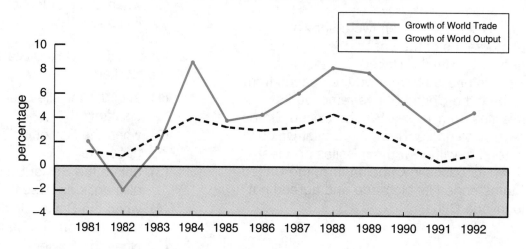

GROWTH OF WORLD TRADE AND OUTPUT

T F **1.** World trade fell below world output in 1982.

T F **2.** The lowest percentage of growth in world output took place in 1992.

T F **3.** The percentage of growth in world trade and world output was about the same in 1984.

T F **4.** The growth in world output reached its highest points in 1984 and 1988.

T F **5.** The percentage of growth in world trade has been above world output ever since 1984.

T F **6.** The percentage of growth in world trade fell below 0 percent in 1982.

T F **7.** The percentage of growth in world output remained at about the same level between 1988 and 1992.

T F **8.** The percentage of growth in world trade reached its highest point at over 8 percent in 1984.

Statement 1 is *true.* The line showing world trade dropped to -2 percent. World output fell only slightly in 1982 to about 1 percent.

Statement 2 is *false.* The lowest percentage of growth took place in 1991, not 1992. World output was moving up in 1992.

Statement 3 is also *false.* In 1984, world trade reached its highest point in the years covered—more than 8 percent. World output grew only 4 percent.

Statement 4 is *true.* The line showing world output is clearly at its two highest points in 1984 and 1988.

Statement 5 is also *true.* Follow the line for world trade. You will see that it is above the line showing world output from 1984 to 1992.

Statement 6 is also *true.* The line for world trade fell to about -2 percent in 1982.

Statement 7 is *false.* The line showing world output consistently fell between 1988 and 1991 and rose slightly in 1992.

Statement 8 is *true.* The line for world trade rose slightly above the 8 percent level in 1984.

EXERCISE 5

Directions: Study the table to see which of the following four graphs matches it. Then put a check in front of the correct answer to the questions that follow.

PER CAPITA INCOME

in constant (1991) dollars

1982	$ 12,794
1983	13,057
1984	13,539
1985	13,940
1986	14,502
1987	14,856
1988	15,109
1989	15,439
1990	14,992
1991	14,617

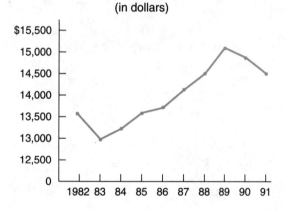

1) PER CAPITA INCOME TRENDS IN THE U.S.
(in dollars)

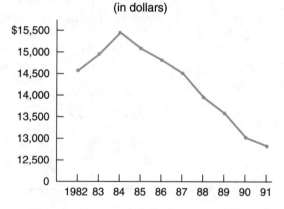

3) PER CAPITA INCOME TRENDS IN THE U.S.
(in dollars)

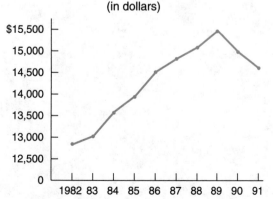

2) PER CAPITA INCOME TRENDS IN THE U.S.
(in dollars)

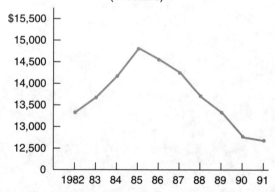

4) PER CAPITA INCOME TRENDS IN THE U.S.
(in dollars)

1. In which year was U.S. per capita income at its highest?

____**(1)** 1983

____**(2)** 1984

____**(3)** 1988

____**(4)** 1989

2. Which line graph sums up the table data most accurately?

____**(1)** graph 1

____**(2)** graph 2

____**(3)** graph 3

____**(4)** graph 4

3. About how much did per capita income increase between 1982 and 1991?

____**(1)** $1,000

____**(2)** $2,000

____**(3)** $3,000

____**(4)** $4,000

4. Which of the following is the best inference based on the data given in the table and the graph that represents it?

____**(1)** Economic problems caused per capita income in the United States to drop in 1990 after steady upward growth in the 1980s.

____**(2)** The number of people receiving unemployment rose during the entire period.

____**(3)** Good times caused U.S. per capita income to rise throughout the period.

____**(4)** The way Americans lived got worse when per capita income began to fall.

ANSWERS ARE ON PAGE 299.

EXERCISE 6

Directions: Study the two graphs below. Then answer the questions in the space provided.

POLITICAL DIVISION IN THE U.S. CONGRESS
1981–1995

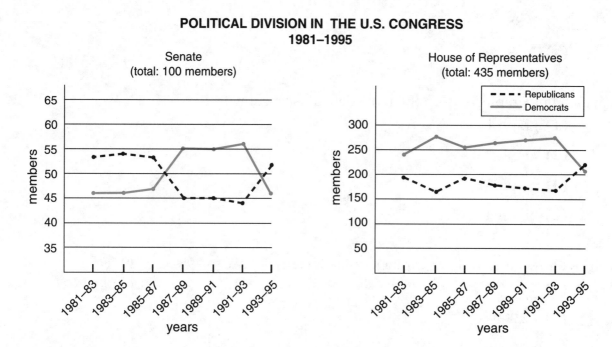

1. During which two-year period did the Democrats first control the Senate?

   _____

2. In which years was the number of Republicans in the House of Representatives the greatest?

   _____

3. Did the Republicans gain control of the House of Representatives at any time from 1981 to 1995?

   _____

4. During which years was Democratic membership in the Senate the lowest?

   _____

5. Did Republican membership in the Senate decline or increase from 1993 to 1995?

   _____

ANSWERS ARE ON PAGE 299.

INFERENCES

In a previous chapter, you learned how to identify the main idea and locate supporting details. This type of reading skill is called **literal understanding**. It simply requires that you go back to the passage and understand information that is stated directly. Making **inferences** requires a reader to go beyond the directly stated information and find a meaning that is only suggested. An inference is a form of "educated guess" based on facts. Before you make an inference, you must be very sure of what the passage is stating directly.

Below is a short paragraph. The question that follows asks for an inference.

There is some evidence that people who take sleeping pills over long periods of time become irritable or depressed. One possible explanation is that sleeping pills inhibit normal dreaming. Thus, many doctors do not recommend the consistent use of sleeping pills.

Based on the passage, what inference can you make about dreaming?

_____ **1.** Dreaming makes people depressed and irritable.

_____ **2.** Too much dreaming is abnormal.

_____ **3.** Not everyone needs to dream.

_____ **4.** Sleeping pills do not affect dreaming.

_____ **5.** Dreaming may be necessary for good mental health.

_____ **6.** The sale of sleeping pills should be banned.

_____ **7.** Most people have normal dreams.

_____ **8.** Some sleeping pills are more harmful than others.

_____ **9.** People often dream in color after taking sleeping pills.

_____**10.** Anyone who takes a sleeping pill gets depressed.

The answer is (5). The paragraph shows a connection between the restraint of normal dreaming and irritability or depression. From this connection, you can infer that normal dreaming promotes mental well-being.

≡ PRE-GED Practice ≡
EXERCISE 7

Questions 1 and 2 are based on the paragraph below.

Until recently, the Catholic Church was tied very closely to the Spanish government. This meant that divorce and abortion were illegal. The Catholic religion was taught in schools. After the death of General Franco in 1975, the ties between church and state came apart. In 1978, a new constitution did away with the church's official position. While the Catholic Church was still an important institution, religion seemed to have become less important in people's daily lives.

1. What can you infer about religion in Spain?

    (1) Catholicism is the religion of a small majority of people in Spain.
    (2) Catholicism is the traditional religion of Spain.
    (3) Only the rich and powerful are Catholic.
    (4) People in Spain have no special religious affiliation.
    (5) Catholicism continues to guide the government of Spain.

2. What can you infer about Franco's government?

    (1) The government supported legal divorce and abortion.
    (2) The government gave the Catholic Church a special place under its constitution.
    (3) The government gave no special place to the Catholic Church under its constitution.
    (4) The government supported legal abortion, but not divorce.
    (5) The government supported legal divorce, but not abortion.

Questions 3 and 4 are based on the paragraph below.

Because of over 400 miles of coastline in Rhode Island, water is its most abundant natural resource. Naragansett Bay forms an open door for trade in the Atlantic Ocean. It is also a popular recreation area that attracts many tourists. Several valuable fisheries are located in this area. Rhode Island is the world's leading costume-jewelry center and the home of the leading silversmiths in the United States. This state is also known for its manufacturing of fabricated metals, machinery, electrical and electronic equipment, and ships and boats.

3. Which of the following is probably NOT a popular sport in Rhode Island?

    (1) water skiing
    (2) swimming
    (3) boating
    (4) fishing
    (5) downhill snow skiing

4. Rhode Island is known for all of the following industries EXCEPT

    (1) silversmithing
    (2) metal fabricating
    (3) machine technology
    (4) foresting timber
    (5) making costume jewelry

ANSWERS ARE ON PAGE 300.

DRAWING CONCLUSIONS

The ability to draw conclusions is an important inference skill. You ***draw a conclusion*** when you predict the outcome of events or determine the relationship of facts in a passage.

What conclusion can be drawn from the following passage?

> The federal government borrows large amounts of money for its spending. This causes the supply of available money for loans to become tightened. Interest rates for borrowing tend to rise. Thus, when companies borrow money, they pay more in interest. Companies usually pass this extra cost along to consumers.

If the government borrows a lot of money to finance a big increase in spending, what might happen to consumer prices?

Put a check in front of the correct conclusion.

_____ **(1)** Prices would fall. ·

_____ **(2)** Prices would rise.

_____ **(3)** Prices would fall and then rise.

_____ **(4)** Prices would rise and then fall.

_____ **(5)** Prices would stay the same.

The correct conclusion is *(2), prices would rise.* The facts show that large-scale government borrowing leads to higher interest rates. Companies must spend more money when they borrow, so they usually raise their prices to make up the difference.

PRE-GED Practice
EXERCISE 8

Questions 1 and 2 are based on the passage below.

Credit Cards

There are advantages and disadvantages to having and using a credit card. On the positive side, a credit card, if used wisely, can be a wonderful convenience. You never have to worry about having ready cash when you want to buy something. You also don't have to pay the full price for an item right away. Instead, you can pay in monthly installments. You always have to pay either the full cost or a part of it when you get your credit card bill each month.

On the negative side, if you pay only part of your credit card bill, you'll be charged interest on the remaining amount. You will continue to pay interest until you pay the total amount you owe. You can end up spending much more for your purchase than if you had paid cash. So think twice before you charge big-ticket items with your credit card.

1. Which piece of advice is based on this passage?
   (1) Use credit cards because they are cheaper.
   (2) Never use a credit card because you pay more.
   (3) Make sure that you can afford to pay monthly installments.
   (4) Always use cash because it is easier.
   (5) Use credit cards as a way to establish good credit.

2. A disadvantage to buying with credit cards is that
   (1) you will never have cash on hand
   (2) you may forget to carry the cards with you
   (3) you may underestimate how much you will pay for an item in the long run
   (4) interest rates are rising
   (5) it is difficult to establish credit

Question 3 is based on the paragraph below.

In the 1920s, psychologists Hugh Hartshorne and Mark May studied the development of honesty by testing 11,000 children. Hartshorne and May saw the children imitating adult and peer models a great deal. In other words, they found that the children did what they saw others do, not what they were told to do. If the children were surrounded by lying, cheating, and stealing, they tended to lie, cheat, and steal. If the people they imitated were honest, they tended to be honest.

3. According to Hartshorne and May, children are likely to be honest if
   (1) they are often in social situations
   (2) the people around them are honest
   (3) they are told they should be honest
   (4) their families have plenty of money
   (5) they are punished for dishonesty

Questions 4 and 5 are based on the graph below.

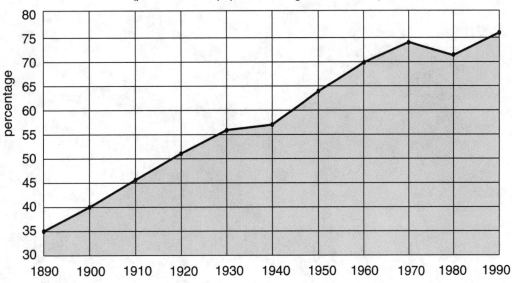

AMERICA MOVES TO THE CITIES
(percent of U.S. population living in urban areas)

Source: *Statistical Abstract of the United States*

4. Which statement about the graph is NOT true?

(1) More people lived in urban areas in 1990 than in 1890.

(2) Fewer people lived in urban areas in 1900 than in 1910.

(3) The percent of people living in urban areas increased by about 4 percent from 1960 to 1970.

(4) The decades with the lowest percent of increase in people living in urban areas were 1970 and 1980.

(5) The percent of people living in urban areas almost doubled between 1900 and 1950.

5. Which of the following conclusions is best shown by this graph?

(1) The percentage of people living in urban areas of the United States has steadily fallen.

(2) The percentage of people living in rural areas of the United States has steadily risen.

(3) The percentage of people living in a few major cities in the United States has risen greatly.

(4) The percentage of people living in urban areas of the United States has risen greatly.

(5) More people lived in the northeastern part of the United States in 1990 than in 1900.

ANSWERS ARE ON PAGE 300.

4 Evaluating Social Studies Materials

When you read, you **evaluate**, or judge the value or logic of an idea. You often ask yourself if you have enough information to answer a question or solve a problem. You also ask if the information you have is what you need.

For example, when you are thinking about buying a new car, you evaluate your financial situation and your transportation needs before you go out and look for the best deal. You judge to see if various cars are well made, how much they cost, and what features are offered with the car and which ones you will have to pay extra for. You ask which repairs are covered under warranty and what the loan rates are.

You also evaluate information when you read social studies passages, charts, maps, graphs, and political cartoons. You decide if the information is accurate or if it is based on sound logic.

In this section, you will learn how to evaluate social studies materials by:

- distinguishing fact from opinion

- identifying faulty logic

- recognizing tone

- interpreting editorial cartoons

FACT AND OPINION

A **fact** is a statement that can be proved. An **opinion** is a personal belief or feeling that cannot be proved. If someone believes that something is true, it still has to be proven to be a fact. Every day you read and hear both facts and opinions. At times you may have to give some thought as to which is which. When you read social studies material, take note of whether a statement you read is fact or opinion. Can a statement be proved? Or is it something the author believes but cannot prove?

One of the following two statements is a fact; the other is an opinion. Write *F* before the statement that is a fact and *O* before the statement that is an opinion.

_____ **1.** The U.S. Constitution is the greatest political document ever written.

_____ **2.** Twenty-six amendments have been added to the U.S. Constitution.

You were right if you thought the first statement was an opinion. The word *greatest* shows that the writer is expressing an opinion. The second statement is a fact that can be checked by looking at a copy of the Constitution.

EXERCISE 1

Directions: Read the statements below. Write *F* if the sentence is a fact, or *O* if the statement is an opinion.

_____ **1.** The United States is a democracy in which people elect their government officials.

_____ **2.** Democracy is the best form of government.

_____ **3.** Local governments mismanage their responsibilities of police and fire protection.

_____ **4.** Local governments have responsibility for the public schools.

_____ **5.** All citizens over the age of eighteen have the right to register and vote.

_____ **6.** The vice president has the most unimportant job in the entire federal government.

_____ **7.** If the president dies in office, the vice president becomes the new president.

ANSWERS ARE ON PAGE 300.

EVALUATION OF LOGIC

After reading a passage ask yourself, "Does the writer make sense? Are the ideas logical?" To answer these questions, you must use ***evaluation of logic***. This is another inferential reading skill, in which you make a judgment of the way writers present and use their ideas. When evaluating logic, you may have to draw on any or all of the reading skills you have learned.

Probably the most important part of evaluating logic is judging the writer's logical consistency. ***Logical consistency*** means the writer's use of sound reasoning in developing an idea. You should especially be aware of the following two points.

- A writer's facts should support his or her conclusions.

- A writer should correctly apply his or her own ideas.

Read the passage below and put a check in front of the statement that is supported by the passage.

Critics of government assistance programs for the poor often claim that such aid does not work. However, nationwide studies show that students who participated in pre-school Head Start programs showed improvement in their school performance in later grades.

_____**(1)** Increased spending on education does not improve performance.

_____**(2)** Early help in education has no relation to later performance.

_____**(3)** Pre-school children do well in later grades without these programs.

_____**(4)** Early help in education can affect later academic performance.

The details in the passage support statement *(4)*. The passage states that children who participated in pre-school Head Start programs showed improved school performance in later grades. The details in the passage do not support any of the other statements.

EXERCISE 2

Directions: Read the passage below and put a check in front of the correct answer to the questions that follow.

The Rising Crime Rate

The soaring crime rate affects everyone in the United States. One explanation for the rise in crime is that society offers too many rewards for the criminal and too few reasons for people to do honest work. Many people turn to crime because they think of it as a quick way to get what they want. Crime must be made less desirable and work more attractive.

Another explanation is that most crime results from economic and social conditions. These conditions affect men and women who are unable to better their lives. They feel hopeless in a society that promises an equal chance for everyone.

1. Which conclusion is supported by the details in the passage?

   _____(1) Crime does not pay.

   _____(2) The rise in the crime rate has more than one cause.

   _____(3) Getting rid of poverty would mean an end to crime.

   _____(4) The crime rate is rising because society is too easy on lawbreakers.

2. According to the passage, different views of the causes of crime reflect different ideas about

   _____(1) work

   _____(2) the influences of society

   _____(3) law enforcement

   _____(4) the criminal justice system

ANSWERS ARE ON PAGE 300.

TONE

A writer uses tone to influence the reader's reaction to a situation. **_Tone_** refers to a writer's own bias or opinion about a subject. Feelings such as delight or anger sometimes can be detected in a piece of writing. However, not all writing gives away the author's feelings. Many writers are straightforward and objective.

To recognize tone in writing, you must analyze the way a selection is written and the feeling that underlies it. Pay careful attention to the writer's choice of words. Look at the two paragraphs below.

Paragraph 1

Starvation is rampant, and hunger haunts the humble hovels of the needy. Will nothing be done about this? How can people continue to support a government that ignores the needs of the poor?

Paragraph 2

Not long ago, concern about hunger focused on the world's poorer nations. Lately, hunger has become an issue in the United States. Many people accuse the government of making the problem worse by cutting back on programs that help the poor. The government denies these charges, saying that it has always provided assistance to the needy.

In paragraph 1, the writer's tone is angry. Notice the writer's words. "Starvation is rampant"; "hunger haunts the humble hovels" (not homes) of the poor; the government "ignores the needs of the poor." The goal of the first writer is to make the reader angry and upset about the hungry poor.

Paragraph 2 has an objective tone. The writer's own feelings are not clear. The words "hunger," "the issue," and "the needy" are not charged with emotion. The writer simply reports the opinions of two different sides on the subject of government responsibility for hunger.

EXERCISE 3

Directions: Read the following passage and put a check in front of the correct answer to the questions that follow.

We could see the two principal characters approaching the Senate chamber from opposite directions. The senator from North Carolina strode briskly and with confidence toward the Senate floor. He chatted amiably with reporters about strategy for the debate. Meanwhile, the senator from New York darted into sight and scurried down the hallway. He paused briefly to huddle nervously with his assistants about maneuvers in the debate.

1. Based on the passage, the writer

_____ **(1)** does not admire either senator

_____ **(2)** likes the North Carolina senator but dislikes the New York senator

_____ **(3)** has no feeling about either senator

_____ **(4)** dislikes the North Carolina senator but likes the New York senator

2. Which word has a positive feel to it?

_____ **(1)** darted

_____ **(2)** scurried

_____ **(3)** amiably

_____ **(4)** nervously

ANSWERS ARE ON PAGE 300.

EDITORIAL CARTOONS

Cartoonists make fun of individuals, governments, and businesses by drawing them in a humorous or ridiculous way. *Editorial* or *political cartoons* express an opinion and bring attention to a social or political problem. Cartoonists make great use of irony—showing things in a way that is the opposite from the way they really are. Editorial or political cartoons have a main idea. They express the opinion of the artist.

When looking at an editorial or political cartoon, pay attention to the following features:

- the title or caption

- the characters (may be real people or symbols such as Uncle Sam for the United States)

- any labels or conversation (shown in balloons with the words printed inside)

Study the editorial cartoon shown below and put a check in front of the correct answer to the questions that follow.

1. What does the large bulldozer represent?

____**(1)** large business

____**(2)** a construction company

____**(3)** the federal government

____**(4)** city hall

2. What can you infer about the cartoonist's beliefs?

____**(1)** Small businesses will stay open no matter what the tax is.

____**(2)** Unfair taxation will hurt small businesses.

____**(3)** High taxes are fair for small businesses.

____**(4)** Small businesses will sweep away taxes.

For question 1, the bulldozer represents choice (3), *the federal government.* The bulldozer is labeled "taxes." The size of the bulldozer is much larger than needed to tear down the small business. The federal government determines the largest share of the taxes that people and small business pay. So the bulldozer represents the federal government.

For question 2, statement (2) is the best choice. The cartoonist believes that *unfair taxation will hurt small businesses.* The label "Fairness Construction Co." represents the government that levies the tax. The cartoonist uses the name "Fairness" to mean just the opposite, unfairness.

≡ PRE-GED Practice ≡
EXERCISE 4

Questions 1–3 are based on the following passage.

(1) The best political system ever developed is the two-party system of the United States. (2) Since the Civil War, no third party has been able to threaten the political power of either the Democratic Party or the Republican Party. (3) Every president of the last one hundred years has been a member of one of these two parties. (4) No third party has been able to gain control of either house of Congress. (5) The country has been spared the chaos that results when there are more than two parties. (6) And the people have not had to endure the tyranny of one-party rule.

1. Which of the following sentences from the passage are opinions?

    (1) sentences 1, 2, and 3
    (2) sentences 2, 3, and 4
    (3) sentences 3, 4, and 5
    (4) sentences 4, 5, and 6
    (5) sentences 1, 5, and 6

2. Which of the following statements is supported by the passage?

    (1) A third-party candidate could win a national election if he or she had enough money to run a campaign.
    (2) The two-party system is outdated and is in urgent need of change.
    (3) The Republican and the Democratic parties are the only political parties that could be successful in the United States.
    (4) The United States is slowly turning toward a one-party political system.
    (5) Both the Democratic and the Republican parties have considerable strength and support in the United States.

3. Which statement best describes the tone of the passage?

    (1) The passage is completely straightforward and objective.
    (2) The passage reflects the author's bias for the two-party system of the United States.
    (3) The passage starts out being objective, then changes to an emotional tone.
    (4) The tone of the passage is angry and hostile.
    (5) The passage is bias-free.

Question 4 is based on the cartoon below.

4. What is the main idea of this cartoon?

    (1) Smoking is bad for your health.
    (2) Only people who live far away from other people should be allowed to smoke.
    (3) There are getting to be far fewer areas where people are allowed to smoke.
    (4) Automobile exhaust and cigarette smoke pollute the air.
    (5) Smokers won't bother anyone in the desert.

Questions 5 and 6 are based on the cartoon below.

5. What is the main idea of this cartoon?

  (1) People have a hard time cashing their Social Security checks.

  (2) The national debt is higher than ever.

  (3) Bankers have a hard time deciding on good credit risks.

  (4) People should stay away from banks.

  (5) People are worried about the Social Security system going broke.

6. You can infer that the cartoonist

  (1) feels that the nation's economy is strong

  (2) has once worked as a banker

  (3) has little faith in the Social Security system

  (4) opposes loans to the federal government

  (5) feels that the Social Security system should be done away with

ANSWERS ARE ON PAGE 301.

WRITING ACTIVITY 4

    Find an editorial cartoon in a newspaper or a magazine. What is the main idea of the cartoon? What symbols are used in the cartoon? Is the cartoon effective in getting its point across to you? Explain why or why not.

ANSWERS WILL VARY.

UNDERSTANDING SOCIAL STUDIES

- U.S. History
- Political Science
- Behavioral Sciences
- Geography
- Economics

5  U.S. History

In this chapter, you will study U.S. history. You study **history** to learn about important events that happened in the past. You often compare what happened in the past to what is happening now. As you read, try to keep in mind events today that are similar to those of the past. You may find that, indeed, history repeats itself.

EXPLORATION OF THE NEW WORLD: 1492–1783

KEY WORD

indentured servant—one who worked for a specific period of time in the American colonies as payment of a debt

Many European powers explored and settled the Americas, North and South, to find new sources of wealth. Columbus represented Spain when he sailed across the Atlantic in 1492. He was trying to find a new route to India and the Far East. Instead, he found the Western Hemisphere, which Europeans called the New World. After that voyage, Spain took over many of the Caribbean islands, Mexico, and most of Central and South America. Spain took home huge amounts of silver and gold it found in its new colonies.

England and France led the settlement of North America. England established colonies along the Atlantic coast in the 1600s in Jamestown, Virginia; Plymouth, Massachusetts; and Massachusetts Bay. France established settlements in what is now Canada, along the Ohio and Mississippi River valleys, and south to New Orleans near the Gulf of Mexico.

The photo at left shows the historic signing of the U.S. Declaration of Independence

Many of the English colonies were started by Englishmen in search of fortunes. But the colonies were populated by people trying to escape prison or poverty in Europe. Between 50 and 75 percent of the colonists became indentured servants, bound to spend a certain number of years serving a master. This service was usually in payment for their passage to the New World. After this period of service, the indentured servants were free colonists. Slaves, on the other hand, were forcibly imported from Africa for cheap labor, often for a lifetime. They also became a large part of the colonial population. Other colonists, like the Puritans, came to establish religious communities.

NORTH AMERICA PRIOR TO 1763

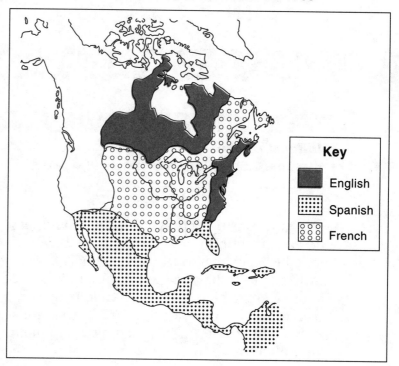

Key

■ English

▦ Spanish

▣ French

EXERCISE 1

Directions: Based on the passage and the map, answer the questions in the space provided.

1. Which person's explorations influenced other countries to explore America?

_____

2. What did Spain find in the New World that was of great value?

_____

3. Why did some people become indentured servants?

_____

4. What is the difference between an indentured servant and a slave?

_____

_____

_____

5. Which country settled in the central part of North America?

_____

6. Which country claimed land in the northern part of North America?

_____

7. Why did the Puritans come to North America?

_____

8. About what percent of the colonists became indentured servants?

_____

9. Which country did Columbus represent when he sailed across the Atlantic?

_____

ANSWERS ARE ON PAGE 301.

DEVELOPMENT OF THE AMERICAN COLONIES

KEY WORDS

mercantilism—seventeenth century practice in which the colonies supplied the mother country with raw materials and became a market for manufactured goods

representative—one who stands or acts for another through delegated authority

The English colonies developed an expanding trade in lumber, tobacco, and other agricultural products. Slave traders also made huge profits from the growing slave trade. The colonists began industries in shipbuilding, textiles, shoes, and iron making. Large and busy towns grew up around the seaports. England controlled trade with the colonies through a policy of mercantilism. England passed laws to slow the growth of colonial industries and to force the colonies to be dependent on England for their manufactured goods.

Each American colony had a governor and an elected representative body to pass laws on taxes and other matters. These representative bodies became the centers of opposition to English colonial policies. As the colonies grew, they tried to expand west. Their expansion was blocked by the French and Indians. The long-standing competition between England and France came to a head during the French and Indian War (1756–1763). France lost the war and almost all of its North American territories to England. France could no longer block westward expansion.

EXERCISE 2

Directions: Put a check in front of the correct answer to the questions that follow.

1. Why did England try to stop the growth of industry in its colonies?

_____**(1)** to make the colonists dependent upon English manufactured goods

_____**(2)** to avoid a war with France

_____**(3)** to make colonists buy English agricultural products

2. Which of the following is true of government in the colonies?

_____**(1)** Governors ran each colony's affairs with an iron hand.

_____**(2)** Representative bodies had no power at all.

_____**(3)** Representative bodies became centers of opposition to English policies.

3. What happened as a result of the French and Indian War?

_____**(1)** The colonists no longer had to pay taxes.

_____**(2)** The policy of mercantilism ended.

_____**(3)** France lost most of its North American territories to England.

4. In the seventeenth century, colonies supplied the mother country with raw materials and

_____**(1)** expanded westward

_____**(2)** bought manufactured goods

_____**(3)** took over Native American territories

ANSWERS ARE ON PAGE 301.

WRITING ACTIVITY 5

Countries often adopted a mercantilist policy to make their economy strong. Colonies existed for the benefit of the mother country. In a few paragraphs, explain how England's colonies in North America did or did not fit into this policy.

ANSWERS WILL VARY.

ROAD TO REVOLUTION AND INDEPENDENCE

KEY WORD

tyranny—a government in which all power is in the hands of a single ruler

---

In 1763, England passed laws to tax the American colonists to help pay for the French and Indian War. The English also believed the colonists should help pay the costs of government. Among the laws were the Sugar Act, the Stamp Act, and the Tea Act. The English also tightened political control over the colonial government and courts. The colonists protested these laws by dumping tea into Boston Harbor (called the Boston Tea Party). Colonial protesters cried out that English rule had become a tyranny. The colonists had no political representation in England, where the tax laws were passed.

The English responded to the Boston Tea Party with the Intolerable Acts. Boston Harbor was closed until the colonists paid for the destroyed tea. Colonists were forced to pay to house English soldiers. The powers of the colonial courts were also cut back. The governor had to approve any town meeting.

In response, the colonists called the First Continental Congress in 1774 to resist English control and to increase their rights. In April 1775, British troops and American colonists fought at Lexington and Concord, Massachusetts. The battles marked the beginning of the American Revolution. The Second Continental Congress met later in 1775. It voted for an army and named George Washington as commander-in-chief. In July 1776, the Congress adopted the Declaration of Independence. The colonists waged a five-year war with England. It ended in 1781, with the surrender of the British at Yorktown, Virginia. Independence was won.

The American Revolution established the principle that government must be based on the consent of the governed. It marked the first time that a European power had lost a colony to an independent movement. The American Revolution influenced the successful slave revolution against the French in Haiti (1795–1803) and later struggles in Latin America against Spanish rule in the early nineteenth century.

EXERCISE 3

Directions: Match the date on the left with the important event that happened in that year on the right. Write the correct letter on the line.

_____ **1.** 1774

_____ **2.** 1775

_____ **3.** 1776

_____ **4.** 1781

_____ **5.** 1795

(a) The British surrendered in Yorktown, Virginia.

(b) The First Continental Congress was called to resist British control over the American colonies.

(c) Slaves began to revolt against the French in Haiti.

(d) The Second Continental Congress voted for an army and appointed Washington as its commander-in-chief.

(e) The Declaration of Independence was adopted.

ANSWERS ARE ON PAGE 301.

EXERCISE 4

Directions: Put a check in front of the correct answer to the questions that follow.

1. The purpose of the Boston Tea Party was to

_____ **(1)** entertain English soldiers

_____ **(2)** celebrate the Tea Act

_____ **(3)** protest unfair British laws in the colonies

2. What effect did the American Revolution have on others?

_____ **(1)** Most other countries took on democratic forms of government.

_____ **(2)** Latin America rebelled against Spain's dominance.

_____ **(3)** The English made several new settlements in colonial America.

ANSWERS ARE ON PAGE 301.

TRIANGULAR TRADE ROUTE

Fifteen million Africans were violently torn away from their homes and forced into slavery in the New World. Many American slave traders followed a triangular trade route. They took rum to Africa to trade for slaves and then sailed across the Atlantic to the West Indies. This second leg of the voyage was the awful "Middle Passage" in which many slaves died. In the West Indies, the slaves were sold for money or traded for molasses. The molasses was taken back to New England and distilled into rum for another trip to Africa.

Slavery proved to be very profitable. Each voyage produced between 100 and 1,000 percent profit. The slave trade provided cheap labor to run plantations in Brazil, the West Indies, and North America. More than 700 American ships were involved, and more than 100 New England distilleries supplied rum for trading. By the eighteenth century, the English controlled the slave trade. Profits were used to finance economic and industrial growth in England during the nineteenth century.

After 1808, it was illegal to bring slaves into the United States. But slavery itself did not end in the United States until after the Civil War.

TRIANGULAR TRADE ROUTE

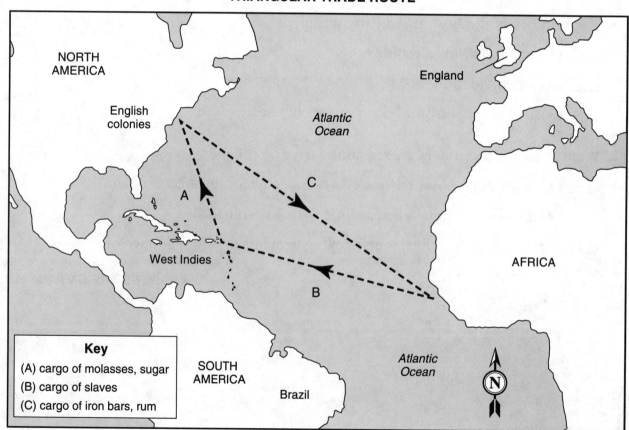

Key
(A) cargo of molasses, sugar
(B) cargo of slaves
(C) cargo of iron bars, rum

EXERCISE 5

Directions: Based on the passage and the map, answer the questions that follow in the space provided.

1. Which three areas formed the basis of the Triangular Trade Route?

   _____

2. Why was molasses important in slave trade business?

   _____

   _____

3. Why were slaves important to the plantation system in colonial America?

   _____

   _____

4. How were American ship owners affected by slavery?

   _____

   _____

5. How did slavery benefit England in the nineteenth century?

   _____

   _____

6. When did slavery end in the United States?

   _____

ANSWERS ARE ON PAGE 301.

WRITING ACTIVITY 6

Write a few paragraphs describing what the Middle Passage might have been like. What hardships did slaves endure? Why would many slaves have died during this leg of the journey?

ANSWERS WILL VARY.

A NEW NATION ESTABLISHES ITSELF

After winning independence from England, great political disagreements took place over how much power should go to the federal government and how much to the states. When a strong Constitution was adopted in 1787, the federal government was able to slowly gain power over the states. The first president, George Washington, organized the various government departments. He also established taxes to pay for running these departments, and set up the federal courts.

The new nation had gained from England most of the land east of the Mississippi River. But disputes continued over forts on the Great Lakes. In 1800, France was back in North America. France got most of the Louisiana Territory from Spain and controlled the Mississippi River. In 1803, President Thomas Jefferson bought the huge territory from the French for $15 million. The area doubled the size of the nation. It also put the Mississippi River firmly under American control.

The War of 1812 was fought over the issue of English interference with American merchant ships. The war ended with no clear winner. U.S. boundaries were unchanged. However, the War of 1812 was important for the United States for two reasons. First, it helped unite Americans by temporarily making national interests more important than sectional, or regional, interests. Second, the war proved that the United States was strong enough militarily to keep its independence. With new land available in the West and the removal of the English threat, the road to westward expansion was finally open.

EXERCISE 6

Directions: Put a check in front of the correct answer to the questions that follow.

1. The new United States faced its most serious problems with

____**(1)** British control of forts along the Mississippi and French control of the Great Lakes

____**(2)** British control of forts on the Great Lakes and Spanish control of the Mississippi

____**(3)** British control of forts on the Great Lakes and French control of the Mississippi

____**(4)** French capture of U.S. merchant ships and British control of the Mississippi

2. As a result of the War of 1812, the United States gained all of the following EXCEPT

____**(1)** a temporary unity around national interests

____**(2)** stronger sectional, or regional, interests

____**(3)** greater military strength

____**(4)** an ability to stay independent

3. Based on the U.S. experience in the War of 1812, you might conclude that governments facing a divided nation have used a war against foreign enemies to

____**(1)** temporarily unite the country

____**(2)** cause more divisions

____**(3)** prevent the growth of nationalism

____**(4)** strengthen the government

ANSWERS ARE ON PAGE 302.

WESTWARD EXPANSION

KEY WORDS

Manifest Destiny—American belief that it was the country's destiny to take over the entire North American continent

annexation—taking over of lands not originally part of a country

From 1800 to 1850, Americans believed that it was their Manifest Destiny to occupy the land from the Atlantic to the Pacific Ocean. The country soon obtained Florida from Spain and Texas from Mexico.

The Mexican government gave grants of land to American settlers in its province of Texas during the 1820s. Later, these settlers rebelled against Mexico. They declared Texas an independent republic in 1836. The brief but fierce war was famous for the battle of the Alamo in San Antonio.

THE UNITED STATES EXPANDS, 1783–1853

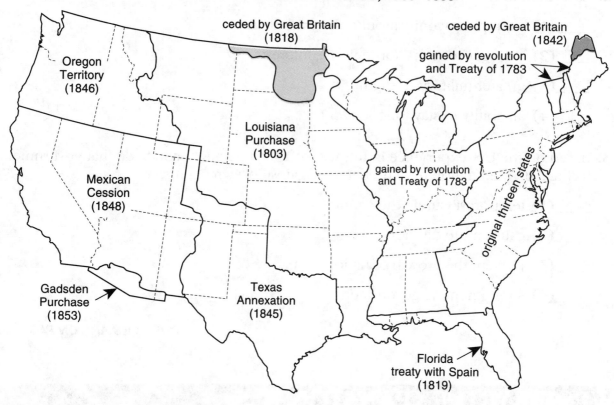

In 1845, the United States annexed Texas as a state. The annexation angered many Mexicans. When U.S. troops occupied a border region claimed by Mexico, the Mexican War began. The United States won the war and took control of even more land. This area now holds California, New Mexico, Arizona, Nevada, Utah, Texas, and parts of Colorado. The United States also reached agreement with England and acquired the Oregon Territory.

The new lands contained rich farmlands and vast pastures for cattle and sheep. There were boundless forests and rich stores of gold, silver, and other minerals. All of these resources contributed greatly to the economic growth of the United States.

ECONOMIC DEVELOPMENT AND SECTIONALISM

KEY WORD

sectionalism—the economic, political, and social differences among the regions of the United States

Economic development was rapid during this period. Canal building and the development of the steamboat gave a big boost to trade and transportation by water. After the 1820s, railroad building became a major economic activity. By 1860, the United States was crisscrossed with 30,000 miles of track.

The growth of the cotton industry brought in more money than all other exports combined. This boom began with Eli Whitney's invention of the cotton gin in the 1790s. The cotton gin cleaned large amounts of cotton so it could be used in manufacturing. The Industrial Revolution had led to the establishment of large, mechanized mills in England and New England to process this cotton. The demand for Southern cotton grew. Cotton was well suited for growing on large plantations. In this way, cotton helped firmly establish slave labor as the basis for the South's economy.

Territorial expansion and the development of different regional economies created political problems. The South was based on slavery and the export of cotton. The West was based on several crops grown on small farms. The North, especially the Northeast, became the region of shipping, finance, and industry. These differences led to the growth of sectional feelings. For example, people were proud to be Southerners or Westerners. Under sectionalism, politicians in each region defended that region's economic interests. The Southern states argued strongly for the rights of states to do as they pleased without federal government interference. The growth of sectionalism was an important cause of the Civil War.

EXERCISE 7

Directions: Study the map. Then put a check in front of the correct answer to the questions that follow.

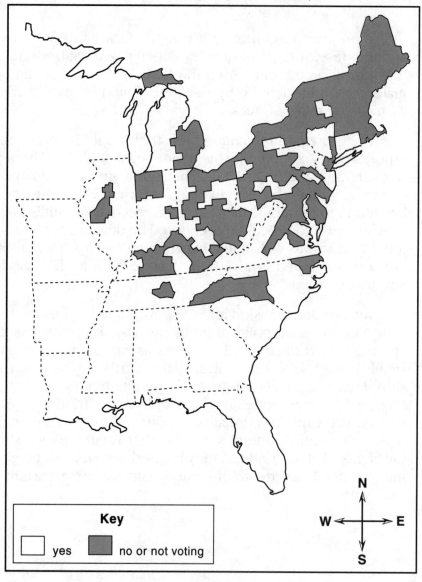

**SECTIONALISM AND THE VOTE IN CONGRESS
ON TEXAS ANNEXATION, 1845**

(vote on passage of joint resolution)

Key

yes no or not voting

1. In which region did most states vote no on the question of the annexation of Texas?

_____**(1)** South

_____**(2)** West

_____**(3)** North

2. Which of the following can you infer from the voting pattern?

_____**(1)** The Northern states were opposed to another slave-owning Southern state in the Union.

_____**(2)** The Northern states supported Mexico's right to Texas.

_____**(3)** The Southern states preferred that Texas stay independent.

_____**(4)** The Northern states feared Texas's industrial competition.

ANSWERS ARE ON PAGE 302.

WRITING ACTIVITY 7

Sectionalism has a long history in the United States. In a few paragraphs, write how sectionalism makes itself known in your region. Explain if sectionalism is more against other regions or more against the federal government.

ANSWERS WILL VARY.

POLITICS AND MOVEMENTS

Modern political parties also developed in the period from 1783 to 1850. They stood for the very real economic and political differences that were developing in the country.

Issues about democratic rights became important during Andrew Jackson's presidency (1829–1837). Before Jacksonian Democracy, most states had required people to own a certain amount of property in order to vote. Now property qualifications for voting were dropped. All white male citizens over the age of twenty-one could vote. Indians, women, and blacks still could not vote.

Reforms of this period also included the popular vote to confirm state constitutions. The filling of public office by elections rather than appointment was another reform. Horace Mann led a movement to establish free public schools. This is a basic right in a democracy.

An unhappy result of national growth was increasing conflict with the Indians. The federal government's policy was to move the Indians west of the Mississippi River. The Indians tried and failed to keep their homelands. Cherokees and Creeks were forcibly moved from the Carolinas, Georgia, and Alabama to the Oklahoma Territory in the late 1830s.

More Americans attacked the system of slavery. These people were called abolitionists. They wanted to abolish, or do away with, slavery altogether. The secret Underground Railroad helped slaves escape to freedom. The abolitionists helped create an antislavery feeling in the North and West. This feeling paved the way for popular support for the Union position in the Civil War.

Women continued to have few rights. But women were active in the early antislavery societies. This experience helped them in the fight for the vote, or women's suffrage. Elizabeth Cady Stanton and Lucretia Mott founded the first national women's organization at Seneca Falls, New York, in 1848. Its goal was women's rights.

≡ PRE-GED Practice ≡
EXERCISE 8

Questions 1 and 2 are based on the passage to the left.

1. The extension of voting rights during Andrew Jackson's presidency
    (1) was limited to white males
    (2) was made to look good but was not successful
    (3) included women with property
    (4) ended the three-fifths rule for counting slaves
    (5) has not been expanded upon since then

2. The emergence of protest movements for social change as early as the 1820s shows that these movements were
    (1) a very important part of U.S. history
    (2) inspired by a handful of radicals
    (3) shortsighted and achieved only limited goals
    (4) not very important to the two-party system
    (5) a threat to the democratic way of life

ANSWERS ARE ON PAGE 302.

EXERCISE 9

Directions: Match the person or term on the left with the description on the right. Put the correct letter on the line.

_____ 1. Jacksonian Democracy

_____ 2. Horace Mann

_____ 3. Oklahoma Territory

_____ 4. Underground Railroad

_____ 5. Elizabeth Cady Stanton

(a) secret network that helped slaves escape

(b) leader of movement for free public schools

(c) nationwide movement concerned with the spread of democratic rights

(d) leader of women's suffrage movement

(e) Creeks and Cherokees were forced to move to this location

ANSWERS ARE ON PAGE 302.

EXERCISE 10

Directions: Read the letter below from an ex-slave and then put a check in front of the correct answer to the questions that follow.

Dear Sir:

We arrived here (St. Jo) on the 14th. All in good order
or as good as could be expected. Some of our animals
were stiffened by standing on the boat. The weather was
very disagreeable and cold until yesterday. We put up
5   in town one week to recruit our animals. . . . We
bought two mules at St. Jo for $120.00. They are as
good or better than an average of our other ones.
After our arrival here, we concluded to sell one of our
wagons and only take three. We sold it to some
10 advantage. We are going to put four mules to two wagons
and two mules to one.

Mules, oxen, corn, and oats can be had to some
better advantage than in St. Louis but nothing else.
They put the screws very tight to emigrants for all
15 small jobs and articles the emigrants are obliged to
get, and upon the whole, I think outfits can be had as
cheap in St. Louis excepting livestock. . . .

There has been teams starting for several days past,
heavy loaded with feed. The grass is very backward, and
20 . . . . for some distance on the prairies, little or no
old grass to be had as it has been eat and burned off.
My intention is to haul feed to do us about 12 or 14
days. Consequently I want to see whether it is warm
enough for grass to grow while we have feed, so that
25 when our feed is out we can have some grass. There has
not been any here yet but it begins to start or make
appearance this morning since the rain. . . . My health
is good at this time and has been since I left. . . .
I have concluded not to go to Council Bluff as the
30 season is late and that point so much north of this.
There is at least 10 days difference in vegetation
between this place and St. Louis. . . . There is large
quantity of cattle starting and emigrants fitted out in
every way, but their wagons are generally heavier than
35 ours. We have as light wagons as any that I have seen
and our teams look as well as any. There is some better
and many not half as good.

From yours respectfully,
A. H. Wilson, 1852

1. You can infer that the route these settlers planned to take was

____**(1)** well-known

____**(2)** unexplored

____**(3)** lightly traveled

____**(4)** a very rough terrain

2. Why did the group have to bring feed for its animals?

____**(1)** The animals got sick from eating prairie grass.

____**(2)** The old grass had been eaten and burned off.

____**(3)** They planned to sell it to other settlers.

____**(4)** They planned to use some of it for seed.

3. What can you infer about merchants in St. Joseph?

____**(1)** They often charged more than merchants in St. Louis.

____**(2)** They earned more money from local townspeople.

____**(3)** They charged much less than merchants in St. Louis.

____**(4)** Their businesses could not handle the settlers.

4. Which things could the group buy more easily in St. Joseph than in St. Louis?

____**(1)** wagons

____**(2)** feed for the animals

____**(3)** heavy clothes

____**(4)** mules, oxen, corn, and oats

ANSWERS ARE ON PAGE 302.

THE PROBLEM OF SLAVERY

KEY WORD

Dred Scott case—the controversial 1857 Supreme Court decision ruling that slaves were not citizens and that slaves were the property of their masters

Sectionalism continued to deepen in the country until 1860. Northern manufacturers wanted to build an industrial country based on manufacturing, free labor, and many kinds of farming. Southern plantation owners preferred a single-crop plantation economy based on slave labor.

The argument over slavery was at the heart of sectionalism. It grew sharper as the sections competed for control over the new western territories. Control of most of the western territories could tip the political balance in the U.S. Congress. The whole future development of the United States was at stake. Peace was kept only through a series of compromises.

The purchase of the huge Louisiana Territory raised the issue of "free soil versus slave soil." Antislavery forces wanted slavery banned. Proslavery forces wanted the future states to decide for themselves whether to be free or slave states. The Missouri Compromise of 1820 admitted Missouri as a slave state and Maine as a free state. Slavery was limited to the land stretching west from the southern border of Missouri. Still, large new areas were opened to the expansion of slavery.

In the *Dred Scott* case of 1857, the Supreme Court ruled that slaves were not citizens. They were the property of their masters. Slave owners' property rights were protected by the U.S. Constitution. So Congress could make no law prohibiting slavery. The *Dred Scott* decision created great anger against the South. People feared the further expansion of slavery.

Antislavery feelings grew with the publication in 1853 of Harriet Beecher Stowe's best-selling novel, *Uncle Tom's Cabin*. In 1859, John Brown, a militant abolitionist, attacked the federal arsenal at Harpers Ferry (now part of West Virginia). He tried to get weapons to arm slaves for rebellion. Brown failed and was hanged. Frederick Douglass, an ex-slave and eloquent spokesman against slavery, toured the North, raising support for abolitionism.

The newly formed Republican Party was opposed to the spread of slavery and in favor of economic growth. This position helped the Republican Party to grow rapidly. In 1860, its presidential candidate, Abraham Lincoln, won the election.

EXERCISE 11

Directions: Circle *T* for each true statement, or *F* for each false statement.

T   F   1. Slavery became the leading problem in sectionalism.

T   F   2. Control over new states created in the western territories could tip the balance of power in the U.S. Congress.

T   F   3. The Missouri Compromise settled the issue of slavery in the territories once and for all.

T   F   4. The *Dred Scott* case protected the rights of property owners.

T   F   5. Harriet Beecher Stowe's novel helped build strong feelings against slavery.

T   F   6. The election of a Republican president in 1860 was not likely to please the South.

T   F   7. John Brown was hanged because he gave weapons to slaves so they could lead a rebellion.

T   F   8. Frederick Douglass attacked the federal arsenal at Harpers Ferry.

ANSWERS ARE ON PAGE 302.

 ## WRITING ACTIVITY 8

Sectional differences increasingly divided the United States in the first half of the nineteenth century. Write a few paragraphs explaining what these differences were.

ANSWERS WILL VARY.

THE CIVIL WAR

KEY WORD

secession—the act of a state seceding, or leaving, a country to which it belongs

The South believed that the balance of power had been permanently tipped against it by the 1850s. Northern political and economic strength grew with the admission of California, Oregon, and Minnesota into the Union. It was only a matter of time before a majority of free states would vote for a constitutional amendment abolishing slavery. The Southern leaders feared Lincoln and quickly moved for secession from the Union. They formed the Confederate States of America.

Lincoln was unwilling to allow the breakup of the Union, and war began in 1861 between the North and the South. The industrial North had more people and more resources to fight a war. The South had excellent military leaders and fought on their own land. However, Lincoln's Emancipation Proclamation in 1863 freed the slaves who lived in rebel territory. In addition, the recruitment of ex-slaves into the Union army helped to undermine the South. The war to save the Union turned into a crusade against slavery.

After four long years, the North's superior ability to maintain a modern army ground down the backward Confederate states. General Robert E. Lee's army surrendered in the spring of 1865.

≡ PRE-GED Practice ≡
EXERCISE 12

Questions 1 and 2 are based on the passage above.

1. Southern leaders seceded from the Union chiefly because they

   (1) underestimated Lincoln
   (2) believed they could win the conflict
   (3) feared a majority of free states would vote to abolish slavery
   (4) wanted to stop abolitionists from provoking slave rebellions
   (5) wanted to extend slavery to the North

2. According to this summary, President Lincoln's Emancipation Proclamation

   (1) turned the war to save the Union into a crusade against slavery
   (2) had no effect on the North's war effort
   (3) had little effect on the Confederacy
   (4) freed all slaves in the North and South
   (5) was welcomed by the Confederacy

ANSWERS ARE ON PAGE 302.

RECONSTRUCTION

KEY WORD

impeachment—the process of charging a public officeholder with a crime or misconduct in office so that the person can be removed from office

The time of rebuilding following the Civil War is known as the Reconstruction era. President Lincoln and Andrew Johnson, his successor, tried to reunite the torn nation quickly. They were willing to let Southerners decide most questions of race relations in the defeated states. Both Lincoln and Johnson were willing to pardon Confederate officers and politicians. Many Confederate officials then returned to Southern legislatures in 1865. These legislatures passed so-called Black Codes. These laws severely restricted the rights of former slaves.

Radical Republicans in Congress were enraged by the actions of Southern state legislatures. They wanted far-reaching social changes in the South. They also wanted protection for the rights of freed slaves. The Radicals were in favor of a tough policy toward the South and former Confederate officials. Their plan was adopted.

The Radicals' conflicts with President Johnson became so heated that impeachment proceedings were brought against him. However, Johnson was not convicted by the Senate.

The Radicals sponsored many important reforms and constitutional amendments. The Thirteenth Amendment (1865) abolished slavery. The Fourteenth Amendment (1868) made blacks citizens who had equal rights under the law. The Fifteenth Amendment (1870) granted black men the right to vote.

The Radicals' Reconstruction plan temporarily forced many former Confederate officials out of office. For the first time, blacks were elected to statewide offices and to the U.S. Senate. In the South, the Freedmen's Bureau set up the first schools for blacks. Reconstruction ended in 1877. It was part of a compromise between conservative Republicans and Southern Democrats in the disputed presidential election of 1876. The compromise agreement gave Rutherford B. Hayes the crucial Southern Democratic support he needed for election. In return, Hayes pulled the remaining U.S. troops out of the South.

Reconstruction made few economic and social changes in the South. Ex-slaves did not receive the "40 acres and a mule" that they had been promised. Large plantations still remained. The freedmen had little land and no economic base from which to defend their newly won freedom. Many issues of justice and equality would not be settled for another hundred years.

EXERCISE 13

Directions: Match the term on the left with its description on the right. Write the correct letter on the line.

_____ **1.** impeachment

_____ **2.** Black Codes

_____ **3.** Thirteenth Amendment

_____ **4.** Fourteenth Amendment

_____ **5.** Fifteenth Amendment

(a) made blacks citizens who had equal rights under the law

(b) abolished slavery

(c) gave black men the right to vote

(d) passed by Southern state legislatures to restrict the rights of former slaves

(e) charging a public official with a crime or with misconduct

ANSWERS ARE ON PAGE 302.

═ PRE-GED Practice ═
EXERCISE 14

Questions 1 and 2 are based on the table below.

COMPARISON OF RESOURCES BETWEEN NORTH AND SOUTH IN 1860

	North	South
population	71%	29%
railroad mileage	72%	28%
iron and steel	93%	7%
farm output	65%	35%

1. In which resource does the North have the greatest advantage compared with the South?

(1) population
(2) railroad mileage
(3) iron and steel
(4) farm output
(5) production of cotton

2. This table illustrates
(1) that the South had a superior railroad system
(2) equal regional economic development before the Civil War
(3) the great agricultural wealth of the South
(4) the economic advantages of the North
(5) the agricultural weakness of the South

ANSWERS ARE ON PAGE 303.

EXERCISE 15

Directions: Read the letter below sent by an ex-slave to his former master. Then answer the questions that follow.

To My Old Master

Sir:

    I got your letter, and was glad to find that you had not forgotten Jourdon, and that you wanted me to come back and live with you again, promising to do better for me than anybody else can. I have often felt uneasy
5   about you. I thought the Yankees would have hung you long before this, for harboring Rebs they found at your house. I suppose they never heard about your going to Colonel Martin's to kill the Union soldier that was left by his company in their stable. Although you shot
10 at me twice before I left you, I did not want to hear of your being hurt, and am glad that you are still living. It would do me good to go back to the dear old home again. . . . I want to know particularly what the good chance is you propose to give me. I am doing
15 tolerably well here, I get 25 dollars a month, with victuals [food] and clothing; have a comfortable home for Mandy, the folks call her Mrs. Anderson, and the children go to school and are learning well. . . . We are kindly treated. . . .

20   As to my freedom, which you say I can have, there is nothing to be gained on that score, as I got my free papers in 1864 from the Provost-Marshal-General of the Department of Nashville. Mandy says she would be afraid to go back without some proof that you were disposed to
25 treat us justly and kindly; and we have concluded to test your sincerity by asking you to send us our wages for the time we served you. This will make us forget and forgive old scores, and rely on your justice and friendship in the future. I served you faithfully for
30 thirty-two years, and Mandy for twenty years. At twenty-five dollars a month for me, and two dollars a week for Mandy, our earnings would amount to eleven thousand six hundred and eighty dollars. Add to this the interest for the time our wages have been kept
35 back, and deduct what you paid for our clothing, and three doctor's visits to me, and pulling a tooth for Mandy, and the balance will show what we are in justice entitled to.

Please send the money by Adam's Express,
40   in care of V. Winters, Esq., Dayton, Ohio. If you fail
to pay us for faithful labors in the past, we can
have little faith in your promises in the future. We
trust the good Maker has opened your eyes to the wrongs
which you and your fathers have done to me and my
45   fathers, in making us toil for you for generations
without recompense. Here I draw my wages every Saturday
night; but in Tennessee there was never any pay-day for
the Negroes anymore than for horses or cows. Surely
there will be a day of reckoning for those who defraud
50   the laborer of his hire.

From your old servant,
Jourdon Anderson

Directions: Put a check in front of the correct answer to the questions that follow.

1. The letter demonstrates that some ex-slaves

_____**(1)** were miserable as freemen and wanted to return to their former homes

_____**(2)** were easily attracted by the appeals of their old masters

_____**(3)** had just as hard a time in the North as in the South

_____**(4)** clearly understood how slavery had exploited them

2. The letter expresses the view that slavery

_____**(1)** had been beneficial to blacks

_____**(2)** had reduced human beings to the level of animals

_____**(3)** was preferable to the life Anderson has found in the North

_____**(4)** had provided a good education for Anderson's children

ANSWERS ARE ON PAGE 303.

CHANGES IN SOCIETY: 1865–1900

KEY WORD

industrialization—the development of large-scale industries and mass-production techniques

During the period from the end of the Civil War to 1900, some great changes occurred across the country. The foundations of modern America were laid in the factories, mills, mines, and cities of the Midwest and the East. The widespread settlement of the West meant the end of the frontier.

Western migration greatly increased after the Civil War. Indians who were pushed off their lands fought the U.S. cavalry from 1865 to 1890. The Indian wars finally came to an end in 1890 following the massacre by federal troops of more than 200 Sioux men, women, and children at Wounded Knee, South Dakota. At about the same time, the last of the western lands were settled and the land rush slowed down.

The eastern United States was rapidly becoming an industrial urban society. Northern businessmen had gained wealth and experience from the Civil War. After the war, they moved quickly to change civilian production. In doing so, they put America on the road to industrialization. Large-scale production began to dominate American economic growth.

EXERCISE 16

Directions: Circle *T* for each true statement, or *F* for each false statement.

T F 1. From the Civil War to 1900, the foundations of modern America were laid in the Midwest and East.

T F 2. The close of the western frontier and the end of the Indian wars took place at about the same time.

T F 3. The massacre at Wounded Knee, South Dakota, brought an end to the Indian Wars.

ANSWERS ARE ON PAGE 303.

TECHNOLOGY, INDUSTRIALIZATION, AND URBANIZATION

KEY WORD

urbanization—the growth of large cities, with a population shift away from rural areas

Inventions revolutionized all areas of life. The national railroad system greatly expanded. The telegraph established nationwide communication. The invention of the Bessemer and open-hearth smelt processes led to the creation of a giant steel industry. Tremendous growth in energy resources took place. New coal fields opened, the electric dynamo was invented, and oil well drilling developed.

Technical advances also revolutionized agriculture by mechanizing the farm. The McCormick Reaper drastically reduced the time and people needed to cut grain. The mechanization of agriculture freed more farm laborers to work in the new factories in the cities.

Industrialization caused a gigantic growth in the population of cities and towns. Americans moved to where the jobs were. The population shift from rural areas to the cities is know as urbanization. Industry centered around sources of raw materials, energy sources, and good transportation. Large cities like Pittsburgh and Chicago took shape around steel mills and factories. Even more new industry was needed to build housing and transportation for the new urban areas.

Immigration from Europe also played an important role in the growth of American cities. About 25 million Europeans were recruited to work in U.S. mines, mills, and forges. Agents were sent to Europe to encourage people to come to the United States. Millions of Europeans faced economic hardship and political repression in their homelands. They were eager to come to the United States to find a better life. Large numbers of Asians came to build the railroads in the West. Most of the new immigrants settled in the big cities. These people often faced poverty and discrimination.

A powerful new group of financiers and industrialists sparked America's industrialization. Andrew Carnegie, John D. Rockefeller, J. P. Morgan, Cornelius Vanderbilt, and others put together the giant companies that ruled American economic life. They created monopolies that centralized control of business in a few hands. This power was often misused to keep prices high and wages low. These company owners used their great economic power to dominate politics. They also got laws passed that were favorable to their businesses.

PRE-GED Practice
EXERCISE 17

Questions 1–6 are based on the passage at the left.

1. Which person was most directly responsible for technological advances in agriculture?

   (1) Andrew Carnegie
   (2) Cornelius Vanderbilt
   (3) Cyrus McCormick
   (4) John D. Rockefeller
   (5) J. P. Morgan

2. Europeans and Asians who came to America expected to find all of the following EXCEPT for

   (1) freedom from economic problems
   (2) a better life in this country
   (3) freedom from political repression
   (4) a chance to work in U.S. factories or on the railroads
   (5) poverty and discrimination in housing and in the workplace

3. Financiers and industrialists did NOT create monopolies to

   (1) keep the control of business in the hands of a few
   (2) lower prices and keep wages high
   (3) dominate the political arena
   (4) have favorable laws passed
   (5) gain economic power

4. The impact of industrialization in America was that it

   (1) affected only industrial technology
   (2) influenced only where people lived
   (3) had little effect on the number of immigrants
   (4) revolutionized the entire country
   (5) affected only agriculture

5. Urbanization in the United States

   (1) caused industrialization
   (2) was caused by the growth and centralization of industry
   (3) took place faster in the South than elsewhere
   (4) took place by simply moving farmers into the cities
   (5) met all the hopes of European immigrants for a better life

6. Which of the following can you infer from this section?

   (1) Large-scale social change is usually very smooth and free of conflict.
   (2) Changes in one part of society, such as the economy, lead to changes in all other areas.
   (3) Change can take place in one part of society, and have little effect on any other part.
   (4) The settling of the West was the most important event of this period.
   (5) Immigration caused America to industrialize.

ANSWERS ARE ON PAGE 303.

THE IMPACT ON THE SOUTH

KEY WORDS

sharecropper—a tenant farmer who pays a portion of the crop as rent for the land

Jim Crow laws—racial segregation laws passed in the South during the late nineteenth and early twentieth centuries

In contrast to the North and West, the urban and industrial growth in the South was slow. Large areas of the South were still characterized by a backward agricultural system of sharecropping. The situation was much like the old plantation because tenant farmer sharecroppers, both black and white, did not own the land. They also had to pay part of their crop as rent. The sharecroppers were in constant debt to the large landowners.

After the end of Reconstruction, a new system of segregation based on Jim Crow laws destroyed any remaining hopes for racial equality. Poll taxes and literacy tests kept both blacks and poor whites from their right to vote. These abuses continued until the civil rights protests of the 1960s led to federal laws outlawing such practices.

EXERCISE 18

Directions: Based on the passage above, fill in the correct answers in the space provided.

1. Sharecroppers paid rent by giving the landowners _____.

2. Racial equality in the South made no progress under the _____.

3. Two things which kept blacks and poor whites from voting

   were _____ and _____.

4. Urban and industrial growth were slowest in the _____.

ANSWERS ARE ON PAGE 303.

THE WORKERS AND FARMERS RESPOND

Workers and farmers saw very little of the new riches from rapid industrialization. Factory, rail, and mine workers often worked more than twelve hours each day for extremely low pay. In reaction to these conditions, workers began to organize. The Knights of Labor was the first truly national federation of trade unions. Local labor disputes were widespread. The first nationwide strikes took place on the railroads. A railroad strike in 1877 affected much of the eastern United States. Street battles took place between troops and labor union supporters in Pittsburgh and Chicago.

Union organizers were only mildly successful. A few skilled craft unions survived to form the American Federation of Labor (AFL). But organizing drives for most unskilled and semiskilled laborers failed. Violence was frequent. In the 1894 Pullman strike in Chicago, unions were defeated by a combination of private police, state militia, and federal troops. Thirty strikers died and labor leaders were put in jail. Meanwhile, rural areas were swept by waves of protests over high credit costs and steep railroad freight rates. Mechanization had increased farm production. Bankers and the monopolies, however, harvested the wealth. Farmers were urged by their leaders to "raise less corn and more hell." They did. Across the country, they organized the Farmers' Alliances to fight for their interests.

Protests against monopoly power led to the passage of the Interstate Commerce Act (1887) and the Sherman Anti-Trust Act (1890). Nevertheless, the influence of the monopolies was great. The antitrust law was eventually enforced more against unions and farmers than against the monopolies. The failure of reform laws such as the Sherman Act led to strong public support for the Populists (People's Party) in the 1890s. This third-party movement aimed to control the monopolies. The Populists won over a million votes in 1892. In 1896, its demands were incorporated into the Democratic Party platform. Republican candidate William McKinley was supported by big business. He defeated Democrat William Jennings Bryan. Later, many Populist ideas were adopted by both parties.

In the last thirty years of the nineteenth century, industrialization and urbanization changed America. Social and political problems created by these changes were not solved. They would come up again in conflicts during the twentieth century.

EXERCISE 19

Directions: Put a check in front of the correct answer to the questions that follow.

1. The Populists' goal was to

	____(1) help establish more monopolies

	____(2) protect the rights of Indians

	____(3) control the power of unions

	____(4) help unions in their struggle with big business

2. Drawing on the experience of America, today's developing countries that try to industrialize should expect

	____(1) a smooth transition to a new society

	____(2) to see little political turmoil

	____(3) widespread changes combined with political and social turmoil

	____(4) unions, farmers, and business to work in harmony

3. Workers' efforts to organize unions in this period

	____(1) got unlimited support from owners

	____(2) were limited to local areas

	____(3) were often met with violent resistance

	____(4) succeeded in establishing large, lasting unions of unskilled workers

4. Which of the following is NOT a reason why workers tried to become unionized?

	____(1) twelve-hour workdays

	____(2) extremely low pay

	____(3) rapid industrialization

	____(4) low credit costs

ANSWERS ARE ON PAGE 303.

EXERCISE 20

Directions: Study the graph below and then answer each question in the space provided.

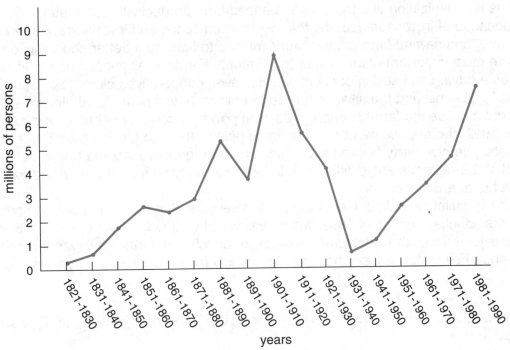

UNITED STATES IMMIGRATION, 1821–1990

Sources: *Immigration and Naturalization Service, U.S. Justice Department*

1. During which ten-year period did immigration reach its peak? _____

2. Which ten-year period had the lowest number of people immigrating to the

United States? _____

3. Put a check in front of the generalization that can be drawn from the passage and the graph.

_____**(1)** Immigration was not important to urbanization.

_____**(2)** Immigration reached its peak during the period of rapid urban and industrial growth.

_____**(3)** Most immigrants did not settle in the city.

_____**(4)** Although immigration reached its peak during the late 1800s and early 1900s, it was not related to industrialization.

ANSWERS ARE ON PAGE 303.

EXERCISE 21

Directions: Read the passage below and answer the question that follows.

Farmers' Protests

The mechanization of agriculture increased farm productivity, but it left the farmers poor because of increased debt, high transportation costs, and low prices. Farmers were desperate, and several farm organizations formed to fight for a better economic deal.

The most important of these was the National Farmers' Alliance. It began in Texas in 1877 as a buying and selling cooperative. However, cooperatives did not solve the farmers' problems, and the alliance turned to politics. It won some local elections, but these did not give the farmers enough political power to control the banks and railroads.

In 1892, the alliance moved into national politics through the People's Party of Populists. The new party favored such things as a progressive income tax, government control of the railroads and utilities, and inflated currency so the farmers could pay off their debts at a cheaper rate.

The Populist candidate, General James Weaver, polled more than one million votes in the presidential election of 1892, which was won by Grover Cleveland. In 1896, the Populists joined with the Democrats in order to run William Jennings Bryan for the presidency. Following his loss, the Populists rapidly faded away as an organized force.

Directions: Match the item on the left with its description on the right. Write the correct letter on the line.

_____ **1.** People's Party

_____ **2.** William Jennings Bryan

_____ **3.** James Weaver

_____ **4.** National Farmers' Alliance

_____ **5.** inflated currency

(a) candidate of the Populist party in 1892

(b) organization that began as a buying and selling cooperative

(c) believed in political reform

(d) candidate who lost the presidential election of 1896

(e) part of Populist program to help farmers pay off their debts

ANSWERS ARE ON PAGE 304.

THE PROGRESSIVE ERA: 1900-1917

KEY WORDS

Progressive Era—a period of many social and political reforms largely backed by presidents Theodore Roosevelt, Taft, and Wilson

social class—a group of people who share a common economic position in society

muckrakers—writers who exposed corruption in business and politics during the early twentieth century

In the last quarter of the nineteenth century, the United States was transformed from a rural, farming society into an urban industrial society. By 1900, the United States had replaced Great Britain as the leading industrial producer in the world. The country was poised for even greater growth when Henry Ford developed the first modern factory production line. However, many Americans were concerned by worsening social conditions brought about by industrialization and urbanization. Labor strife continued. Abuses of child labor were widespread, and living and working conditions deteriorated in the cities.

At the same time, the economy became more concentrated in the hands of a small number of families. This concentration of economic power helped to cause a serious depression in 1907. Political institutions that had been suitable for a nation of farmers and small-business people could no longer deal with the problems of a large-scale industrial society. The developing economic, social, and political crises gave birth to a time known as the Age of Reform, or the Progressive Era. This period lasted roughly from 1900 to America's entry into World War I in 1917.

Industrialization had created a large new class of industrial workers and a very small class of wealthy industrialists and financiers. It also had created a large urban middle class. These people were professionals such as lawyers, doctors, engineers, and teachers. A rapidly expanding group of white-collar workers and small-business people was also created. Each of these social classes had its own ideas about how the country should make reforms. Many middle-class people feared that the large corporations were destroying America's free-enterprise system.

Radical journalists, called muckrakers, influenced many people. Lincoln Steffens exposed in his books and articles the corruption, poverty, and boss-run political systems in the large cities. Upton Sinclair's novel, *The Jungle* (1906), exposed the awful conditions in Chicago's meatpacking industry. This eventually led to the Meat Inspection Amendment and the Pure Food and Drug Act.

EXERCISE 22

Directions: The questions below are based on the passage on page 117. Circle *T* for each true statement, or *F* for each false statement.

T F 1. Industrialization and urbanization brought about many improved social conditions.

T F 2. Industrialization was responsible for creating a large class of industrial workers and a small class of wealthy industrialists and financiers.

T F 3. During the Progressive Era, the wealth of the nation was almost evenly spread among all the social classes.

T F 4. Living and working conditions deteriorated in the cities during this era.

T F 5. Muckrakers, such as Steffens and Sinclair, wrote about the terrible conditions of workers in large cities.

T F 6. In 1900, Great Britain replaced the United States as the world's leader in industrial production.

T F 7. Lincoln Steffens developed the first modern factory production line.

T F 8. America experienced a serious depression in 1907 as a result of having the country's economic power in the hands of the rich.

T F 9. Sinclair's novel was partly responsible for the creation of the Pure Food and Drug Act.

T F 10. Political institutions were well-equipped to handle the problems of a large-scale industrial society.

ANSWERS ARE ON PAGE 304.

PROGRESSIVE REFORMS

KEY WORD

Social Darwinism—the theory that the development of society is based on the survival of the fittest

The growing strength of radicals and the influence of the middle class forced the Democratic and Republican parties to take reform seriously. At first, reforms were carried out at state and local levels. Local reforms included sanitation laws, building codes, and child welfare laws.

Many private settlement houses, like Jane Addams's Hull House in Chicago, were built in poor neighborhoods. These houses provided some social and educational facilities for the poor. However, local reforms and their financial resources were limited. Reformers wanted the federal government to help solve the most serious problems.

Society was deeply divided over what to do. Some people supported Social Darwinism. Its main belief was that society is based on the survival of the fittest. Wealth was a symbol of survival. Nature intended for some people to succeed and for others to fail. Social Darwinists did not want government to take part in social reforms.

Others believed that reforms were necessary to keep the system from falling into economic disorder. Their spokesperson was the Republican President Theodore Roosevelt. He pushed for reforms to control the worst abuses of big business. By 1912, Roosevelt felt that the Republican Party had turned its back on reform. He split from the Republicans and formed the Progressive (Bull Moose) Party. The Republican vote was split. Woodrow Wilson, the Democratic candidate, was able to win.

The Progressive Era produced a long list of legislative reforms. Some of these included regulation of railroads, establishment of the Federal Trade Commission, and child labor protection laws. The basic questions of the Progressive Era centered on what role government should play in regulating economic and social conditions. What Progressive reform led to was the rule of economy by private business. Limited government regulation would protect the general welfare. This solution has governed American society since. The Progressive Era ended with World War I, when the country turned its attention to international concerns.

≡ PRE-GED Practice ≡
EXERCISE 23

Questions 1–4 are based on the prior passage.

1. Why did Theodore Roosevelt run for president in 1912?

   (1) The Progressive Era was over.
   (2) Social Darwinists had taken over the government.
   (3) The unprogressive Woodrow Wilson was the Democratic Party's candidate.
   (4) He believed the Republican Party had turned its back on reform.
   (5) The Socialists had become a major worry.

2. If the ideas of the Progressive Era reform were applied to environmental protection,

   (1) companies could make all decisions about environmental protection
   (2) polluting companies would be run by their workers
   (3) polluting companies would be taken over by the federal government
   (4) polluting companies would be run by their local communities
   (5) the government would regulate the worst abuses of polluting companies, but the owners would still control those companies

3. Why did Progressive Era social reformers turn to the federal government for help in solving problems?

   (1) Reformers always believe in big government.
   (2) They did not want to resolve the problems themselves.
   (3) Private and local resources were limited.
   (4) The government demanded a voice in the situation.
   (5) They thought the federal government would be more sympathetic.

4. Social Darwinism was based on a belief in

   (1) social reforms
   (2) survival of the fittest
   (3) big business
   (4) international concerns
   (5) child labor protection laws

ANSWERS ARE ON PAGE 304.

WRITING ACTIVITY 9

Social workers and muckrakers faced social problems of the Progressive Era head-on. Both achieved considerable success in changing society. What problems would a muckraker write about in today's society? Select a problem and discuss what should be done about it.

ANSWERS WILL VARY.

EXERCISE 24

Directions: Read the speech below and then put a check in front of the correct answer to the questions that follow.

Women's Suffrage Movement

"Women even more than men need the ballot to protect their especial interests and their right to earn a living. . . . We want a law that will prohibit home-work. . . . We hear about the sacredness of the home. What sacredness is there about a home when it is turned into a factory, where we find a mother, very often with a child at her breast, running a sewing machine? Running up thirty-seven seams for a cent. Ironing and pressing shirts seventy cents a dozen, and children making artificial flowers for one cent. . . . These women have had no chance to make laws that would protect themselves or their children.

They [men] discriminate against the class that has no voice. Some of the men say, 'You women do not need a ballot; we will take care of you.' We have no faith in man's protection. . . . Give us the ballot, and we will protect ourselves."

—Inez Haynes Irwin, *Uphill With Banners Flying*

1. What is the writer's position in this passage?

   _____ (1) The ballot will not help the working woman.

   _____ (2) Men cannot be depended on to protect women and children.

   _____ (3) Men should protect the well-being of women and children.

   _____ (4) Giving women the right to vote will destroy the sanctity of the home.

2. The law "that will prohibit home-work" specifically refers to putting an end to

   _____ (1) work on one's home

   _____ (2) schoolwork

   _____ (3) factory-like production at home

   _____ (4) sewing

ANSWERS ARE ON PAGE 304.

FOREIGN AND DOMESTIC POLICY: 1890–1945

KEY WORDS

imperialism—a policy by which a nation extends its control over other lands

gunboat diplomacy—U.S. practice of sending troops into countries of the Western Hemisphere to protect U.S. interests

The Monroe Doctrine of 1823 proclaimed that the United States would not tolerate any new European colonization or interference in the Western Hemisphere. After this doctrine was announced, the United States did little to enforce it. The country was not much interested in world affairs until the 1890s.

By 1890, however, the West was largely settled and the frontier was closed. Then Americans became serious about taking over lands outside the United States. It began the policy called imperialism. European countries were building up large colonial empires in Africa and Asia. The United States did not want to be left out in the race to gain colonies.

The Cuban struggle for independence from Spain gave U.S. imperialists the opportunity they needed. To help Cubans win their struggle, the United States fought a three-month war with Spain in 1898. Cuba became independent but with strong U.S. controls for a number of years. The United States took outright control of the Spanish colonies of Puerto Rico, the Philippines, and Guam.

In 1898, the United States also took over the Hawaiian Islands. After 1900, the United States helped Panama become independent in exchange for a canal through Panama built and controlled by the United States. During the next few years, the United States sent troops to Mexico, Nicaragua, Haiti, and the Dominican Republic. It believed these actions were necessary to protect U.S. interests. But the people in these countries resented this gunboat diplomacy.

Some Americans were against imperialism. They wanted more foreign trade, but they did not want the United States to have a colonial empire. So they founded the Anti-Imperialist League. The writer Mark Twain was one of its most outspoken members.

EXERCISE 25

Directions: Answer the questions below in the space provided.

1. American imperialism became most prominent when the United States fought

   a war with _____.

2. In 1898, the United States annexed a group of islands that today is

   the state of _____.

3. U.S. military intervention, called _____, caused a

   great deal of resentment in the countries of Latin America and the Caribbean.

4. Taking over lands beyond a country's borders is called

   _____.

5. Anti-imperialists wanted _____ but

   not a _____.

6. Part of the Monroe Doctrine of 1823 declared that the United States would not allow

   _____ or _____

   in the Western Hemisphere.

7. European countries built up large colonial empires in

   _____ and _____.

8. The United States fought with _____ to help Cuba

   win its independence.

9. One of the most outspoken members of the Anti-Imperialist League was

   _____.

ANSWERS ARE ON PAGE 304.

EXERCISE 26

Directions: Study the map below and then answer the questions in the space provided.

U.S. INTERESTS IN THE CARIBBEAN, 1903–1994

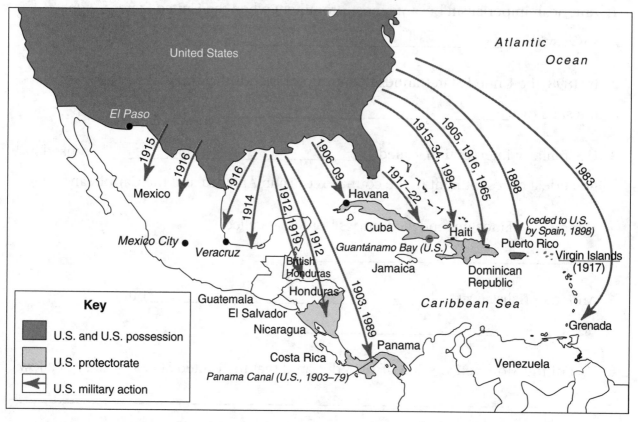

1. U.S. military action in the region is shown by

_____.

2. In what year did the United States invade Grenada?

_____

3. Name the present U.S. possessions in the region.

_____

4. From the number of U.S. military actions in the Caribbean region, a logical conclusion is that the United States

_____(1) had no interest in the region

_____(2) was enforcing the Monroe Doctrine

_____(3) was interested in Cuba but not Haiti or the Dominican Republic

_____(4) was interested only in Mexico

ANSWERS ARE ON PAGE 304.

WORLD WAR I AND AFTER

> **KEY WORDS**
>
> *isolationism*—national policy or attitude that a nation will do better if it pays more attention to domestic matters rather than to international matters
>
> *armistice*—a stopping of fighting between countries

In 1914, Archduke Francis Ferdinand, the heir to the Austro-Hungarian throne, was assassinated. This sparked a war between rival groups of European nations—the Allies and the Central Powers. The United States stayed out of this war until 1917. Then Germany stepped up its submarine attacks on U.S. passenger ships and unarmed merchant ships. These attacks led to the loss of many American lives. The United States was forced into the war on the side of the Allies.

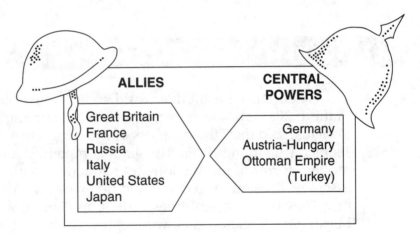

ALLIES

Great Britain
France
Russia
Italy
United States
Japan

CENTRAL POWERS

Germany
Austria-Hungary
Ottoman Empire
(Turkey)

By that time, the warring countries were tired of fighting and neither side seemed able to win. U.S. soldiers helped break this stalemate. On November 11, 1918, the Germans signed an armistice. Today we celebrate that date as Veterans Day.

The war made the United States a major world power. President Woodrow Wilson proposed Fourteen Points to make a lasting peace. However, the other Allied leaders decided that the enemy, especially the Germans, needed to be taught a lesson. The peace treaties were harsh. Republican leaders in the U.S. Senate opposed to Wilson kept the United States from signing the peace treaties and joining the League of Nations. This international body, similar to today's United Nations, was set up to ensure peace and world security. The United States wanted to keep its freedom of action. The country retreated into isolationism, where it stayed until forced into war again in 1941.

≡ **PRE-GED Practice** ≡
EXERCISE 27

Questions 1 and 2 are based on the prior passage.

1. From 1890 to 1941, America

   (1) alternated between active involvement in foreign affairs and periods of isolation

   (2) did not let trade influence its foreign policy

   (3) followed only a policy of isolation

   (4) always followed George Washington's advice of avoiding entangling alliances

   (5) did not use the military in expanding its influence

2. Why did the United States enter World War I?

   (1) Great Britain forced it to do so.

   (2) German submarine attacks led to the loss of American lives.

   (3) It had made too many loans to the Allies and feared it wouldn't get its money back.

   (4) Public opinion favored joining the fight.

   (5) It was reacting to the assassination of Archduke Francis Ferdinand.

ANSWERS ARE ON PAGE 304.

THE ROARING TWENTIES

Isolationism meant that world affairs were quiet for the United States in the 1920s. At home, however, a lot was happening. President Calvin Coolidge said that "the business of America is business." That certainly seemed true in the 1920s. The giant companies developed and expanded modern forms of production and marketing. With mass production assembly lines, more goods could be made and Americans were ready to buy. They bought telephones, radios, and automobiles. When the decade began, only 9 million cars were registered in the United States. By 1930, there were more than 26.5 million cars.

The consumer age was born. Chain stores and department stores replaced many of the small shops. Industrial production rose 64 percent between 1919 and 1923. Many workers' real wages (wages adjusted for inflation) rose 24 percent. Stockholders' dividends often increased by 100 percent. Expanding industry caused changes in the work force. Women took jobs as secretaries and clerical workers. The Nineteenth Amendment (1920) gave women the right to vote.

Black workers continued to migrate from the South to work in factories in the North. There they could earn higher wages. Blacks brought with them African-American music called jazz, which became popular with whites. They danced to a form of jazz, called swing, played by the big bands in the 1930s. Blacks also had their own cultural life in the Harlem Renaissance of New York City. Discrimination, particularly from a revived Ku Klux Klan, and race riots were common. The black nationalist leader Marcus Garvey founded the Universal Negro Improvement Association to combat discrimination and end imperialism in Africa.

Americans distrusted foreigners during this period. Congress followed the public mood by establishing strict quotas and lowering the number of immigrants allowed into the country.

The best-selling nonfiction book in 1926 was Bruce Barton's *The Man Nobody Knows*, a businessman's version of the life of Christ. Many writers during the 1920s were turned off by the emphasis on material things. Some of them, such as Ernest Hemingway and F. Scott Fitzgerald, moved to Europe.

EXERCISE 28

Directions: Circle *T* for each true statement, or *F* for each false statement.

T F **1.** Mass production made more goods available to consumers during the 1920s.

T F **2.** The main business of America during the 1920s was business.

T F **3.** When war production ended, women no longer remained in the work force.

T F **4.** African-American culture remained strictly in the South and had no influence on the rest of the nation.

T F **5.** Immigration was cut back by Congress during the 1920s.

T F **6.** Some American writers disliked the emphasis on material goods and went to Europe.

T F **7.** Swing music has its roots in African-American jazz.

ANSWERS ARE ON PAGE 305.

THE GREAT DEPRESSION AND THE NEW DEAL

KEY WORDS

collective bargaining—meeting between labor representatives and employers to settle disputes about hours, wages, and working conditions

industrial unionism—organizing of unskilled and semiskilled factory workers chiefly by the Congress of Industrial Organizations (CIO)

The era of economic prosperity ended suddenly with the stock market crash of 1929. Manufacturers could not sell their goods. Workers lost their jobs. Farmers lost their farms. Unemployment in some cities rose to 60 percent. People without jobs faced being put out of their homes because they could not pay the rent. When the Depression began, the United States had no unemployment insurance. It had very little public welfare and no Social Security. Private relief agencies had difficulty caring for so many people. Millions of people had no money, no work, and no hope. Farmers killed their livestock and destroyed crops rather than lose even more money by selling at very low prices.

World War I veterans marched on Washington, D.C., to collect their army bonus, which the government had promised them. They were driven out by the army. Councils for the unemployed were formed to keep people from being evicted from their homes.

President Hoover's actions did little to restore confidence or the economy. With the country on the verge of economic collapse, Franklin D. Roosevelt was overwhelmingly elected President in 1932. Roosevelt's New Deal programs, including Social Security and Federal Unemployment Insurance, were designed to prevent the worst features of the Great Depression from taking place again. The Works Progress Administration (WPA) gave public works jobs to thousands of unemployed.

The New Deal did not get the United States out of the Depression. But it did establish the idea that government is responsible for seeing that people are free from economic anxiety through income support programs and the creation of jobs. At the same time, the New Deal greatly increased the government's role in regulating the economy.

Labor unions made great gains during the Depression. New Deal legislation guaranteed workers the right of collective bargaining. The Congress of Industrial Organizations (CIO) was formed in 1935 to promote industrial unionism. The older American Federation of Labor (AFL) was craft-oriented and had paid little attention to unskilled industrial workers. Between 1935 and 1937, the CIO organized four million workers.

EXERCISE 29

Directions: Put a check in front of the correct answers to the questions that follow.

1. The people most hurt at the beginning of the Great Depression were those who

_____ **(1)** received government assistance

_____ **(2)** organized protest movements

_____ **(3)** lived largely by private charity

_____ **(4)** were recent immigrants

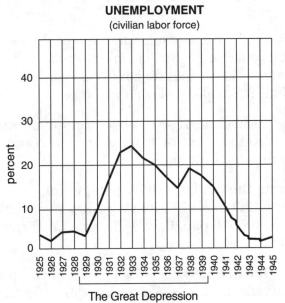

UNEMPLOYMENT
(civilian labor force)

The Great Depression

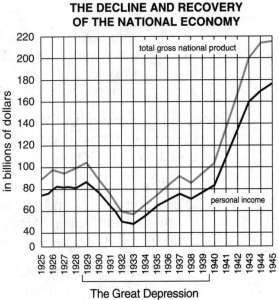

THE DECLINE AND RECOVERY OF THE NATIONAL ECONOMY

total gross national product

personal income

The Great Depression

2. The two graphs show that unemployment

_____ **(1)** increased from 1929 to 1933 and the gross national product declined

_____ **(2)** decreased from 1929 to 1933 and the gross national product decreased in the same period

_____ **(3)** declined continuously since 1933

_____ **(4)** and the gross national product both increased in 1938

3. The most lasting effect of the New Deal was that it

_____ **(1)** brought the country out of the Depression

_____ **(2)** set a policy that government does not interfere in labor disputes

_____ **(3)** established the idea that government was responsible for people's basic economic needs

_____ **(4)** established the policy of creating economic growth by making payments to business and cutting welfare

ANSWERS ARE ON PAGE 305.

THE ROAD TO WORLD WAR II

KEY WORDS

communism—a system practiced in the former Soviet Union in which private ownership of property and the means of production was not permissible

fascism—a political system that always puts the state above the individual, and which usually has a dictator to carry out its social and economic policies

The entire world was gripped by the Great Depression of the 1930s. The dictator Joseph Stalin tried to make the Soviet Union into an industrial power based on communism. The Russian people suffered greatly in the process; the brutal Stalin allowed no opposition.

In Germany and Italy, fascist dictators rose to power on the misery of the people. The dictators believed that fascism, expansion, and conquest could solve their countries' economic problems.

The Japanese military began the road to war by conquering Manchuria in 1931 and invading China in 1937. Italy's Benito Mussolini conquered Ethiopia in Africa in 1935. Japan, Italy, and Germany formed an alliance known as the Axis Powers.

In 1936, Germany's Adolf Hitler started his march to world conquest. He took over the Rhineland, Austria, and Czechoslovakia without a fight. In Germany, Hitler murdered or jailed his opponents and began a systematic extermination of the Jews.

When Germany attacked Poland in 1939, Great Britain and France declared war. Germany quickly conquered most of Europe with its blitzkrieg (lightning war). Hitler next turned on the Soviet Union. The Japanese sneak air attack on the U.S. fleet at Pearl Harbor, Hawaii, brought the United States into the war in December 1941. Japan's Axis allies in Europe then declared war on the United States.

World War II was truly a "world" war. Fighting raged in Europe, Asia, Africa, and in the Pacific islands until 1945. President Roosevelt met with Stalin and British Prime Minister Winston Churchill at several Big Three conferences. They agreed that the Allies would fight until their enemies surrendered unconditionally. The Germans were defeated in May 1945. The Japanese surrendered only after atomic bombs were dropped on the cities of Hiroshima and Nagasaki in August 1945.

EXERCISE 30

Directions: Match the item on the left with its description on the right. Write the correct letter on the line.

_____ **1.** Ethiopia

_____ **2.** Poland

_____ **3.** Big Three

_____ **4.** Axis Powers

_____ **5.** Hiroshima

_____ **6.** Japan

_____ **7.** Manchuria

_____ **8.** Great Depression

_____ **9.** 1937

_____ **10.** Stalin

_____ **11.** Hitler

_____ **12.** 1945

(a) invasion of this country caused England and France to declare war on Germany

(b) alliance of Germany, Italy, and Japan

(c) sneak attack by this country at Pearl Harbor brought United States into World War II

(d) African nation conquered by Italy in 1935

(e) Asian area first conquered by Japan

(f) agreed that Germany and Japan must surrender unconditionally

(g) Japanese city on which an atomic bomb was dropped

(h) when the Japanese military invaded China

(i) introduced a communist system into the Soviet Union

(j) when World War II ended

(k) when the stock market crashed in the 1930s

(l) responsible for a systematic extermination of the Jews

ANSWERS ARE ON PAGE 305.

EXERCISE 31

Directions: Read the passage below and then put a check in front of the correct answer to the questions that follow.

The Flint Sit-Down Strike of 1936

The Flint sit-down happened Christmas Eve, 1936 . . . The second shift had pulled the plant. It took about five minutes to shut the line down. The foreman was pretty well astonished.

We had guys patrol the plant, see that nobody got involved in anything they shouldn't. If anybody got careless with company property . . . he was talked to. You couldn't paint a sign on the wall or anything like that. . . . They'd assign roles to you. When some of the guys at headquarters wanted to tell some of the guys in the plant was what cookin', I carried the message. . . .

We have a ladies auxiliary. They'd visit the homes of the guys that was in the plant. They would find out if there was any shortage of coal or food. Then they'd maneuver [scheme] amongst themselves until they found some place to get a ton of coal. Some of them even put the arm on Consumer Power if there was a possibility of having her power shut off.

Finally we got the word: THE THING IS SETTLED. My God, you had to send about three people, one right after the other, down to some of those plants because the guys didn't believe it. Finally, when they did get it, they marched out of the plants with the flag flyin' and all that stuff.

When Mr. Knudsen put his name to a piece of paper and says that General Motors recognizes the UAW-CIO—until that moment we didn't even exist. That was the big one.

Studs Terkel, *Hard Times: An Oral History of the Great Depression*

1. The Flint sit-down strike shows

____**(1)** the helplessness of business resistance to unionism

____**(2)** manipulation by a handful of outside troublemakers

____**(3)** how to organize a complicated strike

____**(4)** the inability of union workers to influence business

2. You can infer that the company did not try to remove the strikers because

____**(1)** there was public support for the strike

____**(2)** the workers would destroy the plant equipment

____**(3)** the company thought the strikers could be starved out

____**(4)** the company thought the strike would be over quickly

ANSWERS ARE ON PAGE 305.

U.S. FOREIGN POLICY: 1945–1990s

KEY WORDS

Cold War—the period of conflict between the superpowers of the United States and the former Soviet Union and their allies after World War II

containment—U.S. foreign policy to block further expansion of communism after World War II

arms race—a continuous buildup of large amounts of weapons and of a huge military force by one country in order to gain an advantage

The United States became the strongest world power after World War II. Much of Western Europe and Japan was in ruins. The other major world power was the Soviet Union. The two superpowers had joined together during the war to defeat Hitler. When the war ended, they became hostile. This was a struggle between two different social and economic systems. It was also a struggle between two giants competing for spheres of influence. This period of struggle was called the Cold War. It lasted from the late 1940s until the late 1980s.

The Soviet Union set up communist governments in several Eastern European countries. These countries were called satellites because they depended upon Soviet occupation forces and economic ties. Communists also came to power in China by 1949.

The Marshall Plan helped Western European countries rebuild their war-torn economies. Americans feared that the communists might take over the world. Therefore, it drew up a containment policy to limit communism to areas where it was already established. To support containment, the United States, Canada, and the Western European countries formed a military alliance called the North Atlantic Treaty Organization (NATO). The Soviet Union and its satellites formed the Warsaw Pact military alliance.

A long period of open hostility and an arms race began between the two superpowers. The Cold War turned "hot" during the Korean and Vietnam wars, but the United States and the Soviet Union avoided direct military conflict.

EXERCISE 32

Directions: Circle *T* for each true statement, or *F* for each false statement.

T F 1. The United States and the Soviet Union kept up their wartime cooperation for many years after defeating the Axis powers.

T F 2. The countries that the Soviet Union controlled in Eastern Europe were called colonies.

T F 3. The containment policy was supposed to keep Soviet communism from expanding into more countries.

T F 4. The United States and its allies formed the military alliance called the Marshall Plan.

T F 5. The Korean War was fought to prevent communist expansion in Asia.

ANSWERS ARE ON PAGE 305.

THE THIRD WORLD

KEY WORD

Third World—developing nations of Asia, Africa, and Latin America, many of which gained their independence after World War II, and were not allied with either superpower

Outside the conflict between the United States and the Soviet Union, political struggles took place in Africa, Asia, and Latin America. Nationalist movements in European colonies fought for independence. There were also movements against wealthy local elites who upheld unjust social and economic conditions. The Europeans had been weakened by World War II, so they had difficulty trying to hold on to their colonies. The Soviet Union supported local opposition forces in order to gain influence in Third World countries. By the 1960s and 1970s, most Third World countries had become independent.

The Cold War dominated U.S. policy toward the Third World. Once a British colony itself, the United States sometimes found it awkward to support colonial rule rather than a nationalist movement. But when the nationalism movement was supported by the Soviet Union, the United States seemed to have little choice. Most Third World nations tried to steer an independent course between the two superpowers.

The worst fears of the United States were realized in 1959 in Cuba. Fidel Castro overthrew a military dictatorship and set up a revolutionary communist government.

EXERCISE 33

Directions: Put a check in front of the correct answer to the questions that follow.

1. U.S. foreign policy toward the Third World

_____**(1)** stressed foreign aid to Cuba

_____**(2)** linked nationalist movements to communist expansion

_____**(3)** was opposed to all independence movements

_____**(4)** was concerned only with protecting U.S. business interests

2. Third World nations often

_____**(1)** sided with the United States against the Soviet Union

_____**(2)** sided with the Soviet Union against the United States

_____**(3)** had complicated social and economic movements that had no relation to international politics

_____**(4)** were kept in line by whichever superpower gave them the most money

3. U.S. fears of communism in the Third World came true in

_____**(1)** Mexico

_____**(2)** South Africa

_____**(3)** India

_____**(4)** Cuba

ANSWERS ARE ON PAGE 306.

THE UNITED STATES AND VIETNAM

KEY WORDS

guerrilla—a person who fights behind the lines and carries out acts of sabotage, strike-and-run military action, or terror against the enemy

domino theory—the argument noted by President Eisenhower that if one nation faces great danger, so will its neighbor and then the next country until a whole region falls

The containment policy applied to Vietnam as well. When the French left in 1954, Vietnam was divided in two. North Vietnam was a communist country led by Ho Chi Minh. It sponsored guerrilla activity in South Vietnam, a weak country. To stop the domino theory from working, the United States sent aid to South Vietnam so that the communists would not take over the country. American military and economic aid climbed steadily under all presidents from Eisenhower to Nixon.

U.S. troop strength in Vietnam reached 543,000 by 1969. More tons of bombs were dropped by air on North Vietnam than were dropped on Germany, Italy, and Japan in World War II. It did little good. Eventually, the United States signed the Paris Peace Agreement in 1973 and pulled out of Vietnam. Two years later, the communists united Vietnam under their leadership.

The Vietnam War created enormous difficulties at home. Antiwar activism was the greatest in U.S. history. The cost of the war weakened the economy. The war also forced U.S. foreign policy makers to take a new look at how the United States should deal with the Third World.

EXERCISE 34

Directions: Based on the passage, underline the correct answer to the questions below.

1. North Vietnam supported guerrillas in (China, South Vietnam).

2. U.S. military aid to (North Vietnam, South Vietnam) increased steadily through the 1960s.

3. The (containment policy, domino theory) meant that if communism won in one country, the neighboring countries were also in danger.

4. You might infer from the passage that the war in Vietnam caused greater problems for the United States (at home, with its allies) than it did with the Soviet Union.

ANSWERS ARE ON PAGE 306.

WRITING ACTIVITY 10

President Nixon had been a longtime enemy of communism. In 1973, however, he decided to renew U.S. relations with communist China. Write a few paragraphs explaining why Nixon might have done so at that time.

ANSWERS WILL VARY.

THE END OF THE COLD WAR

KEY WORDS

deténte—a policy that called for more peaceful cooperation between the United States and the Soviet Union

market economy—another name for free enterprise where buyers and sellers, not the government, determine prices and output

Both superpowers saw that the Vietnam War was dangerous because it could lead to a direct struggle between the United States and the Soviet Union. President Nixon worked out a policy of deténte with the Soviet Union and met with the leaders of China. By the late 1970s, however, deténte returned to Cold War when the Soviet Union invaded Afghanistan and the communist government in Poland took strong action against the Solidarity workers' movement.

In 1980, President Ronald Reagan decided to build up U.S. forces to overtake the military might of the Soviet Union. By the mid-1980s, a young leader, Mikhail Gorbachev, took charge of the Soviet Union. He realized that the Soviet economy could no longer keep up the arms race. The country withdrew from Afghanistan. By 1990 it allowed the East European satellites to go their own ways. The Berlin Wall was torn down in 1989 and Germany was reunited. The Cold War was over.

Within two years, the Soviet Union broke up into fifteen independent republics. Old-style communism survived in only a few countries such as North Korea and China. Market economies were introduced in nearly every former communist country.

While communism was breaking up, nationalism took its place. Ugly fighting broke out in Yugoslavia, which split into several independent countries. Many African countries faced economic decline, hunger, and heavy debt. The Middle East continued to be a battleground. Acts of terrorism occurred everywhere, even in the United States. All of these things created great problems for the United States because the country was now the only remaining superpower. The United States continues to serve as the world's peacekeeper because the world looks to it for leadership.

EXERCISE 35

Part A

Directions: Match the item on the left with its description on the right. Write the correct letter on the line.

_____ **1.** Cold War

_____ **2.** terrorism

_____ **3.** nationalism

_____ **4.** Berlin Wall

_____ **5.** peacekeeping

_____ **6.** detente

(a) relaxing of tensions and increased cooperation between the U.S. and the Soviet Union

(b) ended in 1989 with the Soviet satellites free to go their own ways

(c) its destruction led to the unification of Germany

(d) became a more important force in world affairs with the breakup of the Soviet Union

(e) a major problem that knows no borders and affects innocent people

(f) role the U.S. often assumes in the post–Cold War period

Part B

Directions: Based on the passage on page 137, answer the questions below in the space provided.

1. President _____ established a policy of detente with the former Soviet Union and met with Chinese leaders.

2. The communist government opposed the _____ movement among workers in Poland.

3. A market economy is a system in which buyers and sellers determine _____ and _____.

4. The person responsible for easing up on the arms race in the former Soviet Union was _____.

ANSWERS ARE ON PAGE 306.

EXERCISE 36

Directions: Study the cartoon below and then put a check in front of the correct answer to the question that follows.

What do you think is the cartoonist's message?

_____**(1)** Germany does not believe in wasting bricks.

_____**(2)** Germans believed the Berlin Wall was a good idea and can be applied to unwanted immigrants.

_____**(3)** Immigration is a major problem in Germany.

_____**(4)** Germany has learned no lessons from the past in facing the current problem of immigration.

ANSWER IS ON PAGE 306.

U.S. DOMESTIC HISTORY: 1945–1990s

Several important themes run through American domestic history since World War II. These themes include the impact of U.S. foreign policy on politics, the appearance of mass movements for social change, and the government's role in the economy and in meeting social needs.

A FAST-CHANGING WORLD

1989	**Germany**—Berlin Wall comes down **Poland**—Solidarity victory in free elections **Afghanistan**—Soviet Union withdraws last troops
1990	**Nicaragua**—Pro-Communist Sandinistas voted from office **Iraq**—invades Kuwait; defeated by U.S.-led coalition
1991	**Soviet Union**—breaks up into 15 independent republics **Yugoslavia**—Croatia and Slovenia declare independence
1992	**El Salvador**—end of 12-year civil war **Bosnia and Herzegovina**—declare independence; civil war **Somalia**—U.S. troops sent to guard food deliveries
1993	**Israel**—signs peace agreement with Palestinian Liberation Organization (PLO) in Washington **Russia**—Boris Yeltsin survives impeachment by former communists
1994	**South Africa**—black majority rule begins with election of Nelson Mandela as president **Rwanda**—civil war, mass flight and death of refugees **Jordan**—ends 46 years of war with Israel **Haiti**—military rulers defy world; refugee problem worsens

Source: *World Almanac 1994*

KEY WORD

McCarthyism—careless and groundless attacks on people suspected of being communists; associated with Senator McCarthy's anti-communist tactics

The fear of communism led to a witch hunt in the 1950s. Senator Joseph McCarthy of Wisconsin and his followers accused many Americans of being communists or communist sympathizers. In Congress, the House Un-American Activities Committee made its own investigations. Thousands of Americans lost their jobs as a result of McCarthyism. In 1954, Senator McCarthy's colleagues in the U.S. Senate condemned his actions.

As we have seen, the government's conduct in the Vietnam War had a widespread effect on the American people in the 1960s and early 1970s. The attempt to contain communism led instead to a large antiwar movement and a discrediting of the presidency and U.S. foreign policy. The cost of American involvement increased inflation and made it difficult to keep up with costly domestic social programs.

Americans seemed to have shaken the trauma of the Vietnam War by the 1980s. The end of the Cold War, however, meant that new thinking about the direction of U.S. foreign policy was needed. It was not clear what long-term direction it would take. Besides, Americans had become more concerned about the U.S. economy and making a living.

≡ PRE-GED Practice ≡
EXERCISE 37

Questions 1 and 2 are based on the previous passage.

1. Why might the U.S. Senate have condemned McCarthy's actions?

   (1) He accused too many senators of being communists.
   (2) He was a discredit to the U.S. Congress.
   (3) The communist threat had ended.
   (4) His charges were proved correct and the accused put in jail.
   (5) The United States had become friendly with the communist countries.

2. Because by the late 1960s polls showed that the majority of Americans disapproved of U.S. involvement in Vietnam, you can infer that

   (1) the cost in American lives and money was too high
   (2) Americans increasingly sympathized with the North Vietnamese
   (3) Americans feared that the Soviet Union would send in troops
   (4) Americans favored isolationism and wanted to pull out
   (5) Americans wanted the troops to be stationed in other countries

   ANSWERS ARE ON PAGE 306.

WRITING ACTIVITY 11

With the end of the Cold War, the United States had to refocus its attention from fighting communism to a great number of other problems and areas, such as terrorism, the international drug trade, renewed nationalism, the Middle East, and Central America. In a few paragraphs, describe what you believe U.S. foreign policy should be.

ANSWERS WILL VARY.

MOVEMENTS FOR SOCIAL CHANGE

KEY WORD

Brown* v. *Board of Education (1954)—the unanimous Supreme Court decision that struck down racial segregation in public schools

---

In the period after World War II, several large protest movements that sought basic changes in society grew up. In 1954, the Supreme Court banned racial segregation in public schools in its *Brown* v. *Board of Education* decision. The court did not consider segregated schools to be equal under the law. Protests against all forms of racial segregation and discrimination developed.

A young and skillful speaker, Dr. Martin Luther King, Jr., became the leader of this civil rights movement. He got black and white support for nonviolent protest against discriminatory laws. Student sit-ins and local boycotts were part of the nonviolent disobedience that produced the Civil Rights Act (1964) and the Voting Rights Act (1965).

Although King was assassinated in 1968, the movement continued. The Voting Rights Act allowed hundreds of African Americans and members of other minorities to be elected to public office. In 1992, thirty-eight African Americans, seventeen Hispanics, and forty-seven women were elected to the House of Representatives. In that same year, one African-American woman (the first ever), five other women, and one Native American were elected to the Senate. The civil rights movement by African Americans led women, Hispanics, Native Americans, gays and lesbians, senior citizens, and other groups to seek similar rights.

By the 1970s, many Americans became interested in protecting or cleaning up the environment. This echoed the concern of the Progressives in the early 1900s and the conservationists of the New Deal of the 1930s. A number of private groups such as the Sierra Club and the National Wildlife Federation lobbied Congress and backed candidates in elections who supported their views. A number of acts of Congress were aimed at curbing pollution, cleaning up the land and water, and disposing properly of toxic and nuclear wastes. The Environmental Protection Agency was set up. The continuing goal is to improve the environment—and thus the quality of life—for all Americans.

EXERCISE 38

Directions: Based on the previous passage, underline the correct answer that completes each statement below.

1. *Brown* v. *Board of Education* was a Supreme Court decision banning (segregation, integration) in (private, public) schools.

2. The civil rights movement led by Dr. King favored (violent, nonviolent) means to obtain racial justice.

3. Judging from the information on the 1992 election, you can infer that the Voting Rights Act was (successful, unsuccessful).

4. The number of private groups and public laws favoring environmental protection indicates that the movement had (little, widespread) support.

ANSWERS ARE ON PAGE 306.

President Lyndon Johnson's Great Society Legislation

Economic Opportunity Act (War on Poverty)

- Head Start
- Job Corps
- Volunteers in Service for America (VISTA)
- Upward Bound

Civil Rights Act

Voting Rights Act

Equal Employment Opportunity Commission

Medical Care Act

- Medicaid (for welfare recipients)
- Medicare (for the elderly)

Immigration Act ended quotas of 1924 act

Public housing and rent supplements

Food stamps

By the 1980s, the government's role in maintaining social programs clashed with the need to cut government spending and reduce the national debt. Inflation made programs with built-in cost-of-living increases very costly, and many of them were cut.

By the 1990s, millions of Americans were without medical insurance because the country had no national health insurance program. The Clinton administration's proposed universal coverage ran into great opposition in Congress. In addition, people who need public assistance but are not covered by a particular government program must seek private help or depend on limited local or state funds. The AIDS epidemic and the revival of other diseases thought to be under control (such as tuberculosis) put further strains on the nation's health care system.

EXERCISE 39

Directions: Study the political cartoon below and then put a check in front of the correct answer to the questions that follow.

1. What is a likely meaning of this cartoon?

   ____ **(1)** Clinton is chiefly concerned that people know the health care plan is his.

   ____ **(2)** Taxpayers have no idea how much Clinton's health care plan will cost them.

   ____ **(3)** Clinton is not concerned about the cost of his plan.

   ____ **(4)** Clinton has not worked out the details of his health care plan.

2. What does the cartoonist think of Clinton's health care plan?

   ____ **(1)** He favors it somewhat.

   ____ **(2)** He is 100 percent for it.

   ____ **(3)** He is concerned about its cost.

   ____ **(4)** He is worried about the details of insurance coverage.

ANSWERS ARE ON PAGE 306.

GOVERNMENT'S ROLE IN THE ECONOMY

KEY WORDS

national debt—the total amount of money owed by the federal government of the United States to its creditors

trade deficit—an excess of the value of imports over the value of exports; also called unfavorable balance of trade

The United States emerged from World War II with a strong economy that led the world in output. Pent-up demand for goods brought prosperity at home that continued through the 1950s and 1960s.

During the 1970s, however, the U.S. economy faced great inflation. This was caused in part by the Vietnam War spending and rising oil prices. The national debt increased enormously.

The American love for large, gas-guzzling automobiles forced the country to import much larger amounts of oil from overseas. This worked well until the Organization of Petroleum Exporting Countries (OPEC) decided to raise the price of oil and take a greater share of the profits for themselves. In addition, U.S. manufacturers faced powerful competition from Japanese and West German products. These countries had rebuilt their industries and used the most modern technology. The United States, on the other hand, continued to use old factories with outmoded equipment. The U.S. trade deficit, particularly with Japan, worsened.

U.S. businesses downsized, or cut back, in order to be more efficient. This worked well for the companies, who then became more competitive in the world market. But thousands of Americans lost their jobs. President Bush's lack of attention to the economy probably cost him the election in 1992.

People continue to question government intervention in the economy. Despite wide differences, the consensus is that government must provide some degree of economic regulation and some form of economic security for its citizens.

EXERCISE 40

Directions: Study the graph below and then put a check in front of the correct answer to the questions that follow.

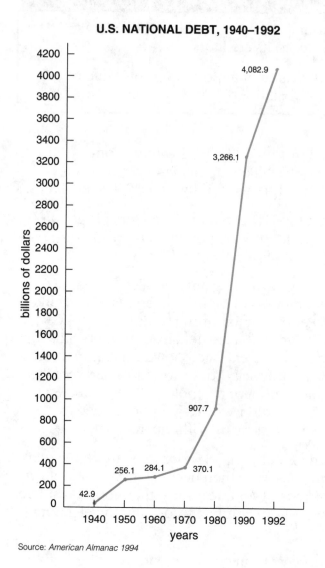

U.S. NATIONAL DEBT, 1940–1992

billions of dollars

4,082.9

3,266.1

907.7

370.1

256.1   284.1

42.9

1940 1950 1960 1970 1980 1990 1992

years

Source: *American Almanac 1994*

1. During which ten-year period did the national debt show the largest dollar increase?

_____ **(1)** 1940–1950

_____ **(2)** 1960–1970

_____ **(3)** 1970–1980

_____ **(4)** 1980–1990

2. Spending on which of the following accounted for the rapid growth of the national debt between 1940 and 1950?

_____ **(1)** New Deal

_____ **(2)** World War II

_____ **(3)** Social Security

_____ **(4)** Korean War

ANSWERS ARE ON PAGE 307.

≡ PRE-GED Practice ≡
U.S. HISTORY

Questions 1–3 are based on the passage below.

Cleaning Up America's Rivers

The Nashua's pollution grew up with America. For more than a century wood, wool, shoe, cotton, and paper mills had dumped waste into its quiet flow. By the mid-1960s, the river was classed as unfit even to receive sewage. Because of dumped dyes, people used to bet on whether it was going to be red, orange, blue, green, or white the next day. Then a woman named Marion Stoddart started a campaign to restore the Nashua and its tributaries. It's been called a one-woman crusade, but in many ways it worked because it wasn't. . . .

Stoddart built coalitions with businessmen, labor leadership, and paper companies—the worst polluters. She focused on economic as well as environmental issues. She gave bottles of dirty river water to key officials. At a hearing before the state water-pollution–control board to reclassify the river's quality rating, which would force the cleanup, she demanded a goal many thought unthinkable: water safe for swimming. "Come on, be realistic," she was told. She didn't back down.

Within a few years people cleaned up their businesses, changed state law, and testified before Congress. And with federal help eight treatment plants have been built or upgraded, and a broad conservation buffer zone called a greenway has been created along about half of the Nashua and two major tributaries. Today most of the industry is still there—and many parts of the river are safe for swimming.

Michael Parfit, *National Geographic,*
November 1993

1. Marion Stoddart's goal was to
   (1) drive the paper companies out of business
   (2) set up water treatment plants throughout New Hampshire
   (3) make the Nashua River and its tributaries safe for swimming
   (4) build dams on the Nashua River
   (5) lobby in Washington for the Clean Water Act

2. How did Marion Stoddart go about achieving her goal?
   (1) making coalitions with business, labor, and the companies that caused the pollution
   (2) making coalitions with government and labor against the polluting companies
   (3) writing a series of articles in the newspaper on water pollution
   (4) making demands and, when those were met, making further demands
   (5) dumping varied colored dyes into the river to attract attention

3. Based on the passage, you could infer that
   (1) one person can accomplish major changes in the environment
   (2) environmental changes can be made only by the federal government
   (3) companies that pollute the environment refuse to change their ways
   (4) people working together can bring about environmental change
   (5) state and local government will do nothing about the environment unless private citizens take action

ANSWERS ARE ON PAGE 307.

6 Political Science

Political science is the study of the institutions of government and how they work. Political scientists study governmental structure and policy making, political parties, political behavior, interest groups, and international relations.

A *political system* is an institution that organizes power relationships in a society. People have created a wide variety of political systems from simple tribal organizations to very complex nation-states like the United States. The earliest political systems had no formal governmental structure. Important decisions were often made by one person or a council. As societies became more complex, people created more complicated governmental structures.

A *government* is the body or institution that makes and administers society's laws. The police and the courts are the part of government that maintain order in society. Armed forces provide security against attack by other countries. Most governments promote some form of general welfare in health, safety, education, and help to the needy.

Three necessary functions underlie all governments:

- executive (administers the operations of government)

- legislative (makes the laws)

- judicial (interprets the laws)

All governments possess the power to make decisions and carry them out. Some rule by direct force or by the threat of force against its citizens. Others rule with the support of their citizens.

When the people believe that the government is not working in their interest, governmental authority can break down. If a government uses force against the people, the struggle can escalate. Some governments have been overthrown by revolution, such as the American colonists' fight against the English government.

Governments may also be overthrown by a small group rather than by a popular uprising. This kind of action is called a *coup d'état*, meaning a "blow against the state."

People try to influence the government in many ways. For example, political parties are a part of the American political system, but they are not a part of the government. Citizens also can become involved in the American political system by petitioning, demonstrating, and lobbying.

TYPES OF GOVERNMENT

KEY WORDS

absolute monarchy—a type of government in which the king or queen's word is the law

constitutional monarchy—a limited monarchy that has constitutional checks upon the ruler

direct democracy—a democracy in which the people have a direct voice and vote in the government

representative democracy—a democracy in which people select delegates or substitutes to represent them

oligarchy—a type of government in which a small group of people rule

totalitarianism—an extreme type of dictatorship that controls the political, economic, and social life of a country

There are four main types of government. They are monarchy, democracy, oligarchy, and dictatorship.

MONARCHY

Monarchies are one of the oldest forms of government in the world. A king or a queen is the head of the government. Queen Elizabeth II of Great Britain and Queen Beatrix of the Netherlands are monarchs. Countries that have constitutions, such as the United States, but also have monarchs, are called constitutional monarchies. Great Britain is a constitutional monarchy. The queen's tasks are chiefly ceremonial. She reigns but does not rule. Instead, the queen has a prime minister, a cabinet, and a permanent civil service who carry out the day-to-day job of governing according to the laws passed by Parliament, the legislative branch of government.

Countries where the monarch's word is the law are called absolute monarchies. King Fahd of Saudi Arabia is an absolute monarch. The country has no constitution, no parliament, and no political parties.

France and Russia used to be absolute monarchies, but the people overthrew King Louis XVI during the French Revolution in 1792 and Tsar Nicholas II in the Russian Revolution of 1917. Sometimes absolute monarchs claim to rule by divine right, which means that they believe their right to rule comes from God.

DEMOCRACY

A second type of government is a democracy. The power to rule in a democracy comes from the people. (In Greek, *demos* means people, and *cracy* means power or form of government.) The United States is a democracy in which the people take part in the government. Other countries, such as France and India, are also democracies.

Democracy has deep roots in Western political tradition. It can take different forms ranging from the direct democracy, or participatory democracy, of the Greek city-states or the representative democracy found in the United States.

The United States is too large for everyone to gather to discuss and vote on laws. The people elect representatives to carry out the wishes of the people according to the Constitution. In a representative democracy, all people over a certain age have the right to vote. This was not always so. In the United States, only white men could vote until after the Civil War. Then black men had this right according to the Fifteenth Amendment (1870). Women did not get the right to vote until 1920, when the Nineteenth Amendment was passed.

The largest democracy in the world is India, which has a population of 900 million. However, the country is divided by many ethnic groups, languages, and religions. The result is that India is difficult to govern.

OLIGARCHY

A third type of government is an oligarchy, which means government by a few. Before the Industrial Revolution, England was considered an oligarchy. Even though it had a monarch whose powers had by then become limited, the real power was in the hands of a few members of Parliament. Voting was limited to people with a certain income. So the aristocracy and rich merchants—the upper class—controlled the government.

Some of the ancient Greek city-states were oligarchies ruled by a few leading families. The seafaring Republic of Venice was ruled by a merchant elite. The rest of the people had no say in the government.

Some countries today might be considered oligarchies even though they would not call themselves that. Although conditions change rapidly, certain developing countries, particularly in Latin America, have long been ruled by the leading families who control the economies of these countries.

DICTATORSHIP

A widespread form of government is the ***dictatorship***. A dictator is a person who has complete control. A dictator rules somewhat in the manner of an absolute monarch but does not use royal titles like king or emperor. In modern times, dictators have become totalitarian rulers. Under totalitarianism, the dictators have complete control over all political, economic, and social life in the country. Joseph Stalin and Adolf Hitler were totalitarian dictators. Both ruled through a secret police that terrorized people to keep them from opposing the dictators. The Communist Party in the Soviet Union had this role from 1918 to 1990. The Nazi Party in Germany supported Hitler from 1933 until Allied victory in World War II ended his rule.

At the present time, many developing countries are dictatorships, particularly in Africa and Asia. Iraq's Saddam Hussein is a dictator. North Korea is one of the last communist dictatorships. Although countries with dictators often have constitutions and legislative bodies, the wishes of the dictators are always carried out.

EXERCISE 1

Directions: Match the type of government on the left with its description on the right. Write the correct letter on the line.

_____ **1.** direct democracy

_____ **2.** representative democracy

_____ **3.** absolute monarchy

_____ **4.** constitutional monarchy

_____ **5.** oligarchy

_____ **6.** totalitarianism

(a) has checks on the ruler

(b) people select delegates to represent them

(c) people vote on government issues

(d) the king or queen's word is law

(e) an extreme form of dictatorship

(f) a small group of people rule

ANSWERS ARE ON PAGE 307.

THE AMERICAN POLITICAL PROCESS

KEY WORDS

plurality—the greatest number of votes in an election

simple majority—50 percent of the votes plus a minimum of one vote

electoral college—a special group of voters from each state that elects the president and vice president

---

At the heart of democracy are the concepts of consent and majority rule. Majority rule is the only practical way of achieving consensus, or group agreement. A unanimous vote (100 percent) is unlikely, and minority rule does not truly represent a consensus.

In a representative democracy such as the United States, a candidate for public office needs to win a majority of the votes cast. Sometimes a candidate needs to win only a plurality, the greatest number of votes cast, to win.

Candidate Bill Clinton won only 43 percent of the popular (people's) vote for president in 1992, but he won 370 electoral votes. It is the electoral college that elects the president. Each state has its own number of electors, depending on the size of each state. The candidate who gets the most votes from the people of a particular state also wins all the electoral votes from that state. Clinton got well over the majority of electoral votes needed to win the election.

Most bills submitted to Congress need a simple majority (50 percent plus a minimum of one vote) to become laws. In special cases, majorities of two-thirds or three-fifths may be required.

The importance of a majority in American politics does not mean that the minority viewpoint is totally ignored. Compromise is often needed to get a simple majority of votes to pass legislation in Congress. Senators and representatives also take public opinion into consideration.

PRE-GED Practice
EXERCISE 2

Question 1 is based on the vote totals shown below.

In the election for mayor in Metropolis, Alfred Johnson was elected. The vote totals for the three candidates were:

Johnson	101,700
Alvarez	93,201
Lee	45,718

1. What term best describes Johnson's vote total?

   (1) plurality
   (2) majority
   (3) simple majority
   (4) consensus
   (5) three-fifths majority

Questions 2–4 are based on the passage on page 154.

2. In a council vote, 30 of the 50 members voted to ban smoking in all the city's restaurants. The vote is an example of

   (1) compromise
   (2) simple majority
   (3) three-fifths majority
   (4) consensus
   (5) two-thirds majority

3. The owners of a condominium high-rise meet each month to discuss and decide on the business of their building. This meeting closely resembles a direct democracy. Which of the following is required to reach a consensus?

   (1) The condominium board president makes decisions.
   (2) All owners must agree for consensus to be reached.
   (3) A majority of owners must approve any actions.
   (4) The five richest owners decide for the others.
   (5) The elected officers of the board make all decisions.

4. The owners of another condominium building have an elected board of five members. Which of the following is required to make a decision binding?

   (1) The condominium board president makes decisions.
   (2) All owners must agree for a decision to be binding.
   (3) A majority of owners must approve a decision.
   (4) The five richest owners decide for the others.
   (5) The elected officers of the board make all the decisions.

ANSWERS ARE ON PAGE 307.

INTEREST GROUPS AND POLITICAL PARTIES

Elected representatives play an important role in the American political system. As soon as these representatives take office, people try to influence their decisions. Individuals, groups, and organizations have interests that can be aided by government decisions. There are many stages of political activity between the desires and needs of citizens and final government decisions.

INTEREST GROUPS

Organized interest groups, such as labor unions and business groups, usually have active political programs. Single-issue groups, such as anti-smoking supporters, have become increasingly important. U.S. history has a long record of single-issue movements from Shay's rebellious debtor farmers in Massachusetts in the 1780s to today's environmental movement. Individuals believe they can be more effective if they join others with similar interests.

Interest groups have more power than individuals acting alone. They bring their numbers and influence into politics. They may raise campaign funds to aid a candidate who supports their position and provide volunteers for the candidate's election campaign. They may also put pressure on officials by writing letters, making visits, and demonstrating as a group.

POLITICAL PARTIES

The U.S. Constitution did not provide for political parties. However, the leaders of the young nation had many conflicts over national policy. Various organizations channeled the efforts of different interest groups into political action.

Two major parties, the Republicans and Democrats, have dominated the U.S. political system since the 1860s. They have effectively organized into interest groups. Compromise programs have united broad coalitions that campaign for the party's candidates.

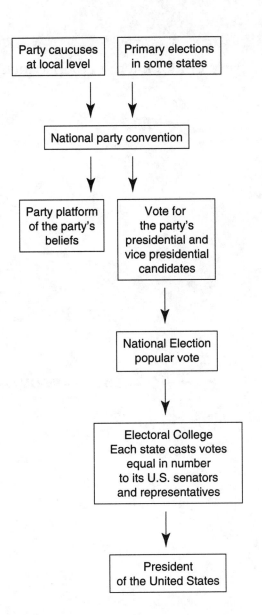

Political parties select presidential candidates at national conventions. The chart at left outlines the process by which political parties choose a presidential candidate.

In a complex society such as the United States, the individual citizen cannot have much influence on the direction of politics without becoming part of an organized political group. Citizens should exercise their right to vote. Only through group participation in defining issues can citizens meaningfully affect the choices they will have at election time.

Politicians play an important role in the political process. They build coalitions needed to get things done. They are not always liked by the public, but they are necessary in the American political process.

The majority of people usually vote for the same political party at each election. Others consider themselves "independents," who switch from one major party to the next, depending on the issues or candidates. Sometimes they support third parties.

Besides the two major parties, a wide variety of third parties have appeared from time to time in U.S. history. They include the Libertarian, Communist, American Independent, Prohibitionist, Socialist, and Populist parties. Nevertheless, the two major parties have managed to dominate politics and also have a far broader appeal to voters than the third parties with their narrower interests.

The activities of political parties, single-issue movements, and interest groups have expanded the limits of American democracy to allow more people to participate. In the process, they have formed election coalitions capable of winning power and acting on those interests.

EXERCISE 3

Directions: Write *P* for political party, *T* for third party, or *I* for interest group to identify the groups listed below.

_____ **1.** anti-smoking lobby

_____ **2.** political caucus

_____ **3.** Republicans

_____ **4.** Populists

_____ **5.** Libertarians

_____ **6.** Save the Whales

_____ **7.** Americans for Democratic Action

_____ **8.** isolationists

ANSWERS ARE ON PAGE 307.

EXERCISE 4

Directions: Read the passage below and then put a check in front of the correct answer to the questions that follow.

Voter Turnout

The low voter turnout in this country is due to the relatively small number of voters who control elections. Most close congressional races are decided by fewer than 7,000 votes. Primary elections and state and local races are often decided by much smaller margins.

Senior citizens have protested every hint of cuts in Social Security. Elected officials know this, and Social Security is untouched because senior citizens vote.

On the other hand, surveys show that only 25 to 35 percent of eligible low-income people vote. This figure would be even lower if people with low incomes but substantial assets were counted separately. The voter turnout rate stands in sharp contrast to the 70 to 75 percent turnout among people making over $25,000 a year. When low-income people fail to vote in numbers that match their total population, their interests are ignored.

1. As a result of voter turnout patterns, the writer believes that

_____ **(1)** the elderly do not have much influence

_____ **(2)** the poor have too much influence on elections

_____ **(3)** poor people do not have much influence on elections

2. Based on this passage, if lower-income people voted in large numbers, what could you conclude?

_____ **(1)** Social welfare programs would probably be expanded.

_____ **(2)** Social welfare programs would probably be decreased.

_____ **(3)** Social Security payments would be decreased.

ANSWERS ARE ON PAGE 307.

WRITING ACTIVITY 12

Think of a special interest group you would like to join. The group can be for or against any cause that interests you or that you think is important. In one sentence, state clearly the focus of your interest group. Then write four or five suggestions about how your group might accomplish its goal.

ANSWERS WILL VARY.

THE U.S. CONSTITUTION

> **KEY WORDS**
>
> **federal system**—the sharing of power between the states and the central government
>
> **checks and balances**—a system among the branches of the federal government that prevents any one branch from dominating the other two
>
> **Bill of Rights**—the first ten amendments to the U.S. Constitution that state the freedoms and rights of individuals

The years after the Revolutionary War (1783-1789) are often called the "time of troubles." The American economy was in a serious economic depression. The Articles of Confederation were adopted in 1781. They did not provide for an executive branch or a court system. The national government had no power to tax or regulate commerce between the states. Interstate commerce was carried on with the greatest difficulty because each state could issue its own currency, or paper money, and often charged their own taxes on goods.

In Massachusetts, armed farmers who were heavily in debt took part in Shay's Rebellion (1786). They seized courtrooms to prevent mortgage foreclosures. The rebellion was finally put down with little bloodshed. However, it pointed to the need for a strong central government that could put down such internal uprisings. The problems facing the new American nation made it clear that the Articles of Confederation needed to be changed drastically or dropped altogether.

Some aspects of the economic crisis—especially problems of interstate commerce—had to be dealt with. Meetings were held among some states in 1785 and 1786. These meetings led to a call for a Constitutional Convention. Its purpose was to amend the Articles of Confederation. The convention call was endorsed by the Confederation Congress. The Constitutional Convention opened in Philadelphia in May 1787.

A main issue in the Constitutional Convention concerned the division of power between the central government and the states. The final Constitution represented a victory of centralized power over states' rights. The government in Washington increased its powers and gained the right to tax, create an army and navy, control foreign trade, make treaties, and control currency. The states, however, still maintained substantial responsibilities. The kind of arrangement that divides power between a central government and the states is called a federal system.

The convention attempted to protect against overcentralization of power by basing the new government on the separation of powers. A legislative branch, made up of a House of Representatives and the Senate, was to enact laws. An executive branch, headed by the president, was to administer the government. A federal judicial (court) system was created to settle disputes and legal matters. Thus, a system of checks and balances was created in order to prevent any single branch of government from dominating the others.

Another important issue at the convention was the fair distribution of power between large and small states. This was resolved by giving each state equal representation in the Senate and basing representation in the House of Representatives on the size of the state's population. In this way, the House protected the rights of large states and the Senate protected the rights of small states.

The question of whether slaves should be counted in population totals was another issue at the convention. If slaves were counted, the Southern states, which had fewer people, would have greater representation in the House. Southern delegates argued that slaves should be counted. Northern delegates said that if slaves were counted for representation, they should be counted for taxation and taxed the same as free people.

They agreed that for both representation and taxation all free people would be counted along with three-fifths of all slaves (known as the Three-fifths Compromise). It strengthened the power of slave states in the House of Representatives. The Constitution also protected the slave trade for at least 20 years. Runaway slaves would also have to be returned to their owners.

The Constitution addressed other areas of government. There were sections on choosing the president, structuring the federal court system, and amending the Constitution. The finished Constitution was sent to conventions in each of the thirteen states. In order to become law, it needed to be ratified by nine states.

There was some opposition to the document. Many Americans believed that it gave too much power to the national government. Many people also opposed the Constitution because it did not guarantee the rights of individual citizens—an objection that resulted in the Bill of Rights, the first ten amendments to the Constitution. The supporters of the Constitution, known as the Federalists, were led by Alexander Hamilton, James Madison, and John Jay. They wrote a series of articles, *The Federalist Papers*, arguing for ratification. A majority of the leaders of the Revolution, including George Washington and Benjamin Franklin, also supported the Constitution. Eleven states finally ratified the Constitution. It became effective March 1789.

EXERCISE 5

Directions: Match the item on the left with its description on the right. Write the correct letter on the line.

_____ **1.** checks and balances

_____ **2.** federal system

_____ **3.** *The Federalist Papers*

_____ **4.** Three-fifths Compromise

_____ **5.** Bill of Rights

(a) the first ten amendments to the Constitution

(b) gave slave states a greater representation in the House of Representatives

(c) prevents one branch of government from dominating the others

(d) sharing of power between the states and the central government

(e) a series of articles that argued for ratification of the Constitution

ANSWERS ARE ON PAGE 308.

AMENDMENTS TO THE CONSTITUTION

The protection of individual citizens' rights dominated the first session of the new Congress in 1789. During the drive for ratification, the Federalists had been forced by popular pressure to support a Bill of Rights in the form of amendments to the Constitution. Congress submitted the first ten constitutional amendments to the states for ratification. They were approved by 1791.

These first ten amendments, known as the Bill of Rights, form the basis of individual rights and liberties. These amendments guarantee the following:

- freedom of speech and the press
- the right to assemble and petition the government
- the right to keep and bear arms
- protection against unreasonable search and seizure

- the right to trial by jury
- the right to due process and protection against self-incrimination
- the right to a public trial
- the right to have an attorney
- protection against excessive bail or unusual punishment
- separation of church and state

Since the Bill of Rights, seventeen more amendments have been added to the Constitution. Only one amendment has been repealed. The Eighteenth Amendment (1919), prohibition, was repealed by the Twenty-first Amendment (1933). The procedure for changing the Constitution was purposely made difficult. Amendments must be proposed by a two-thirds majority vote of both houses of Congress. Otherwise, two-thirds of the state legislatures can ask Congress to call a convention for proposing amendments. Any amendment must be approved by either the legislatures or special conventions in three-fourths of the states. Many proposed amendments have never been ratified because of this difficult procedure. For instance, the Equal Rights Amendment was defeated in 1982 because it fell several states short of the required thirty-eight states needed for ratification.

All amendments that have been adopted have originated in Congress and have been ratified by the state legislatures. Among the more important are the Thirteenth (1865), abolishing slavery; the Fourteenth (1868), granting citizenship to the former slaves; the Fifteenth (1870), guaranteeing black males the right to vote; the Sixteenth (1913), establishing the federal income tax; the Nineteenth (1920), giving women the right to vote; and the Twenty-sixth (1971), lowering the voting age to eighteen.

The Constitution, even with amendments, is a short document, probably shorter than the bylaws of many organizations. It has vague guidelines concerning the powers and functions of the different levels of government. However, its flexibility has allowed it to survive as a symbol of national unity. The concrete meanings of its various paragraphs have constantly evolved as the country has grown and changed.

EXERCISE 6

Directions: Answer the questions below in the space provided.

1. All adopted amendments to the U.S. Constitution have originated in _____.

2. The first ten amendments to the Constitution that list individual rights and freedoms are called the _____.

3. The _____ of the Constitution makes the document as effective today as it was more than 200 years ago.

4. A new amendment must be approved by _____ of the states.

5. After the Bill of Rights, _____ more amendments have been added to the Constitution.

6. The _____ Amendment, prohibition, was repealed by the _____ Amendment in 1933.

7. Any new amendment that is proposed must receive a _____ vote from both houses of Congress.

8. The Thirteenth Amendment abolished _____.

ANSWERS ARE ON PAGE 308.

≡ PRE-GED Practice ≡
EXERCISE 7

Questions 1 and 2 are based on the passage below.

Many Supreme Court decisions have upheld the freedoms in the Bill of Rights. The Supreme Court has defined, limited, or expanded upon the meanings of the amendments. Below are some brief examples from the court battles over the amendments in the Bill of Rights. The examples are from the First Amendment.

". . . Congress shall make no law abridging . . . the right of the people peaceably to assemble, and to petition the government for redress of grievances."

In 1937, in the *DeJonge* v. *Oregon* case, the Supreme Court ruled that freedom of assembly was not limited only to those who wished to petition the government.

". . . Congress shall make no law . . . abridging the freedom of speech or of the press."

This amendment has become the central issue in the debate over what some perceive as obscene or pornographic materials. In 1946, the Supreme Court prevented the Postmaster General from denying second-class postal rates to *Esquire* magazine. In 1962, the court overturned a government practice of treating gay magazines as obscene matter and barring them from the mails. However, the Supreme Court has left the issue of what constitutes pornography up to what are called "community standards."

1. The main idea of this passage is that

    (1) Supreme Court decisions have upheld the constitutional rights of people with controversial opinions or preferences
    (2) freedom of speech has always been upheld by governmental bodies
    (3) freedom of assembly was not clearly defined in the Bill of Rights
    (4) the Bill of Rights should have clearly spelled out individual rights and freedoms
    (5) the courts have always ruled in favor of the Bill of Rights

2. The Supreme Court's decisions on obscene materials have been based on its interpretation of freedom of

    (1) assembly
    (2) religion
    (3) political beliefs
    (4) sexual preference
    (5) speech and the press

ANSWERS ARE ON PAGE 308.

BRANCHES OF GOVERNMENT

> **KEY WORDS**
>
> **veto**—the presidential power to refuse to sign into law a bill that has been approved by Congress; can be overridden by Congress
>
> **pocket veto**—an automatic veto of a bill not signed by the president within ten days of a congressional adjournment

The new Constitution set up a national government with three different branches. To prevent an excess of power, the Constitution divided power and functions among the executive, legislative, and judicial branches. The Constitution also instituted a sophisticated system of checks and balances. This would prevent one branch of government from dominating any other branch.

The chart below shows the branches of government in the United States.

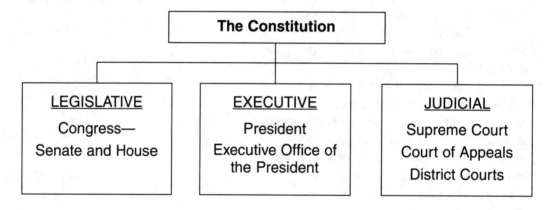

THE EXECUTIVE BRANCH

The executive branch administers the day-to-day activities of the government. The president, who is the head of the executive branch, must be at least thirty-five years old and a natural born citizen of the United States. The presidential term is four years. An individual is limited to two terms by the Twenty-second Amendment (1951). Another amendment allows the vice president to become president if the president dies or resigns while in office.

With the advice and consent of the Senate, the president appoints all of the major executive positions. He also appoints his own Cabinet officers, called secretaries, who are the heads of major government agencies. Some of these are State, Defense, Justice, Agriculture, Labor, and Education. The executive branch also includes federal agencies, such as the Environmental Protection Agency (EPA).

Article II of the Constitution gives the president the power to see that "the laws be faithfully executed." The executive branch is responsible for enforcing acts of Congress, court decisions, and treaties. The president also can issue proclamations and executive orders. These are legislative or lawmaking powers that have been delegated to the president either by law or by court decision. Lincoln's Emancipation Proclamation, which freed all slaves in Confederate states, is one of the most famous examples of this power of the presidency.

All bills passed by Congress must be sent to the president. If he signs the bill, it becomes law. However, he can refuse to sign the bill and return it to Congress; this action is called a veto. Congress may override the president's veto by a two-thirds vote of both houses of Congress. However, if the president does not return the bill within ten days, it automatically becomes a law, unless Congress adjourns during that period. If Congress adjourns during that ten-day period and the president does not sign the bill, he has effected a pocket veto, which cannot be overridden by Congress. The president's veto power shows how the executive branch checks the legislative branch. By using congressional override, the legislative branch checks the executive branch.

Both the president and the vice president are chosen by the electoral college. This body is made up of electors from each state. They have pledged to cast their votes for a certain candidate. When the voters cast a ballot for a presidential candidate and running mate, they are really choosing a slate of electors pledged to vote for the candidate in the electoral college in December. It is possible for a person to receive the most popular votes but fail to be elected president by the electoral college. This has occurred three times in American history: when John Quincy Adams became president in 1824, when Rutherford Hayes was elected in 1876, and when Grover Cleveland became president in 1888.

EXERCISE 8

Directions: Put a check in front of the correct answer to the questions that follow.

1. Which of the following is a lawmaking power of the president?

   ____(1) judicial review

   ____(2) joint resolution

   ____(3) executive order

2. If the president should die in office, who is next in line to become president?

   ____(1) senate majority leader

   ____(2) vice president

   ____(3) secretary of state

   "The President of the United States is to have power to return a bill, which shall have passed the two branches of the legislature for reconsideration; but the bill so returned is not to become a law unless upon reconsideration, it be approved by two-thirds of both houses."

   Alexander Hamilton, *The Federalist Papers*

3. To which of the following processes was Hamilton referring?

   ____(1) pocket veto

   ____(2) presidential veto and congressional override

   ____(3) executive order

4. A president is limited to how many years in office?

   ____(1) four years

   ____(2) eight years

   ____(3) twelve years

ANSWERS ARE ON PAGE 308.

THE LEGISLATIVE BRANCH

KEY WORDS
bicameral—composed of two houses or legislative parts
subpoena—a written order requiring someone to appear in court

The legislative branch of the federal government, the Congress, is responsible for writing the basic laws of the country. The Congress is a bicameral legislature, made up of two houses: the House of Representatives and the Senate. The Senate is made up of two senators from each state. The Senate has 100 members. The number of representatives from a state is determined by the number of people in the state. The House of Representatives has 435 members, a number that Congress has limited since 1910.

A representative in the House is elected for two years, must be at least twenty-five years of age, and also must have been a U.S. citizen for seven years. A senator is elected for six years, must be at least thirty years old, and must have been a U.S. citizen for nine years.

Powers

Congress is responsible for taxing people. The money is used to provide services to people, to defend the country, and to pay the government's debts. Congress has the power to coin money, to declare war, and to override a presidential veto with a two-thirds vote of both houses. Congress proposes amendments to the Constitution, has the power of impeachment, and organizes the federal court system.

Congress operates as a check on the executive branch. It defines the functions of the departments in the executive branch and controls the money set aside for those departments. Congress has the power to investigate numerous areas inside and outside of the government, including the executive branch. A congressional committee, like the court system, has the power to subpoena witnesses and can cite uncooperative witnesses for contempt of court. When Congress actually assumes a "watchdog" role over the executive branch, it can exert a great deal of influence.

Organization

The Speaker of the House presides over the meetings of the House of Representatives and is generally responsible for organizing its activities. The Speaker is a member of the majority party. The Senate is presided over by the vice president, who has little real power to direct the Senate and can cast only tie-breaking votes. The majority party elects a Senate Majority Leader, who leads the legislative activity in the Senate.

Both houses of Congress are organized into committees to carry out the tasks of researching, holding hearings, and writing legislation. All legislation must go through a committee before it can be considered for a vote. A committee chairperson can try to prevent a piece of legislation from reaching a vote or may speed the legislation through the committee and onto the floor. Two important committees are the House Ways and Means Committee, which considers revenue bills, and the Senate Committee on Foreign Relations, which reviews all treaties.

EXERCISE 9

Directions: Based on the passage, circle *T* for each true statement, or *F* for each false statement.

T F **1.** Congress is made up of the Senate and the House of Representatives.

T F **2.** Congress has the powers to make laws, impose taxes, coin money, and declare war.

T F **3.** Congress does not have the power to actually investigate the executive branch in the case of suspected wrongdoing.

T F **4.** A senator is elected for a term of six years, and a representative in the House is elected for two years.

T F **5.** The vice president presides over the meetings of the House of Representatives.

ANSWERS ARE ON PAGE 308.

THE JUDICIAL BRANCH

> **KEY WORD**
>
> *judicial review*—the power of the Supreme Court to rule on the constitutionality of laws

The judicial branch of the federal government is responsible for interpreting laws. The primary responsibility of the federal court system is to hear cases involving federal law.

At the head of the federal courts is the Supreme Court in Washington, D.C. It consists of a chief justice and eight associate justices. These justices are appointed by the president with the approval of the Senate. They serve for life and can be impeached only for misconduct. The major function of the Supreme Court is to hear appeals of lower federal court decisions and from state courts when the questions may involve points of law or constitutionality. The Constitution gives the Supreme Court the right to hear a case first in "all cases affecting ambassadors, other public ministers, and those in which the State shall be a party."

Below the Supreme Court are the federal circuit courts of appeals. They hear appeals and review decisions of the federal district court and federal administrative bodies. At the lowest level are the federal district trial courts. All federal judges are appointed by the president.

The single most important power of the Supreme Court is its power of judicial review. The Supreme Court rules on the constitutionality of laws passed by the legislative branch or on actions taken by the executive branch. The power of judicial review was first used by the Supreme Court in 1803 in *Marbury* v. *Madison*. In that case, the court refused to enforce a law that it believed was unconstitutional.

The power of the Supreme Court to rule on the constitutionality of certain laws and practices has become an important part of our system of government. The judicial branch has become an equal partner in the three-way separation of powers in the federal government. American law has changed over the years as a result of various Supreme Court interpretations of the law and the Constitution.

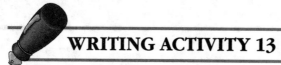

WRITING ACTIVITY 13

In three paragraphs, write a brief summary of what the responsibilities of the three branches of U.S. government are.

ANSWERS WILL VARY.

EXERCISE 10

Directions: Underline the word or words that best complete each statement.

1. Federal judges obtain their positions by (presidential appointment, popular election).

2. The U.S. Constitution (is, is not) open to significant interpretation.

3. The Supreme Court consists of (eight, nine) justices.

4. Immediately below the Supreme Court are the federal (district trial courts, circuit courts of appeals).

5. The power of judicial review allows (the president, the Supreme Court) to rule if a law is constitutional.

6. Supreme Court Justices can be impeached for (misconduct, questionable decisions).

7. The Supreme Court hears appeals from lower federal and state courts in questions of law and (interpretation, constitutionality).

8. Supreme Court Justices are approved by the (House, Senate).

ANSWERS ARE ON PAGE 308.

EXERCISE 11

Directions: Read the passage below and then put a check in front of the correct answer to the questions that follow.

The Supreme Court Reverses Itself

People make the laws and interpret them according to their own beliefs and those of society. Laws are always affected by changing conditions. What the Constitution "really means" is affected by those beliefs and is subject to judicial review at any given time. The political and historical character of court decisions has led to some stunning reversals of earlier Supreme Court rulings.

The influence of surrounding conditions has figured prominently in the Supreme Court's decisions on racial segregation. Consider the two cases below:

(1) In 1896, in the midst of a period marked by extreme expressions of white supremacy, the Supreme Court ruled, in *Plessy* v. *Ferguson*, that segregation in public facilities, including public schools, was constitutional so long as the facilities were "separate but equal." At this time, many social scientists promoted theories about the superiority of whites and the inferiority of non-whites.

(2) In 1954, the Supreme Court reversed the *Plessy* v. *Ferguson* decision in its new decision arising from the *Brown* v. *the Board of Education* case. In the *Brown* decision, the Supreme Court declared that "separate but equal" schools were unconstitutional and violated provisions granting equal protection under the law. The written Constitution had not substantially changed since 1896. The political situation in the United States and in the world, however, had changed.

1. According to this passage, the decisions of the Supreme Court are

 _____ **(1)** influenced by politics and by historical developments

 _____ **(2)** based entirely on the written Constitution

 _____ **(3)** not subject to major revisions

2. The passage argues that the *Plessy* v. *Ferguson* decision was very heavily influenced by

 _____ **(1)** politicians

 _____ **(2)** white supremacist beliefs

 _____ **(3)** the civil rights movement

ANSWERS ARE ON PAGE 308.

STATE AND LOCAL GOVERNMENT

KEY WORDS

home rule laws—state laws that provide local governments with a great deal of self-government

direct initiative—the process that allows citizens to draft laws by obtaining enough signatures on a petition to present the law directly to the voters

referendum—the process by which voters can approve or reject legislation

recall—a procedure that permits voters to remove an elected official from office before his or her term is over

The central government and the states share political power under the American federal system. The central federal government has the power to tax, make war, and regulate interstate and foreign commerce. In addition, it has the right to "make all laws which shall be necessary and proper for" carrying out the powers granted to it under the Constitution. Those powers not specifically granted to the federal government are reserved for the states.

While the Constitution set a general framework, the actual relations between local governments and the central government have evolved over time. The general trend has been toward increasing power for the central government. The rise of a national economy, several major wars, the trauma of the Depression, complicated international relations, and serious urban problems have all helped to create a strong federal government.

STATE GOVERNMENTS

State governments are organized in a way that is similar to the federal government. Each state has a written constitution and a governor, the chief executive officer. States have a bicameral (two-house) legislature, except Nebraska, which has a unicameral (one-house) legislature. All states have court systems, but there are wide variations in how state governments operate. One common trend is toward increased power in the hands of governors.

States provide a wide range of public services. They maintain highways and regulate intrastate (within the state) commerce. States also provide for both education and public welfare.

One of the most important powers of the state is the creation of laws that govern the formation and powers of local governments. Counties, towns, and cities are the legal creations of the states. Many states have strong home rule laws that provide the local governments with a great deal of freedom.

Many states also provide for initiative and referendum voting. The direct initiative allows citizens to draft proposed laws. If citizens can obtain the required number of signatures on a petition, they can have the law decided on directly by the state's voters. The referendum allows voters to repeal legislation that has already been passed by voting on it in general elections. Several states also provide for recall, a special election that permits citizens to vote an official out of office before his or her term is over.

LOCAL GOVERNMENTS

Local governments include counties, municipalities (cities, towns, villages), and special districts. County governments enforce state law and perform whatever other duties the state may assign. In county governments, power is usually vested in an elected board of supervisors or commissioners. County governments collect taxes, maintain roads, and manage county property such as jails, hospitals, parks, and forest preserves. County governments also protect the public health by helping to stop the spread of disease or by passing public health ordinances. Counties record documents such as deeds, mortgages, and marriage licenses. Some counties provide water and sewage service, operate airports, and maintain recreational facilities.

Counties are divided into smaller units of local government. These can include cities, towns, villages, and boroughs. Cities provide services that include police and fire protection, schools, public utilities, libraries, street and sidewalk repairs, and garbage collection.

A city is governed under a charter that is granted by the state legislature. There are three forms of city government. The first is strong mayor–weak city council (the mayor has wide authority to run the local government and to veto council actions). The second form is weak mayor–strong city council (the mayor is usually reduced to a figurehead). The third is city manager–city council (an elected council appoints a city manager and retains the power to make all policy).

The governing bodies in towns, villages, and boroughs provide some of the services that cities do but only on a smaller scale. Local government also includes special districts that serve schools, public transportation, and housing, and maintenance of parks, bridges, and airports.

EXERCISE 12

Directions: Underline the word or words that best complete each statement.

1. Conditions such as major wars, complicated international affairs, and serious problems in major cities have led to a strong (state, federal) government.

2. Nebraska is the only state that has a unicameral, or (one-house, two-house), legislature.

3. States regulate intrastate (between states, within the state) commerce.

4. Citizens can draft proposed laws through a process known as (referendum, direct initiative).

ANSWERS ARE ON PAGE 308.

PRE-GED Practice
EXERCISE 13

Questions 1–6 are based on the passage on pages 175 and 176.

1. Local governments are established by home rule laws enacted by

   (1) state governments
   (2) the U.S. Congress
   (3) the U.S. Constitution
   (4) federal courts
   (5) the president

2. A group of citizens became angered by a law that the state legislature passed. They circulated a petition to have the law put to a vote by the people of the state. This is an example of

   (1) direct initiative
   (2) recall
   (3) referendum
   (4) home rule
   (5) local autonomy

3. A state legislator with one year left in her term goes against overwhelming public opinion in her district and votes for a state income tax. Voters who wish to remove the legislator before the next general election could set in motion the process for

   (1) petition
   (2) referendum
   (3) impeachment
   (4) initiative
   (5) recall

4. The mayor of a city tries to start a project to build a new sports stadium, and the city council overrules him. The form of local government is probably

   (1) manager–council
   (2) strong council–weak mayor
   (3) strong mayor–weak council
   (4) bicameral
   (5) federal

5. The federal government does NOT regulate

   (1) interstate commerce
   (2) war
   (3) taxes
   (4) public utilities
   (5) foreign commerce

6. County governments perform all of the following duties EXCEPT

   (1) passing public health laws
   (2) recording deeds and licenses
   (3) regulating intrastate commerce
   (4) repairing sidewalks
   (5) collecting garbage

ANSWERS ARE ON PAGE 308.

INTERNATIONAL RELATIONS

KEY WORDS

treaties—formal agreements among nations

diplomatic recognition—a government's formal recognition of another country's government, including the exchange of ambassadors

Today's turbulent world has made the entire field of international relations more important than in any previous time. Different branches of the federal government have important roles to play in making and implementing foreign policy.

The Constitution grants the president three important foreign policy responsibilities: to act as commander-in-chief of the armed forces, to make treaties, and to appoint ambassadors. Over the years, many presidents have expanded the powers of the presidency in foreign affairs.

The president can negotiate treaties, but they require the approval of the Senate. The president can also make use of executive agreements with other nations that do not require Senate approval. Such agreements pledge the word of a particular president, but do not bind his successors to follow any earlier agreements.

Presidents can also extend diplomatic recognition to new governments or nations. In some cases, U.S. presidents have withheld diplomatic recognition in order to show disapproval of a particular nation's system of government. For example, the U.S. government withheld recognition of the former Soviet Union for sixteen years.

The chief executive's position as commander-in-chief of the armed forces has been used by presidents to order military intervention without a formal declaration of war by Congress. Without congressional authorization, President Truman sent troops into Korea in 1950. During the 1960s, Presidents Kennedy and Johnson sent troops to Vietnam. In 1983, President Reagan sent troops to Grenada. President Bush sent troops to Saudi Arabia in 1990, and President Clinton sent them to Haiti in 1994. To restrain presidential activities that could involve the country in an undeclared war, Congress passed the War Powers Act in 1973.

The Department of State is the section of the executive branch directly responsible for foreign affairs. The State Department is also responsible for the U.S. diplomatic service. Strong-willed secretaries of state can play an influential role in foreign affairs. At times they have competed with the head of the National Security Council for influence with the president.

In foreign policy matters, Congress exerts its influence through its ability to approve or disapprove appropriations, treaties, and ambassadors and by exercising its sole right to declare war. Many of the domestic bills that Congress reviews, including tariffs, immigration, and import quotas, can have far-reaching international effects.

EXERCISE 14

Directions: Match each term on the left with its description on the right. Write the correct letter on the line.

_____ **1.** treaty

_____ **2.** diplomatic recognition

_____ **3.** War Powers Act

_____ **4.** executive agreement

_____ **5.** Department of State

_____ **6.** executive power of commander-in-chief

(a) allows president to intervene militarily without the approval of Congress

(b) a president's pledge to other nations, which does not need Senate approval

(c) the part of the executive branch that is responsible for foreign affairs

(d) a formal agreement with another nation, which requires Senate approval

(e) protects the United States from becoming involved in an undeclared war

(f) a formal acceptance of another country's government

ANSWERS ARE ON PAGE 309.

INTERNATIONAL ORGANIZATIONS

International organizations have played an increasingly important role in the foreign policy of nations. One of their most important roles is the prevention of global conflict. International organizations fall into three different categories: diplomatic, economic, and military.

Diplomatic Organizations

Diplomatic international organizations have emphasized the promotion of better understanding among nations and the prevention of serious conflicts. Two important organizations have been the League of Nations (1919–1939) and the United Nations (1945–present). The League of Nations was formed after World War I as an organization of sixty-five countries. The United States never joined the league because of a political policy of favoring isolationism. The organization lacked any power to enforce its decisions. It finally collapsed with the onset of World War II.

The United Nations (UN) was formed at the end of World War II. At this time the United States changed its focus from isolationism to involvement in world affairs. The United States was the first to ratify the UN charter in 1945.

The UN was established to maintain international peace and to encourage friendly interaction among all the nations of the world. The UN helps countries cooperate to solve economic and social problems. As of 1994, the UN was composed of 184 members who worked together to help promote basic human rights throughout the world.

The General Assembly of the UN is composed of all the member nations. They vote on questions of world peace and other issues. Most of the UN's real decision-making power resides in the powerful Security Council. It consists of fifteen members, five of which are permanent: the United States, the United Kingdom, China, Russia, and France. The Security Council investigates any disagreements in the world that might threaten world peace.

The United Nations has provided an international forum for nations to air their disputes and grievances and for diplomats to communicate with one another. The UN has also organized international peacekeeping forces to oversee settlements of local disputes.

The United Nations has sponsored many important international agencies. These include the World Health Organization (promotes higher levels of health); the Food and Agricultural Organization (increases food production and distribution); the Educational, Scientific, and Cultural Organization (provides education about people and cultures); and the United Nations Children's Fund (provides assistance to programs for children in developing countries).

Economic Organizations

The Organization of Petroleum Exporting Countries (OPEC) attempts to control the production of oil by setting world oil prices. The European Union (EU) assists in economic, social, and political developments. It also tries to establish a common foreign policy for its twelve members. International economic organizations encourage world trade, find loans for economic development, and obtain better markets for exports.

Military Alliances

Countries with common interests join military alliances for mutual defense and security reasons. The North Atlantic Treaty Organization (NATO) is a military alliance made up of the United States, Canada, and allied European nations. They have agreed to settle disputes peacefully and to help one another in the event of attack from another country.

WRITING ACTIVITY 14

Do you think the United Nations is an effective organization? Remember that its purpose is to promote international peace. Also, since the UN began in 1945, there have been many wars and conflicts all over the world, including some in which the United States was involved. Write a few paragraphs explaining if you think the UN is effective in what it is doing.

ANSWERS WILL VARY.

EXERCISE 15

Directions: Answer the following questions in the space provided.

1. What are the three categories of international organizations?

_____

2. Why was the United Nations established?

_____

_____

3. What does the Security Council of the UN do?

_____

4. What is one reason a nation might join an economic organization?

_____

5. Responding as if "an armed attack" against one or more of them in Europe or in North America were "an attack against them all," would be describing one of the functions of which organization?

_____

6. How many members belonged to the UN in 1994?

_____

7. Which country is considered a permanent member of the Security Council of the UN besides China, Russia, France, and the United States?

_____

ANSWERS ARE ON PAGE 309.

PRE-GED Practice
POLITICAL SCIENCE

Questions 1–3 are based on the following passage.

Metropolitan Government

Metropolitan forms of government and administration are a relatively recent development. Many metropolitan functions, such as mass transit, are too big for one town to handle. So new forms of organization have been created.

The most common of these new forms are the various special districts. These are administrative agencies set up to handle a single function, such as fire protection, health planning, or transportation.

Special districts have been criticized as undemocratic because their governing boards are often appointed instead of elected. Many critics feel that this removes the districts from direct popular control. Those holding this view want democratically elected metropolitan governing boards.

The creation of these single-function districts has helped integrate the separate services. But there has been no movement to integrate all these services into metropolitan governmental structures. Local governments are reluctant to give up power to more centralized metropolitan government. Many citizen groups feel that such a form of government would be too large to influence.

The debate over the role and form of metropolitan-wide government is sure to continue as a part of the ongoing debate over centralization versus decentralization.

1. The growth of special districts has
   - (1) integrated metropolitan government into state government
   - (2) integrated particular government functions on a local level
   - (3) solved the problem of centralization
   - (4) started a strong trend toward metropolitan government
   - (5) established the power of city mayors over suburban areas

2. The author seems to believe that the debate over centralization versus decentralization
   - (1) has been settled
   - (2) will be settled soon
   - (3) will probably always be with us
   - (4) is not an important debate in this country
   - (5) is a new development in American politics

3. A major reason given by people opposing special districts is a belief that they are
   - (1) inefficient
   - (2) too costly
   - (3) too large
   - (4) undemocratic
   - (5) too centralized

ANSWERS ARE ON PAGE 309.

7 🌎 Behavioral Sciences

The **behavioral sciences** study how people behave. There are three fields in the behavioral sciences: psychology, sociology, and anthropology. Each of these sciences looks at human behavior in a slightly different way.

Psychology is the study of individual behavior.

Psychologists study

- how a person thinks, learns, remembers, and makes decisions
- how an individual forms a personality
- what causes a person's feelings and emotions
- what causes a person to behave in certain ways

Sociology is the study of the behavior of groups of people. A sociologist is interested in groups such as families, organizations, social classes, occupational groups, and ethnic groups.

Sociologists study

- how groups form
- why groups behave in certain ways
- why groups have certain beliefs
- why people in groups share certain characteristics
- how groups interact

Anthropology is the study of the origin and development of human beings. Anthropologists study the changes that humans experience. These changes might be physical, such as the physical characteristics that differ in various humans, races, or societies. More often, however, anthropologists study changes in society and in human culture and compare cultures of the past with those of today.

Anthropologists study

- how the human body evolved, or changed, through time
- why and how humans formed cultures and societies
- how human society changed through time
- how cultures change when a group comes in contact with new societies and cultures

Anthropologists continue to study Mexico's Mayan ruins, shown at left. Located in the northwestern Yucatán state, they are one of the best examples of pre-Columbian architecture remaining in Mexico.

PRACTICAL USES OF THE BEHAVIORAL SCIENCES

The behavioral sciences contribute to our daily lives in many ways. For example, companies often use behavioral science to learn what people like and want. Products are created and packaged to meet those wants. Behavioral science is used to create advertising to sell those products.

The government's decision to allow women to fly fighter jets in combat was based partly on behavioral science. Laws to control crime, as well as the counseling and retraining of criminals to become good citizens, also depends upon the work of behavioral scientists.

Many public policies rely on generalizations and theories provided by behavioral scientists. Scientists have studied why homeless people live on the street and what their needs are. Public officials use those theories to learn more about how to help these people.

EXERCISE 1

Directions: Underline the correct answer for the questions that follow.

1. Suppose a remote village in South America had been recently discovered. Which behavioral scientist would most likely want to study the area?

    psychologist   sociologist   anthropologist

2. The owner of a bicycle factory has noticed that her employees are not getting along well with one another. Which behavioral scientist might she hire to advise her on what to do about the employees?

    psychologist   sociologist   anthropologist

3. Prison officials want to help prisoners learn to control their anger. The officials should hire which kind of behavioral scientist?

    psychologist   sociologist   anthropologist

4. A city is planning new services to help senior citizens. What kind of behavioral scientist would study their needs as a group?

psychologist   sociologist   anthropologist

5. The people of a small country have always had bad government. The people are poor and there is much violence. The U.S. government wants to help this country succeed with a new democratic government. What kind of behavioral scientist should the government hire to study the culture and its patterns?

psychologist   sociologist   anthropologist

ANSWERS ARE ON PAGE 309.

PSYCHOLOGY

KEY WORDS

personality—the special qualities that make a person an individual

character—the personal values that make a person decide how to behave

temperament—the emotions that affect how a person acts

Psychologists use research and objective observation. They set up experiments to observe behavior. Their conclusions are based on scientific research and as many facts as they can collect.

Psychologists work in many specialized fields. Developmental psychologists, for example, study how people's emotions and behavior change throughout life. Industrial psychologists work with businesses. They look at how to improve work habits, how to train workers, and so on.

No matter what their specialty, psychologists study individual behavior. Aspects of behavior are personality, motivation, and abnormal behavior.

PERSONALITY

The special qualities or characteristics that make a person an individual form one's personality. It can be seen in the ways people react to events and other individuals. Characteristics include being outgoing, curious, cautious, funny, quiet, or bold.

When psychologists study personality, they look at two things: character and temperament. Character is a person's values. It is what helps someone decide how to behave. Character causes a person to think, "This is right, so this is what I'll do." Temperament is determined by a person's emotions and is not subject to control.

People are born with certain personality characteristics. These often appear at birth and stay with us for life. Genes are the coded messages that are carried in our cells. Like genes that determine eye color and height, genes that decide personality never change.

We form many of our personal characteristics in childhood. The experiences can be good or bad. Bad childhood experiences, like neglect or abuse, often cause learning or behavior problems later on.

Expectations—both those we have for ourselves and those others have for us—can affect our personalities. Behavior problems sometimes result from a failure to achieve expectations.

EXERCISE 2

Directions: Circle *T* for each true statement, or *F* for each false statement.

1. **T   F** A major factor in the development of our personality is what our parents expect us to achieve in life.

2. **T   F** Jevon began playing the violin when he was three. When he was eleven, he gave public concerts. Jevon's violin-playing abilities are an example of genetic characteristics.

3. **T   F** A person relies on temperament when deciding whether to cheat on a test.

4. **T   F** Maria is very fearful of being alone. She worries whenever her husband goes away on business for even a day or two. Her anxiety could be a result of being neglected as a child.

5. **T   F** Noriko keeps her friends laughing by telling funny stories. Her sense of humor is an example of character.

ANSWERS ARE ON PAGE 309.

MOTIVATION

> ### KEY WORDS
>
> ***motivation***—reasons why a person starts, stops, or continues an activity
>
> ***primary motives***—biological reasons (such as thirst and pain) for behavior
>
> ***secondary motives***—reasons a person learns for behaving in certain ways

An important aspect of behavior is the motivation a person has for doing something. There are two kinds of motives: primary motives and secondary motives. Primary motives are physical reasons for actions. Hunger, thirst, and pain are examples. Secondary motives are learned reasons for doing things. Friendship, greed, and ambition are examples. We want friends, so we behave in ways that make people want to become our friends.

Secondary motives can be taught by providing good and bad experiences. A child who is praised and rewarded for good work in school is likely to continue working hard in order to keep getting that reward. A child who does poor work and is not allowed to watch television for a week may try harder next time.

Psychologists debate whether rewards or punishment are the best ways to encourage good behavior. Our criminal justice system is an example of the effects of this argument. Some psychologists say that criminals should be punished so they won't repeat their crimes. Other psychologists argue that rewarding criminals for good behavior will work better. They think criminals need counseling, education, and training to be better prepared to re-enter society.

WRITING ACTIVITY 15

Which method for treating criminals do you agree with? Does punishment effectively motivate criminals to give up their criminal behavior? Should criminals be given education, training, and counseling so that they are prepared to re-enter society? State your position in two or three paragraphs giving reasons for your point of view.

ANSWERS WILL VARY.

EXERCISE 3

Directions: Read the passage below and then put a check in front of the correct answer to the questions that follow.

What motivates people to work? Theory X says that people dislike work. They have little ambition and do not want responsibility. In order for people to work, they must be bribed, threatened, or forced.

Theory Y states that people are creative and want responsibility. Working is a natural process that rewards people's curiosity and creativity. It makes people feel good about themselves. If a job fulfills these needs, people do not need to be bribed, threatened, or forced to work.

Many businesses function according to Theory X. They try to get people to work harder by rewarding them with higher pay and more vacation time.

Other businesses follow Theory Y. They organize workers into teams. Each person works on a part of the product from beginning to end. Team members take more pride in their work, become good friends, and develop team spirit. Workers take less sick time, stay with their jobs longer, and care about the quality of their work.

1. Theory X and Theory Y take different views of

   (1) the value of rewards
   (2) human nature
   (3) the effect of punishment

2. If Theory Y is correct, a workplace with the most productive workers would

   (1) not reward good workers with higher pay
   (2) pay overtime for all weekend work
   (3) encourage workers to look for more creative and efficient ways of doing the job

3. If a classroom were organized according to Theory Y, it would

   (1) include lots of drill to help students remember facts
   (2) use punishment for poor performance
   (3) encourage students to work in small groups and to choose their own report topics

4. The manager of a grocery store told one of the stock clerks that if she did not finish stocking the shelves she would not be able to take the next day off. The manager probably believes in

   (1) Theory X
   (2) Theory Y
   (3) both Theory X and Theory Y

ANSWERS ARE ON PAGE 310.

EXERCISE 4

Directions: Study the graph and the cartoon below and then put a check in front of the correct answer to the questions that follow.

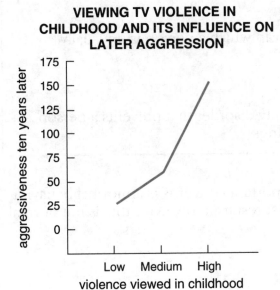

VIEWING TV VIOLENCE IN CHILDHOOD AND ITS INFLUENCE ON LATER AGGRESSION

aggressiveness ten years later

violence viewed in childhood

"This will teach you to hit your sister!"

1. The graph shows that children who were exposed to little TV violence

 _____(1) never became aggressive adults

 _____(2) were less likely to become aggressive adults than children who watched TV violence

 _____(3) were very likely to become aggressive adults

2. From the cartoon, you can tell the cartoonist believes that

 _____(1) parents should physically punish their children

 _____(2) the child in the cartoon will never hit his sister again

 _____(3) parents who use violence encourage their children to be violent

3. Together, the graph and cartoon show that violence and aggression are

 _____(1) learned behaviors

 _____(2) genetic behaviors

 _____(3) primary motives

ANSWERS ARE ON PAGE 310.

ABNORMAL BEHAVIOR

One of psychology's most important concerns is abnormal behavior. Abnormal behavior is an illness that results in behavior that is not normal. It is also called mental illness.

Normal Behavior

People behave in all kinds of ways. Some of this behavior may not seem normal. For example, people vary in their thinking, dress, or life-style choices. But a psychologist considers a person's behavior normal if the person has a strong sense of reality, can manage his or her personal life, and can hold up in stressful situations.

Neuroses

Neuroses are kinds of abnormal behavior that affect a person's goals or sense of self-worth. Under pressure, normal people do things to make themselves feel better and to protect their self-image. People with neuroses, however, may lose sight of reality. Their abnormal behavior can seem strange and unpleasant to others. It can ruin friendships and put strain on families. People with neuroses can usually manage their daily affairs. Most psychologists believe neuroses have emotional, not physical, causes.

Phobias are a type of neurosis. A phobia is a strong, unreasonable fear. Claustrophobia, for example, is a fear of being in a closed place, such as an elevator.

Psychoses

Psychoses are more complicated and serious than neuroses. People with psychoses are out of touch with reality. They often cannot manage their daily lives and are sometimes placed in mental hospitals.

There are two kinds of psychoses: organic and functional. Organic psychosis causes disturbed behavior that results from damage to the nervous system, including the brain. Damage can result from illness, drugs, or alcohol. Functional psychosis also causes disturbed behavior, but it is not the result of physical damage.

EXERCISE 5

Directions: Fill in the blanks with the correct answers from the prior passage.

1. A neurosis can be brought on by _____ from a new job.

2. One cause of psychosis is physical _____ to the nervous system.

3. One difference between psychosis and neurosis is that neurosis is caused

   by _____.

4. Julie always wears yellow dresses with polka dots, carries an open umbrella, and loves to watch trains. Her friends think Julie is odd, but they enjoy her company anyway. Julie likes to dress so people notice her and she has a very strong sense of reality. This

   is a description of someone who probably has _____ behavior.

5. There are two kinds of psychosis, organic and _____.

6. People without neuroses do things to protect their _____.

7. A phobia is a strong, unreasonable, and irrational _____.

8. Functional psychosis is NOT the result of _____.

ANSWERS ARE ON PAGE 310.

SOCIOLOGY

> ### KEY WORDS
>
> ***institution*** –a system that society uses to fill the needs of its people and to teach patterns of behavior
>
> ***peer group*** –a group of people who share some common characteristic, such as working together or being on the same team
>
> ***role*** –expected pattern of behavior in a group or in society
>
> ***socialization*** –the way in which a person learns the normal behavior, habits, and beliefs of a society
>
> ***society*** –a group of people with shared values and organized patterns of behavior

Sociology is the study of group behavior. Two particularly important groups are society and institutions. Society is a group of people who share certain values. The group has organized patterns of behavior, so each person knows how to act. Often the group lives under one government and has shared traditions and a history as a group.

An institution is a system organized by a society to fill the needs of its people. It helps teach people behavior that is expected by society. Major institutions in the United States include the family and religious, political, economic, and educational institutions.

TYPES OF GROUPS

Humans are social animals. We all belong to groups. In fact, each of us belongs to many different groups. Sociologists divide these groups into two major groups: primary groups and secondary groups.

Primary Groups

Primary groups are usually small and members know each other very well. Primary groups include families, peer groups, and even small groups of close, personal friends. Most people belong to several primary groups. They are deeply and emotionally attached to each other. The two most important primary groups are families and peer groups.

The family is the most important primary group. Families may be nuclear or extended. A nuclear family is usually made up of one or two parents and unmarried children. When a family includes the nuclear family plus married children with their partners and children, grandparents, and even aunts and uncles, it is called an extended family.

The family is the most important group in society. In this group, children undergo the socialization process—learning the normal behavior, habits, and beliefs of society.

Usually socialization is informal. Children learn by watching and listening to other family members and by taking part in family activities. Through this process, children learn their role (expected pattern of behavior in the group and in society).

Another important group is the peer group. This is a group of people who share some common characteristic. It might be a group of people who are the same age. This group might work together or play on the same softball team. Members of a peer group have close, personal friendships.

EXERCISE 6

Directions: Based on the passage above, put a check in front of the correct answer to the questions that follow.

1. A thirty-five-year-old man would be in a primary group with which of the following persons?

   ____ **(1)** his employer

   ____ **(2)** his banker

   ____ **(3)** his daughter

2. "Like mother like daughter" is a phrase that reflects what idea?

   ____ **(1)** peer pressure

   ____ **(2)** socialization

   ____ **(3)** an extended family

3. Which of the following is NOT an institution?

   ____ **(1)** a family

   ____ **(2)** a Little League baseball team

   ____ **(3)** a street gang

ANSWERS ARE ON PAGE 310.

Secondary Groups

Members of a **secondary group** are formed for a specific purpose. They have less personal relationships than those in primary groups. Secondary groups include political, religious, and business organizations. Secondary groups are characterized by the following:

- leaders give the groups their direction
- responsibilities and work are divided among members
- members can change roles or jobs and leave or join the organization without affecting the working of the group

Voluntary associations are groups that people join willingly. These groups tend to be informal. Members join and leave when they wish and become as involved as they like. Examples include the PTA, League of Women Voters, and National Audubon Society.

Bureaucracies are formal groups with specific rules and levels of leadership. They can be very large. People sometimes complain that they are impersonal and the rules too strict. However, bureaucracies often are well-organized, efficient, and useful. They are found in large corporations, universities, the armed forces, and government.

EXERCISE 7

Directions: Write a *P* for each of the following that is a primary group, or *S* if it is a secondary group.

_____ **1.** workers at an auto assembly plant

_____ **2.** members of the U.S. Senate

_____ **3.** players on the Knights bowling team

_____ **4.** parents and children

_____ **5.** members of a labor union

_____ **6.** members of the local chapter of the Sierra Club

_____ **7.** the crowd at a Cleveland Indians baseball game

_____ **8.** firefighters from Firehouse Number 3

_____ **9.** members of the Republican party

_____ **10.** four neighborhood teens who shoot baskets together every night

ANSWERS ARE ON PAGE 310.

SOCIAL STRATIFICATION

People are grouped by social rank, or class. These groups are based on income, ancestry, education, profession, and race. The class people are born into generally provides them with their friends, opportunities, and education. Although people can move between classes, they generally do not. This division of society into classes is called **social stratification**.

Social Class

In the United States, **social class** is decided mainly by how much money and power a person has. There are three broad classes: upper, middle, and lower class. The upper class is made up of the richest and most powerful people. The lower class is made up of those persons who are poor and living in poverty. Both the upper and lower classes are relatively small. The middle class is much larger. There are great differences in income, education, and occupation within the middle class. However, compared to the upper and lower class, these differences seem small.

Social Status

Social status is slightly different than social class. A person's status is more difficult to determine. It is mainly based on income, occupation, education, and ethnic background. A person with a high income generally has high social status. However, a person's occupation is also important. Doctors, lawyers, and judges have high status because of their occupations. Even an attorney with a modest income will have a high status. Truck drivers, bartenders, and farmers usually have lower status, even if they have good incomes. A high level of education also provides high social status. A university professor, for example, usually has high status even without a high income. A manual laborer, on the other hand, may have a very good income, but lacking higher education, has a low status.

Ethnic Background

Ethnic background is the racial or cultural origins of people. In spite of advances in civil rights, many African Americans are still not given equal status with white Americans. African Americans do not always have the same educational, business, and income opportunities as white Americans. Although some African Americans have moved into the middle class, many are still part of the lower class. They continue to have higher rates of unemployment than many other groups.

Hispanic Americans also have trouble improving their social status. The number of Hispanics in skilled and professional jobs is small. Many Hispanics do not speak English well, which keeps them from getting better jobs. Some also are not U.S. citizens. They have moved here from Mexico, Puerto Rico, Cuba, and other countries and have not received citizenship and so they have low status.

A physician with a large income and advanced education normally has high status. But if the physician is an African American, a Native American, or a Hispanic, he or she may have trouble buying a house in some exclusive neighborhoods because of low status.

EXERCISE 8

Directions: Read the passage below and then put a check in front of the correct answer to the questions that follow.

The Life of Joe Kuhn

Joe Kuhn is born to Mike, a factory worker, and Sylvia, a housewife. Joe goes to a Catholic church and a Catholic school. Joe joins a gang called the Steel City Blues. Joe takes a job in an auto plant. He joins the union. Joe marries Linda and they have children. Joe still goes out with his buddies on Friday nights. He plays with the kids, goes fishing, and takes care of the car.

Linda washes clothes, cleans house, fixes meals, cares for the kids, and helps with Girl Scouts. Linda joins a women's group and learns more about sexual equality. She convinces Joe to help more around the house.

1. Linda's activities in the women's group caused

   _____**(1)** Joe to go fishing

   _____**(2)** Linda to change her view of sex roles

   _____**(3)** Linda to do all the housework

2. To help the Steel City Blues and other gangs stay out of trouble, the police need good knowledge of

   _____**(1)** peer groups

   _____**(2)** secondary groups

   _____**(3)** institutions

3. When Joe joined the union, he became part of a

_____**(1)** primary group

_____**(2)** secondary group

_____**(3)** social stratification

4. Joe's living group is a(n)

_____**(1)** secondary group

_____**(2)** extended family

_____**(3)** nuclear family

5. Joe probably belongs to the

_____**(1)** upper class

_____**(2)** middle class

_____**(3)** lower class

6. The Girl Scouts group that Linda helps out with is a

_____**(1)** peer group

_____**(2)** socialization group

_____**(3)** voluntary association

7. Joe's church and school are NOT examples of

_____**(1)** peer groups

_____**(2)** socialization groups

_____**(3)** extended family

8. Joe's buddies who get together with him every Friday night are an example of a(n)

_____**(1)** primary group

_____**(2)** secondary group

_____**(3)** institution

ANSWERS ARE ON PAGE 310.

EXERCISE 9

Directions: Study the graph and then fill in the correct answer to the questions that follow.

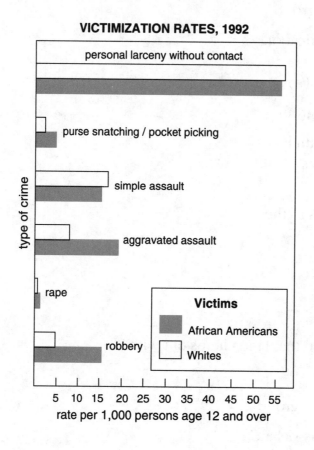

VICTIMIZATION RATES, 1992

personal larceny without contact

purse snatching / pocket picking

simple assault

aggravated assault

rape

Victims

African Americans

Whites

robbery

type of crime

5 10 15 20 25 30 35 40 45 50 55

rate per 1,000 persons age 12 and over

1. Were more African Americans victims of aggravated assault or simple assault?

_____

2. Were more whites victims of robbery or simple assault?

_____

3. Both whites and African Americans are most likely to be victims of which crime?

_____

4. About 4.7 whites are victims of robbery. This means 4.7 people out of how many?

_____

5. How many more African Americans are victims of robbery than are victims of rape?

_____

ANSWERS ARE ON PAGE 311.

ANTHROPOLOGY

KEY WORDS

physical anthropology—the study of the physical characteristics of humans

cultural anthropology—the study of the social and cultural differences among humans

---

Anthropology is the scientific study of humans. Anthropologists look at the physical, social, and cultural aspects of human beings. Of all the behavioral sciences, only anthropology studies human beings as a whole. In fact, anthropology uses many of the physical sciences—such as biology—to learn more about people.

Anthropology is divided into two types: physical anthropology and cultural anthropology.

Specialists in physical anthropology study the physical characteristics of humans. They observe and measure the human body. They may compare the bodies of modern human beings with those of ancient times to see how people have changed over thousands or millions of years.

Because of anthropology, we know a great deal about the physical changes humans have gone through. For example, fossils of early humans have been found in East Africa. They show that humans have existed for at least 5.5 million years.

Some anthropologists study human cultures and societies. They are specialists in cultural anthropology. Their goal is to learn how people organize their lives and activities. They may study individual cultures or they may compare the cultures of different societies. They may even compare present societies with those of the past.

When cultural anthropologists study past cultures, they often use information gathered by ***archaeologists***. These are scientists who study human history by looking at the things left by ancient peoples. For example, they may dig up an ancient town. They will look at how the town was built and study the tools, clothes, and other things that remain.

EXERCISE 10

Directions: Fill in each blank below with the term that best fits the anthropologist described—*physical* or *cultural*.

1. Margaret Mead lived among the people of the South Pacific island of Samoa. There she studied how adolescents became socialized into the culture.

Margaret Mead was a _____ anthropologist.

2. Don Johanson discovered the skeleton of an ancient human in Africa. It is more than 3 million years old. Johanson concluded that the smaller brain and apelike features of the skeleton proved it was not a modern human but a much older ancestor.

Don Johanson is a _____ anthropologist.

ANSWERS ARE ON PAGE 311.

CULTURE AND VALUES

KEY WORDS

culture—all the beliefs, values, ideas, customs, knowledge, and traditions of a society

values—standards of behavior or beliefs set by a society

norms—the normal accepted behavior society expects of a person

ethnocentrism—the act of judging another society by one's own standards

cultural relativity—the act of respecting the values of other societies without judging them

To anthropologists, culture is all of the beliefs, values, ideas, customs, knowledge, and traditions of a society. It is a way of thinking and feeling that is shared by people in a group. These important ideas are passed from one generation to the next.

Anthropologists look at every part of a culture. They look at how the different parts fit together. Anthropologists also look at values. These are the standards that society sets for behavior. Values include honesty, equality, politeness, and justice.

Anthropologists also look at norms—the normal, accepted behavior society expects of a person. For example, a norm might be to tell the truth to one's parents. This is based on a cultural value that calls for honesty.

Two kinds of norms are folkways and mores. *Folkways* are common ways of doing things. When you say thank-you to a bank teller, you are following a folkway that is expected by society.

Mores (mor-ays) are types of behavior society enforces. One of our society's mores is monogamy—marriage to one person at a time. Laws are used to enforce this behavior.

Values become folkways or mores through a process called *institutionalization*. When a society decides certain behavior is necessary, it creates ways to enforce it. A value might be enforced by a frown from a parent. Or it might be enforced by a law passed by Congress.

Every culture has its own values and norms. Someone who looks at another culture might think the other culture's values are wrong. This way of thinking is called ethnocentrism. It is caused by thinking that one's own set of values is the only correct one. Ethnocentrism leads to racial and cultural prejudice.

Cultural relativity is the act of respecting the values of other societies without judging them. Anthropologists, in particular, must look at other cultures and values objectively.

EXERCISE 11

Directions: Circle *T* for each true statement, or *F* for each false statement.

T F **1.** A law against public nudity is a result of society's mores.

T F **2.** Ethnocentrism is a value in our society.

T F **3.** Society enforces folkways more strongly than mores.

T F **4.** Norms are behaviors that grow out of a society's values.

T F **5.** An anthropologist takes a broader view of culture than a psychologist does.

T F **6.** Mores are created from values through the process of institutionalization.

ANSWERS ARE ON PAGE 311.

CHANGES IN CULTURES

KEY WORDS

material culture—the level of tools and technology in a given society

cultural diffusion—the spreading of ideas, values, beliefs, and other parts of a culture to other societies

All cultures change. Sometimes they change quickly, sometimes very slowly. Material culture is the tools and technology in a given culture. It also includes the knowledge needed to make those things. Material culture usually changes because of an invention. The invention may come from within a society or it may be borrowed from another culture. Modern society places high value on new inventions. Many companies have departments whose main job is to develop new inventions. In primitive, or simpler, societies, inventions are more likely to occur by accident or by borrowing from another society. An invention that is borrowed from another society is an example of cultural diffusion. Most societies borrow far more inventions than they create themselves. During the past fifty years, transportation and communication have improved tremendously. These advances have sped up the process of cultural diffusion. Major changes have occurred in many cultures around the world. For example, you can probably choose to have Chinese food, Mexican food, or Italian food tonight. Someone in Mexico City can listen to American rock music on a radio made in Japan.

A major question anthropologists ask is why cultures change. Many cultures seem to change in similar ways. Other cultures seem to change in different ways and at different speeds. There isn't any one explanation for change. However, anthropologists point out that certain inventions seem to spark additional changes. The wheel, for example, caused many advances.

Imagine what our society would be like without the wheel. It is used in cars, watches, elevators, in-line roller blades, and all kinds of machinery. Societies that never developed wheels seem to have stopped evolving. The ancient Aztecs of Mexico are an example. The Aztecs were highly developed in many ways. However, their civilization stalled at a certain point, perhaps because their only use for the wheel was in children's toys.

EXERCISE 12

Directions: Based on the prior passage, put a check in front of the correct answer to the questions that follow.

1. Most societies

    _____ **(1)** invent very little for themselves

    _____ **(2)** do not change

    _____ **(3)** did not find a use for the wheel

2. An example of cultural diffusion is the

    _____ **(1)** use of computers to diagnose disease

    _____ **(2)** celebration of St. Patrick's Day, an Irish holiday, in the United States

    _____ **(3)** Aztecs' use of the wheel in children's toys

3. Most of the world's societies are changing rapidly because

    _____ **(1)** the use of the wheel is widespread

    _____ **(2)** modern transportation and communications spread inventions quickly

    _____ **(3)** companies are working at developing more inventions

4. Material culture includes not only tools and technology, but also

    _____ **(1)** the necessary knowledge to make those things

    _____ **(2)** transportation methods

    _____ **(3)** communication techniques

ANSWERS ARE ON PAGE 311.

PRE-GED Practice
BEHAVIORAL SCIENCES

Questions 1–4 are based on the passage below.

The Nacirema

According to mythology, the Nacirema came from the East. Their nation was created by a great hero, Notgnihsaw. This hero is also known for two great feats of strength. He threw a piece of wampum across the Po-To-Mac River, and he chopped down a cherry tree. This tree was the home of the Spirit of Truth.

The most basic belief of the Nacirema involved a curious dislike and distrust of the body. They used powerful body customs to protect themselves from the evils of the body. For example, every house had one or more shrines, or religious places. In these shrines, people practiced their customs for protecting themselves from the body's evils. The most powerful people in Nacirema culture had several of these shrines in their houses.

The daily body customs were done by everyone. One such custom was the mouth-rite. This rite seems very disgusting to us today. It involved putting a small bundle of hog hairs in the mouth along with magical powders. The bundle was then moved about in the mouth for many minutes.

In addition to the mouth-rite, people went to a holy-mouth-person once or twice a year. These holy people have terrible-looking tools. They use these objects in cleaning out the evils in the mouths of the people. The use of these tools is very painful to the people.

1. Who are the Nacirema?
   (1) a prehistoric culture
   (2) a modern, but primitive society
   (3) a group of anthropologists
   (4) modern Americans
   (5) dentists

2. What is the most basic belief of the Nacirema?
   (1) Every house should have a shrine.
   (2) Everyone should perform a daily custom using hog hairs.
   (3) The human body is evil.
   (4) The hero Notgnihsaw was their god.
   (5) People must go to a holy-mouth-person once or twice each year.

3. The household shrine described here is probably located in
   (1) an ancient village in the Middle East
   (2) a medieval peasant's hut
   (3) a South American village
   (4) the western Pacific
   (5) an American home

4. The author of this passage is trying to get us to
   (1) see our own culture as an outsider might view it
   (2) make fun of an obviously primitive culture
   (3) show how cultural relativity is used in observing strange cultures
   (4) understand the customs of an underdeveloped culture
   (5) look at the roots of Nacirema's religious rites

Questions 5–7 are based on the passage below.

Inuit Culture

The Inuit, or Eskimo, once had a very unusual legal system. Inuit society was organized into local groups. These groups did not have any real form of government. However, they did have a headman who led the group. The headman had no legal or judicial power, and there were few laws. The Inuit did not even recognize many crimes against property. Few Inuit owned land. The custom of freely borrowing goods from each other discouraged stealing.

In the past, some Inuit cultures allowed certain kinds of murder. Disabled persons, sickly infants, and sick elderly people might be killed. These murders were allowed so that the society could give its attention to caring for the healthy. Today, modern transportation and medicine has changed this custom.

In the Inuit culture, wife stealing was not a crime. It was usually done by a man who wanted to gain social rank over the man whose wife he stole. Legal disputes, such as wife stealing, were settled in two ways. One was to murder the offender. The second was in a song contest in which each party insulted the other. The winner was decided by the applause of the group gathered to hear the songs.

5. Based on the passage, a society that has little private property probably

   (1) is run by socialists
   (2) has few crimes against property
   (3) treats wives as public property
   (4) strongly punishes crimes against property
   (5) has a very strong government

6. The practice of wife stealing in Inuit society shows that

   (1) women were little more than property
   (2) the Inuit believed in equal rights for women
   (3) there were too many women in the society
   (4) women held important positions in the culture
   (5) the family was not a strong institution

7. Because the Inuit culture allowed murder as one way of settling a legal issue, this may mean that

   (1) no strong government existed to enforce laws
   (2) the Inuit culture lacked specific laws
   (3) Inuit headmen lacked the power to decide guilt
   (4) the Inuit did not have private property
   (5) the Inuit had very little culture and no mores

ANSWERS ARE ON PAGE 311.

8 Geography

This chapter introduces you to *geography*—the study of Earth and the places on it. Geography is concerned with the physical structure of Earth—its climate, soil, natural resources, waterways, and other important features. Geography is also a social science because of the very important relationship between Earth, on which people live, and the society they create.

For example, it is not likely that the people who live on the dry desert will become expert shipbuilders. You might guess that people who live along rivers and large lakes will learn shipbuilding and navigation skills. The food we grow and the livestock we raise depend on the climate and soil.

People are thus clearly influenced by their environment. But they also can change it. Engineers level hills to build highways and dam rivers to generate power. You know that industrial wastes can pollute the land, water, and air. The interactions of people and their environment make up geography.

ELEMENTS OF GEOGRAPHY

KEY WORDS

latitude—line that measures distance north and south of the equator

longitude—line that measures distance east and west of the prime meridian

equator—0° of latitude that divides Earth into Northern and Southern Hemispheres

prime meridian—0° of longitude that divides Earth into Eastern and Western Hemispheres

All geographers use maps and globes to study Earth. A **map** presents some part of Earth and its features on flat paper. A **globe** is a round model of Earth's surface. Globes are important for the study of how one part of Earth relates to another. They are also important because they show distances between places accurately. The following map shows half of Earth. On it are a series of lines that form a grid pattern. This grid is based on the 360° of a circle.

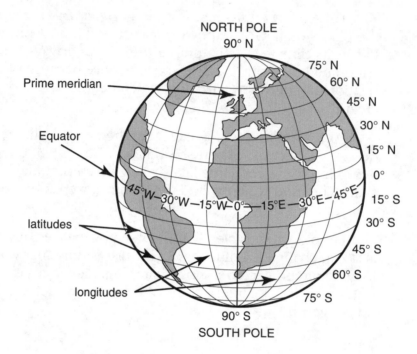

LATITUDE AND LONGITUDE

The lines on the globe are called lines of latitude and longitude. Lines of latitude and longitude divide Earth into the Northern Hemisphere, the Southern Hemisphere, the Eastern Hemisphere, and the Western Hemisphere. Lines that run parallel around the globe are called lines of latitude. The equator is in the middle. Latitude is measured north and south of the equator, which is the 0° line. The North Pole is 90° north, while the South Pole is 90° south.

Lines of longitude circle the globe from the North Pole to the South Pole. The 0° line of longitude is called the prime meridian. It runs through Greenwich, England. Locations east and west of the prime meridian are measured by degrees between 0° and 180° east and west. If you followed the circle of the 0° line from Greenwich over the North Pole, you would come to the 180° line in the Pacific Ocean. These measurements allow geographers to find the exact location of anyplace on Earth.

HEMISPHERES

The lines of latitude and longitude divide Earth into four hemispheres: Northern, Southern, Eastern, and Western. The United States lies in both the Northern Hemisphere and the Western Hemisphere. That's because it lies west of the prime meridian, or 0° of longitude, and north of the equator, or 0° of latitude.

EXERCISE 1

Directions: Complete the statements below in the space provided.

1. The line marking 0° of latitude is called the

_____.

2. The line marking 0° of longitude is called the

_____.

3. The lines of latitude and longitude divide Earth into four

_____.

4. What place would you find at 90° north latitude?

_____.

5. The United States lies in both the Northern Hemisphere and the Western Hemisphere

because it lies north of the _____ and west of the

_____.

ANSWERS ARE ON PAGE 311.

MAP DIRECTIONS

Most maps tell you directions with either a ***compass rose*** or a ***direction arrow*** that points north. A compass rose is shown below. It uses the abbreviations N, S, E, and W for the four main directions north, south, east, and west. It also uses the abbreviations NE, NW, SE, and SW for the intermediate directions northeast, northwest, southeast, and southwest.

TYPES OF MAPS

KEY WORDS

topography—the physical features of a land surface, including mountain ranges, plateaus, and lowlands

contour map—shows changes in elevation of a land surface by a series of lines representing different heights

Maps come in many varieties. They can show natural resources, political boundaries, and cities. You have probably seen the weather map in your daily newspaper or studied a road map to find the direction and distance from one town to the next. This section examines physical, contour, and information, or thematic, maps.

PHYSICAL MAPS

The physical map of South America below shows rivers and elevations of the continent. The map also labels the countries and some major cities of South America. Notice the key on the lower right. It shows four different elevations and the symbol for rivers.

SOUTH AMERICA

Key

over 5,000 feet

2,000–5,000 feet

1,000–2,000 feet

0–1,000 feet

major river

boundary

CONTOUR MAPS

Geographers use the term ***topography*** to define a region's land features such as mountain ranges, plateaus, and lowlands. Contour maps are a type of physical map. They can show topography with a series of lines representing different heights from sea level. When the lines are far apart, the rise in the land is gradual. When the lines are close together, the rise is steep.

On the left below is a contour map of a fictional island. On the right is a vertical view—or elevation—of the same island. The map shows that each interval between contour lines is 10 feet. Counting from the bottom, you can see that the island rises from sea level to 60 feet at the top. If you are a hiker on this island, a contour map would be very useful.

CONTOUR MAP

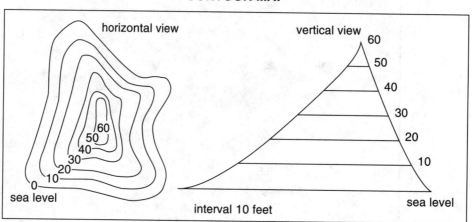

INFORMATION OR THEMATIC MAPS

Some maps give the geographer information such as population distribution, battles, areas where certain diseases are common, climate patterns, or types of farming. It is important that you study the title and the key on an information map. The key tells you what the symbols stand for. The time zone map below is an example of an information map.

TIME ZONES ACROSS NORTH AMERICA

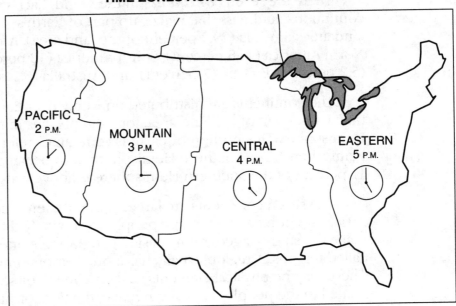

REGIONS

region—an area of land having characteristics that make it different from another area of land

There are seven ***continents*** in the world. Each continent is a large continuous landmass that makes up part of Earth's surface. These large land areas are Asia (29.9 percent of the land area), Africa (20.6 percent), North America (14.8 percent), South America (12 percent), Antarctica (5.2 percent), Europe (7 percent), and Australia (5.2 percent).

The continents are distributed unevenly over Earth's surface. More than 65 percent of the land area, for example, lies in the Northern Hemisphere. This portion of Earth is sometimes referred to as the "land hemisphere." The Southern Hemisphere is an oceanic realm. Only about 11 percent of the Southern Hemisphere is above water.

The seven continents are large. Some of them, such as Asia and Africa, are populated by many people with widely differing cultures. To make the study of geography easier, geographers often write about areas called regions. A region usually has a number of common elements. These may be physical elements such as climate or soil. Or they may be related to the people, such as language, religion, or population—**cultural geography**.

Regions have no uniform size. Some are small and others are quite large. Their boundaries do not have to be strictly defined by any physical features such as mountains or rivers. They can be defined by the kind of people who live there. This kind of region is called a *cultural region*.

Examples of regions include the Midwest and the South in the United States, and Central America, Scandinavia, and the Middle East elsewhere in the world. What region do you live in?

EXERCISE 2

Directions: Study the map of Central America shown below. It uses a key showing three levels of land elevation. Fill in the correct answers to the questions that follow in the space provided.

CENTRAL AMERICA

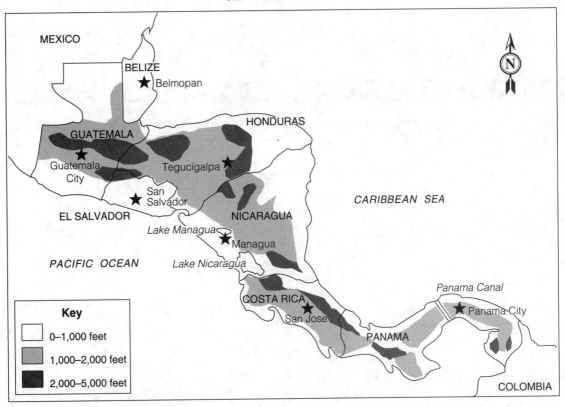

1. Which country has no land above 1,000 feet—Honduras, Nicaragua, or Belize?

   _____

2. Where would you find the highest mountains in the Central American nations—along the Pacific Ocean? along the Caribbean Sea? or toward the center of each nation?

   _____

3. Which direction would you travel to fly in a straight line from San Jose, Costa Rica, to Panama City, Panama?

   _____

4. Which country in the region has a large lake?

   _____

ANSWERS ARE ON PAGE 311.

WRITING ACTIVITY 16

Select one of the regions of the United States and describe in two or three paragraphs the characteristics that make this region different from other regions in the country.

ANSWERS WILL VARY.

EXERCISE 3

Directions: Study the map of East Asia shown below. Then put a check in front of the correct answer to the questions that follow.

EAST ASIA

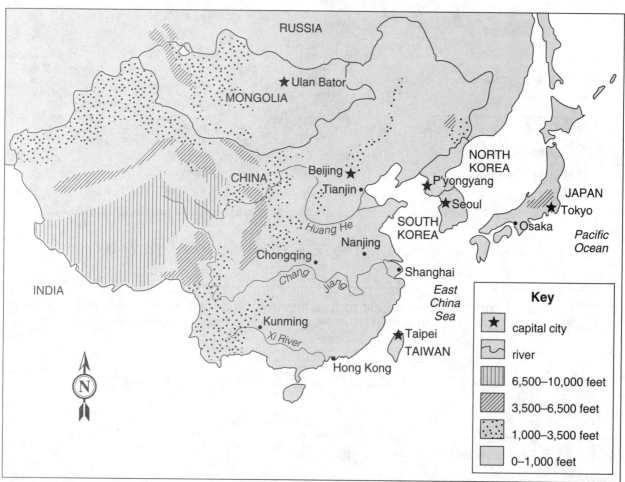

1. Most of the land in Mongolia is what elevation above sea level?

____**(1)** 0 feet

____**(2)** 1,000 feet

____**(3)** between 350 and 3,500 feet

____**(4)** between 0 and 3,500 feet

2. The highest mountains in China are located

____**(1)** toward the western part of the country

____**(2)** just west of Hong Kong

____**(3)** to the east of Beijing

____**(4)** in eastern China

3. Which of the following statements is true?

____**(1)** Taiwan is an island off the coast of Korea.

____**(2)** Most of East Asia is more than 3,000 feet above sea level.

____**(3)** Beijing is located directly to the south of the East China Sea.

____**(4)** Russia borders China on the north.

4. All of the following are part of the region of East Asia EXCEPT

____**(1)** India

____**(2)** North Korea

____**(3)** Japan

____**(4)** China

5. What is the capital city of China?

____**(1)** Tianjin

____**(2)** Nanjing

____**(3)** Beijing

____**(4)** Chongqing

ANSWERS ARE ON PAGE 312.

POPULATION AND MIGRATION

KEY WORDS

demography—the statistical study of the size, growth, movement, and distribution of human population

ecological system—the relationships between living things and their environment

mortality rate—the rate of deaths in a particular time and place

fertility rate—the rate of births in a particular time and place

migration—the movement of people from one country or location to another

The field of geography includes demography, which is the statistical study of the size, growth, movement, and distribution of people in various parts of the world. Geographers find the study of demography important because it shows how people relate to the land they inhabit.

In Central America, for example, the physical environment of highlands and lowlands can decide which areas of land will support more people and which will not. Any population puts pressure on its environment, including its physical features, natural resources, and the other living things that inhabit the same environment.

The ordered relationship between living things and their environment is called the ecological system. Any change in one part of this ecological system can affect changes in other parts. If farmers till the soil harder to produce more crops (intensive farming), many small animals and birds that live in the area may be destroyed. Intensive farming may also lead to soil erosion, a lowering of the water table, and the end of farming in that area.

POPULATION GROWTH

The human species has been very successful in reproducing itself. In 1750, the estimated world population was 725 million. In this century, the population has grown greatly, from 1.6 billion in 1900 to 5.6 billion in 1994. The population projected for the year 2020 is 7.9 billion. This rapid growth is called the population explosion.

Great increases in population growth usually come about from a reduction in mortality rates (death rates), particularly of women and infants, while high fertility rates (birth rates) are maintained. The decline in infant mortality affects population growth in two ways. More people live to become adults and more women reach childbearing age. However, family planning (birth control), famine, or war may check population growth.

The Western industrial countries no longer have a population explosion because of lower birth rates. Population grows more slowly. In countries with developing economies, mortality rates have fallen but fertility rates have not. This has created a population explosion in the developing countries.

MIGRATION

Population migration has been a constant feature of human life. People have migrated to all parts of the globe for a number of reasons, including poor economic conditions at home, the attraction of better conditions elsewhere, and the need for political and religious freedom. Since 1820, 60 million people have emigrated to the United States for all of these reasons.

Most people have been free to migrate as they please. But sometimes people have been forced to move. Millions of African Americans were forced to come to North America and South America, where they were sold as slaves. When Pakistan and India became separate nations in 1947, millions of Muslims feared for their safety in India and fled to Pakistan. At the same time, millions of Hindus in Pakistan left for India. Refugees have been an enormous problem in the twentieth century. Not only were there millions of people displaced by the changes in Europe after World War II, but more recent political strife has created huge numbers of refugees in Rwanda and the former Yugoslavia.

Whatever the cause, migration creates **cultural diffusion**, or the spread of cultural traits from one part of the world to another. The United States has absorbed the customs of many people who have settled in the country.

Those who study demography gather statistics on births, deaths, marriages, divorces, immigration, occupations, and family income. The U.S. census is conducted every ten years by the federal government. State and local agencies also gather vital statistics. Demographers frequently use maps and graphs to illustrate, for example, population distribution according to age, sex, and racial background.

EXERCISE 4

Directions: Circle *T* for each true statement, or *F* for each false statement.

T F 1. Migration is the movement of people from one country or location to another.

T F 2. The mortality rate is the number of births in a particular time and place.

T F 3. The fertility rate is the increase or decline in crop production per acre.

T F 4. Economic conditions, the search for political and religious freedom, wars, and famine are reasons for human migration.

T F 5. A change in one part of the ecological system will have no effect on any other part.

T F 6. The decline in infant mortality is a cause of the population explosion because it enables more people to live to become adults and more women to reach childbearing age.

ANSWERS ARE ON PAGE 312.

EXERCISE 5

Directions: Read the passage below and study the map and graph on the next page. Then underline the correct answer to the questions that follow.

Geographers can reconstruct the demography of a region during a historical period. The map shown on the next page is based on the U.S. census of 1860. Symbols representing four population ranges show where blacks lived in the slaveholding states on the eve of the Civil War. The graph (lower right corner) shows the total population of slaves and free blacks in each state.

THE BLACK POPULATION 1860

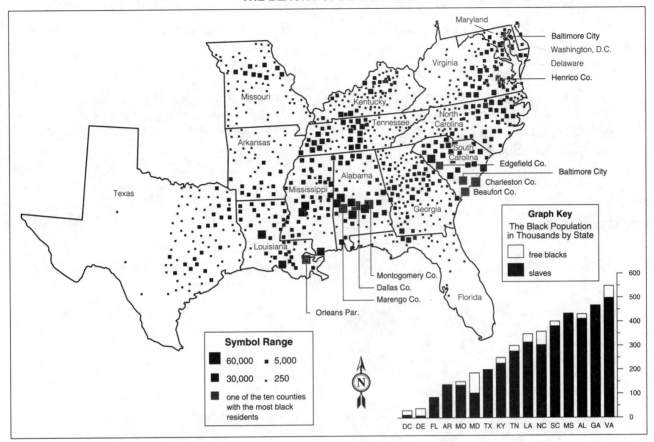

1. Most blacks in Texas lived in the (eastern, western) part of the state.

2. South Carolina had a (larger, smaller) black population than Texas in 1860.

3. A greater number of free blacks lived in (Maryland, Virginia).

4. Four counties in (South Carolina, Georgia) were among the ten counties with the most black residents in 1860.

5. There were more black slaves living in (Alabama, Mississippi) in 1860.

6. There were no free blacks living in Texas, Mississippi, Arkansas, Florida, and (Missouri, Georgia).

7. More blacks lived in Alabama than in (South Carolina, Florida).

ANSWERS ARE ON PAGE 312.

EXERCISE 6

Directions: Based on the passage and map below, circle *T* for each true statement, or *F* for each false statement.

South of Egypt and west of the Arabian Peninsula lies a region whose 100 million people suffered greatly during the 1980s and 1990s. This region is called the Horn of Africa because of its shape. Five nations make up this region: Djibouti, Eritrea, Ethiopia, Somalia, and Sudan.

THE HORN OF AFRICA

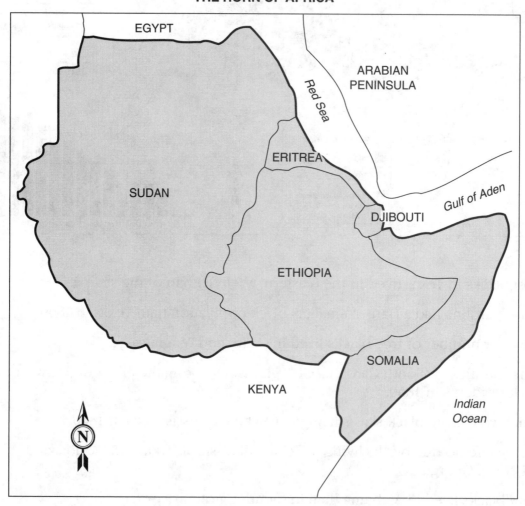

Geography has had a great impact on the lives of the people in this region. Drought, floods, and wars have killed millions of people. Many people became refugees, displaced from their homes. The United States intervened in Somalia in December 1992 to end mass starvation. It ended the famine but got caught up in the internal strife. U.S. troops were pulled out in 1994.

For many years, the region received even less rainfall than usual. Food supplies dwindled to nothing. Heat and sun burned the crops. Farm animals had neither grazing land nor enough water and wasted away or died.

The agony of this situation was heightened by skyrocketing birth rates. The population grew faster than food production. Feeding thousands of refugees increased the problems of already overburdened countries.

T F **1.** The Horn of Africa has suffered from war, drought, and floods.

T F **2.** The United States sent forces to Somalia to help feed the people.

T F **3.** Famine took place in the region only because of greatly reduced rainfall.

T F **4.** The growth in population has been greater than the production of food in the Horn of Africa.

T F **5.** The five nations in the Horn of Africa are Egypt, Eritrea, Somalia, Saudi Arabia, and Sudan.

T F **6.** Through U.S. intervention, Somalia's civil wars were brought to an end.

T F **7.** The Horn of Africa is located east of the Arabian Peninsula.

T F **8.** Many farm animals in the region died due to insufficient grazing land.

ANSWERS ARE ON PAGE 312.

URBAN GROWTH

KEY WORDS

location—the exact point on Earth where a place is found; can be expressed in degrees of latitude and longitude

suburb—a settlement that lies outside a city but within commuting distance to it

A city is an inhabited place of greater size, population, or importance than a town or a village. People in a city work in a variety of jobs. In contrast, rural settlers live in farming areas outside of the city. Many rural residents work in agriculture and grow crops or raise livestock. In the twentieth century, cities have become larger and more numerous as people moved from the countryside.

A city's location explains its importance, growth, and, sometimes, decline. Access to water routes—rivers, large lakes, and oceans—has been of prime importance. For example, Chicago originally grew up where boats or goods had to be carried overland between the Great Lakes and the rivers that drain into the Mississippi. Later, Chicago's location made it an ideal center for rail transportation.

Cities grow at locations like Chicago's because travelers have to change types of transportation, either from land to water or from rivers to oceans. These changes require warehouses, laborers, merchants, banks, repair shops, and all the other businesses associated with trade. Access to transportation also means access to raw materials. The steel-making city of Pittsburgh is located near Pennsylvania's rich coal fields. Pittsburgh's location is ideal for the growth of manufacturing and industry.

Location also influences the choice of cities as political centers, such as state capitals and county seats. Once these cities became political centers, governmental activities caused them to grow. The nation's capital of Washington, D.C., is an excellent example of how location determined its selection and growth. Washington was midway between the thirteen Northern and Southern states and also close to George Washington's home at nearby Mount Vernon.

Climate can also affect city growth. Without air-conditioning and a sure supply of water, the desert city of Phoenix, Arizona, probably would not have become the ninth largest city in the United States.

SUBURBS

Before the development of railroads, the growth of cities was limited by how far people could travel on foot or on animals. Modern transportation changed that. Trains, trolleys, and the automobile allowed people to work in one place and live in another. Suburbs are smaller towns that grew up within commuting distance around cities. Trucking further speeded up the growth of suburbs. Industry could move to the suburbs, bringing workers and their families from the cities.

Many cities are working hard to bring businesses back from the suburbs to restore the life of central city areas. Cities have many attractions, such as art galleries, symphony orchestras, theaters, sports events, zoos, and shopping, that draw residents and visitors. On the other hand, poverty, crime, pollution, overcrowding, and the aging of highways, bridges, schools, and other public works also demand bold solutions.

EXERCISE 7

Directions: Fill in the blanks with the correct answers from the passage in the space provided.

1. The city of _____ is a good example of how location influences the choice of cities as political centers.

2. In the twentieth century, more cities have grown up and become larger as people moved there from _____.

3. The city of _____ grew larger because technology helped it overcome harsh desert conditions.

4. Smaller communities that grow up around a large city are called

   _____.

5. The revolution in _____ allowed people to live in one place and work in another.

ANSWERS ARE ON PAGE 312.

≡ PRE-GED Practice ≡
EXERCISE 8

Questions 1–7 are based on the passage below.

Denver, Colorado

You may picture Denver, Colorado as a spotlessly clean city built high in the clear mountain air of the Rocky Mountains. This was true in the past. But today the influence of people on their environment is shown by Denver's having become one of America's most polluted cities.

The brown cloud that cloaks the city of Denver for an average of 100 days each year is made up primarily of carbon monoxide—the poisonous gas given off by industrial smokestacks and automobiles. Because Denver has not developed a good public transportation system, automobiles are a major cause of air pollution. This cloud poses a critical health risk for Denver's inhabitants. The rate of lung cancer may be anywhere from 10 to 21 percent higher than in other cities.

Geography plays a role, too. Denver is located one mile above sea level and has considerably less oxygen in its atmosphere than cities at lower altitudes. Automobiles work less efficiently and produce increased levels of carbon monoxide. People are breathing in this poisonous gas. Many people with respiratory diseases have been forced to move out of Denver to suburbs at lower altitudes.

1. The problem of air pollution in Denver is
   (1) primarily caused by the city's high altitude
   (2) the result of both natural factors and those caused by people
   (3) not necessarily affecting its citizens' health
   (4) caused by its transportation system
   (5) not serious enough to be concerned about

2. You can infer from the passage that
   (1) if Denver had a better location, pollution would not be a problem
   (2) Denver is the worst city in America in which to live
   (3) industry does not affect air pollution in Denver
   (4) improvements in Denver's public transportation system might help ease air pollution
   (5) Denver's public transportation system is adequate

3. According to the passage, which of the following is true?
   (1) There are two automobiles for every citizen of Denver.
   (2) The cloud of carbon monoxide cloaks the city of Denver an average of 100 days out of the year.
   (3) The cloud of carbon monoxide over Denver has existed for a total of 100 days.
   (4) The rate of lung cancer in Denver is at least 33 percent higher than any other city.
   (5) Denver is located two miles above sea level.

4. The high level of carbon monoxide in Denver is caused by

   (1) its low altitude
   (2) gas from cars and smokestacks
   (3) lack of car emissions testing
   (4) brown clouds that cloud the city
   (5) lack of concern about pollution

5. Because Denver is located one mile above sea level,

   (1) less oxygen is in the air
   (2) the level of poisonous gas is lower
   (3) more respiratory problems occur
   (4) fewer inhabitants should live in this area
   (5) it is easier to breathe in this city

6. According to the passage, Denver is primarily known today as a city that is

   (1) spotlessly clean
   (2) filled with clear mountain air
   (3) beautiful because of its Rocky Mountain vistas
   (4) the ski capital of the world
   (5) more polluted than most other cities

7. The writer believes that many of Denver's residents move to the suburbs because the suburbs

   (1) are less crowded
   (2) have fewer industries
   (3) are at lower altitudes
   (4) have better transportation systems
   (5) have lower rates of lung cancer

ANSWERS ARE ON PAGE 312.

 WRITING ACTIVITY 17

Do you live in the city, a suburb, or in a rural area? Has your area grown or stayed about the same in the past ten years? In a few paragraphs explain why.

ANSWERS WILL VARY.

≡ PRE-GED Practice ≡
GEOGRAPHY

Questions 1–6 are based on the information and the graphics shown below.

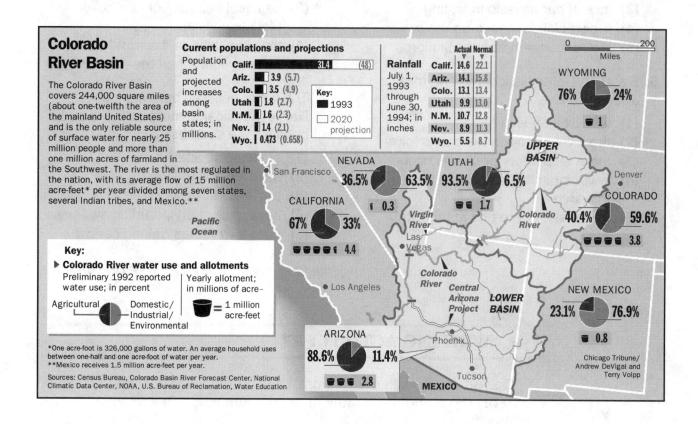

Colorado River Basin

The Colorado River Basin covers 244,000 square miles (about one-twelfth the area of the mainland United States) and is the only reliable source of surface water for nearly 25 million people and more than one million acres of farmland in the Southwest. The river is the most regulated in the nation, with its average flow of 15 million acre-feet* per year divided among seven states, several Indian tribes, and Mexico.**

Current populations and projections

Population and projected increases among basin states; in millions.

Calif.	31.4	(48)
Ariz.	3.9	(5.7)
Colo.	3.5	(4.9)
Utah	1.8	(2.7)
N.M.	1.6	(2.3)
Nev.	1.4	(2.1)
Wyo.	0.473	(0.658)

Key:
■ 1993
☐ 2020 projection

Rainfall July 1, 1993 through June 30, 1994; in inches

	Actual	Normal
Calif.	14.6	22.1
Ariz.	14.1	15.8
Colo.	13.1	13.4
Utah	9.9	13.0
N.M.	10.7	12.8
Nev.	8.9	11.3
Wyo.	5.5	8.7

Key:

▶ **Colorado River water use and allotments**

Preliminary 1992 reported water use; in percent

Agricultural — Domestic/Industrial/Environmental

Yearly allotment; in millions of acre–

🪣 = 1 million acre-feet

*One acre-foot is 326,000 gallons of water. An average household uses between one-half and one acre-foot of water per year.
**Mexico receives 1.5 million acre-feet per year.

Sources: Census Bureau, Colorado Basin River Forecast Center, National Climatic Data Center, NOAA, U.S. Bureau of Reclamation, Water Education

Chicago Tribune/ Andrew DeVigal and Terry Volpp

1. Which three of the seven states have the largest yearly allotments of Colorado River water?

   (1) Nevada, New Mexico, Wyoming
   (2) Arizona, California, Colorado
   (3) Arizona, Colorado, Utah
   (4) California, Nevada, Utah
   (5) California, Colorado, New Mexico

2. Which state's rainfall fell below normal by the greatest amount from July 1, 1993, through June 30, 1994?

   (1) New Mexico
   (2) Utah
   (3) Colorado
   (4) Nevada
   (5) California

3. Which two states use the greatest amount of Colorado River water for agriculture?

   (1) Arizona, California
   (2) California, Wyoming
   (3) Nevada, New Mexico
   (4) Arizona, Utah
   (5) Utah, Wyoming

4. Based on the map, which of the following statements is true?

   (1) Las Vegas, Phoenix, and Tucson are all in the Lower Basin.
   (2) Colorado, Wyoming, and Mexico are all in the Upper Basin.
   (3) San Francisco, Los Angeles, and Las Vegas are all in the Lower Basin.
   (4) Las Vegas is in the Upper Basin while Phoenix and Tucson are in the Lower Basin.
   (5) Denver and Tucson are in the Upper Basin while Los Angeles is in the Lower Basin.

5. Based on population projections for the year 2020, what is the most likely effect that continued below-normal rainfall would have on the states in the Colorado River Basin?

   (1) The river will provide enough water to handle the population increase.
   (2) Strict cutbacks in both agriculture and domestic, industrial, and environmental water will be likely.
   (3) More dams will have to be built on the Colorado River to save water for years of low rainfall.
   (4) The government will have to persuade New Mexico to give up more of its share of water.
   (5) California will have to get its water from the Pacific Ocean so there is enough water remaining for the other six states.

6. Based on population increases, which state is the least likely to be affected by the need for Colorado River water in the year 2020?

   (1) California
   (2) Utah
   (3) Wyoming
   (4) Colorado
   (5) New Mexico

Questions 7–13 are based on the following passage.

El Niño is an occasional warming in the tropical Pacific that develops every four to seven years. Scientists have learned that El Niño and its cool counterpart, La Niña, exert influences far beyond their local neighborhood. Like a rock dropped into a pond, the Pacific's hot and cold spells send ripples spreading through the world's atmosphere, altering weather around much of the globe. For instance, the El Niño that simmered [in early 1993] inundated southern California with unusually heavy winter rains but dried out northeastern Brazil. The warming even contributed to the summer floods in the Midwest.

In strength, this El Niño pales in comparison to the biggest of the century, which struck in 1982 and 1983. The record warmth in the equatorial Pacific those years redirected normal jet stream patterns, generating floods and droughts that left thousands dead worldwide and caused more than $13 billion in damages.

Spurred by that event [El Niño] . . . scientists have developed computer models for predicting when the tropical Pacific will swing toward warm or cool temperatures. Nature still has the upper hand, however, . . . but major warmings and coolings advertise themselves much more openly, and the computer models have started to exhibit skill at detecting such events as many as twelve to eighteen months ahead of their actual arrival.

Excerpted from
"The Long View of Weather"
by Richard Monastersky

7. The main idea of this passage is that
   (1) El Niño is a temporary occurrence and is unlikely to take place again
   (2) computer models have had some success in predicting weather twelve to eighteen months ahead of time
   (3) computer models now can accurately predict El Niño one year in advance with 100 percent accuracy
   (4) computer models are useless in predicting long-range weather patterns
   (5) El Niño has a cool counterpart named La Niña

8. According to the passage, the waters of the tropical Pacific warm up every
   (1) summer
   (2) twelve to eighteen months
   (3) four to seven months
   (4) four to seven years
   (5) year

9. Scientists know that the hot and cold spells in the Pacific can change the weather
   (1) around much of the world
   (2) only along the Pacific coast of North America and South America
   (3) during the winter months only
   (4) during the summer months only
   (5) only when the winds reach sixty miles per hour

10. The great El Niño of 1982–1983

   (1) proved useless for scientific measurement
   (2) made major changes in the weather but caused little loss of life or damage
   (3) was caused by record warmth in the Pacific Ocean
   (4) had no effect on jet stream patterns
   (5) caused scientists to believe it marked a permanent change in climate

11. If 1992–1993 were years of El Niño, when would you expect the next one to begin?

   (1) 1994 to 1997
   (2) 1997 to 2000
   (3) 1999 to 2003
   (4) in 10 years from those dates
   (5) There is no pattern upon which to predict when the next El Niño will occur.

12. The El Niño of 1993 was unusual because it

   (1) caused temperatures to drop rapidly throughout the Pacific
   (2) sent heavy winter rains to southern California and caused a dry period in Brazil
   (3) caused a hot spell in the Pacific
   (4) ended the floods in the Midwest
   (5) caused heavy rains in northern California

13. According to the passage, the cost of damages due to the El Niño of 1982 and 1983 was

   (1) under $20 million
   (2) about $50 million
   (3) around $10 billion
   (4) more than $13 billion
   (5) more than $20 billion

ANSWERS ARE ON PAGE 313.

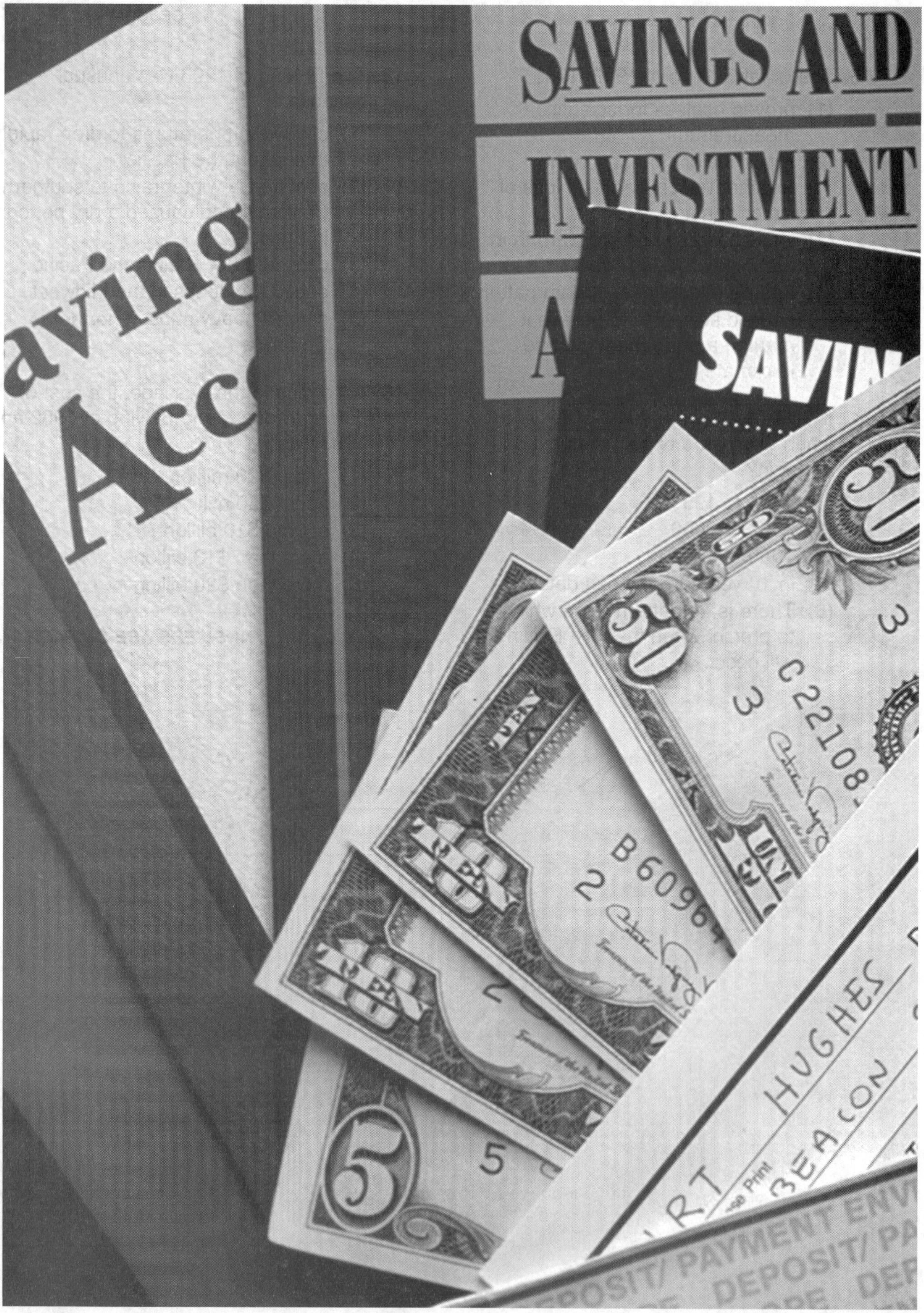
SAVINGS AND
INVESTMENT
HUGHES
PAYMENT
DEPOSIT/

9 Economics

An *economy* is the organized way in which a society produces, distributes, and consumes goods and services. In other words, the economy is the way people make things, ship them, sell them, and use them. *Economics* is the study of how these systems work.

There are various kinds of economies. Different countries may manufacture and distribute goods, or products, in slightly different ways. A small, primitive society will have a different kind of economy than a large, industrial society. Economists study how these different systems work.

WHAT ECONOMISTS STUDY

Economists often specialize in one area. For example, some economists study how a whole economic system, like the U.S. economy, works. Other economists may study one small part of the economy, such as how the trucking industry in Utah works.

Economists today have an important role in guiding government policy. Economists work in such organizations as the president's Council of Economic Advisors, the General Accounting Office, and the Bureau of the Budget.

Government economists predict what will happen if different economic decisions are made. For example, if interest rates are increased, will companies lay off workers? If inflation increases, will people stop buying new cars? The advice economists give Congress and the president can have long-lasting effects on citizens.

Economists also work in private business. They make long-range economic plans for companies. They analyze how businesses operate and advise them on how to become more profitable. Economists advise labor unions on contracts and on trends in the economy.

EXERCISE 1

Directions: Put a check in front of the best answer to the questions that follow.

1. *Economy* can best be defined as a system

   ____(1) for exchanging goods and services

   ____(2) for producing goods and services

   ____(3) of producing, distributing, and consuming goods and services

   ____(4) for producing goods and guiding government policy

2. Congress might ask an economist to advise them on

   ____(1) the effects of increasing trade with Mexico

   ____(2) how to reduce the Internal Revenue Service's paperwork

   ____(3) how to improve safety in interstate trucking

   ____(4) how to reduce the chance of war in the Middle East

3. An economist might help an electric power company by

   ____(1) analyzing the safety of a nuclear reactor

   ____(2) explaining why nuclear energy is too costly

   ____(3) hiring staff to bill for electric service

   ____(4) studying health claims against the company

ANSWERS ARE ON PAGE 313.

EARLY ECONOMIC SYSTEMS

Economists study the history of economics as well as the economies of today. Knowing how economies formed and changed over time helps them better predict the effects of current events.

The earliest economies developed in primitive hunting and gathering societies. Nearly everything produced was immediately consumed. This simple economy began to change with the development of agriculture. Because people raised crops and animals, they often had surplus, or extra, food. This surplus was stored, traded, or sold. These extra activities created new jobs and services. Stores were opened to sell the surplus. Ships were built to move the surplus. Cities grew up around the trade centers. Governments began taxing and protecting the new economies.

In medieval Europe (A.D. 600–1500), the economy was based on agriculture. This economy was known as a feudal economy. Peasants didn't own land, yet they were tied to it. They farmed land that belonged to nobles and to the Catholic Church. The little economic activity that did not involve farming was carried out by craftsmen in the towns. Throughout this period, all economic activity was strictly controlled by tradition. People lived as they always had. Few people thought of trying to do anything different.

Economic conditions began to change with the colonizing of the New World during the sixteenth century. Gold and silver flooded into Europe and financed economic expansion. World trade began to grow. This great wealth led to developments in science and technology. By the late eighteenth century, the way people lived and worked began to change. This was the start of the period known as the Industrial Revolution.

THE INDUSTRIAL REVOLUTION

The Industrial Revolution brought large numbers of people together in towns. They worked in businesses and manufacturing plants. In this new society, there were many buyers and sellers who competed for commodities, which are goods and services for which ownership can be traded or exchanged. This new economic system became known as a market economy. This term refers to the competition for goods, services, land, labor, and other resources.

The market now regulated economic life. Workers were no longer tied to a piece of land. In fact, they could now own land or businesses. They could move from job to job, selling their labor to the highest bidders.

From the 1600s through the 1900s, industrialization and the accumulation of wealth changed industry, agriculture, and society in general. Many people enjoyed great prosperity. However, other people remained in extreme poverty. Many people and governments have tried to change the system to correct what was wrong. Sometimes they tried to change it completely. Sometimes laws were passed to correct abuses without getting rid of the system.

TYPES OF ECONOMIC SYSTEMS

KEY WORDS

capitalism—an economic system based on private ownership of property

commodities—goods and services for which ownership can be traded or exchanged

market economy—another name for free enterprise where buyers and sellers, not the government, determine prices and output

socialism—an economic system that is based on government control of the market

Today, there are three main types of economic systems: capitalism, socialism, and mixed. Capitalist, or market, economies are based on private ownership and market competition.

Socialism is based on government control of the market. The government controls production, distribution, and profit. The goal of socialism is to ensure that all members of society benefit from economic activity, not just those who compete the most successfully.

Mixed economies combine capitalism and socialism. Certain industries, like transportation or mining, may be controlled by the government. Other industries may be allowed to operate in a market economy.

No country's economy is purely of one type. The United States is capitalist, but many controls have been placed on the market. Sweden is a mixed economy. Once there were many socialist economies, such as those of the former Soviet Union and of China. Now most of these socialist economies have been changed to market or mixed economies.

EXERCISE 2

Directions: Circle *T* if the statement is true, or *F* if it is false.

T F 1. Under capitalism, labor is controlled by the government.

T F 2. The U.S. economy will probably not change much but will remain a pure capitalist economy.

T F 3. If the U.S. economy changed, it would probably lead to changes in the political system as well.

T F 4. A socialist economy gives private business owners an unfair advantage.

T F 5. In a market economy, workers can take a job with a new company whenever they think they will be better off.

ANSWERS ARE ON PAGE 313.

HOW THE ECONOMY WORKS

KEY WORDS

demand—the desire and ability of consumers to buy a product or service

equilibrium—the price at which supply equals demand

supply—the quantity of goods and services available for sale at all possible prices

Supply and demand is the basis for the U.S. economy. Businesses must know that there is a demand for the goods or services they want to provide. At the same time, consumers must not only want something, they must also be able to purchase it. Price is what makes this system work.

You see supply and demand working every day. If the price for a certain item goes up, demand usually goes down. If the prices go down, demand usually goes up. For example, when airline tickets are too expensive, fewer people travel, and the demand goes down. When airline ticket prices are reduced, more people travel, and the demand goes up. If airline ticket prices are reduced for too long a period, however, the supply becomes greater than the demand, and some flights have empty seats.

Producers try to control price; they also try to control supply. If there is too much of an item available, the extra product sits in warehouses, or the producer has to reduce the price so that more items can be sold. If there is too little of an item, the price may become too high, and then consumers may stop buying it altogether. Producers, however, have only limited control of either price or supply.

Prices are mainly controlled by the marketplace. Each company tries to sell its products at a lower price than its competitors so that consumers will buy from it. At the same time, the company must keep the price high enough so that it can earn a profit. The continual competition and need for profit keeps prices from getting out of control. The following graph shows the relationship between supply and demand.

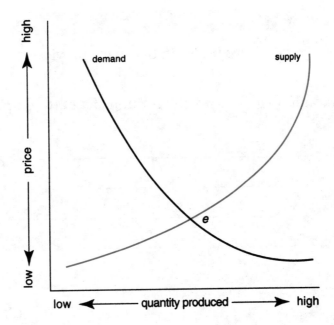

The curve labeled *demand* shows that there is low demand when prices are high. The demand increases as the price goes down. The curve labeled *supply* moves in the opposite direction. Supply is low when prices are low, but supply increases as prices increase. The more income a producer gets from a product, the more he or she is encouraged to produce it.

Price works to bring supply and demand into balance, or equilibrium. On the graph, the point of equilibrium is labeled *e*. Equilibrium is the point at which supply and demand match exactly. If the producer charges too much, demand decreases. If the producer charges less than the equilibrium price, demand will increase and a shortage will occur.

Every product or service has a supply-and-demand relationship. The market for the product is constantly at work to keep supply and demand in balance. If prices go too high, demand is reduced, so producers lower prices again. If demand is high and the supply is low, prices will go up. However, other producers may see that there is a high demand and high prices for this item, so they begin producing it. Eventually, the prices go down again.

EXERCISE 3

Directions: Answer the questions below in the space provided.

1. Which of the graphs below shows the relationship between price and demand? Explain why.

   _____

   _____

   _____

   _____

1) price → h
    I ← demand → h

2) price → h
    I ← demand → h

3) price → h
    I ← demand → h

2. Every holiday season, some toy almost always becomes especially popular. As quickly as a shipment arrives in the store, it's sold out. Many customers are willing to pay much more than the regular price in order to get one. An economist would say there was a

   _____**(1)** surplus of toys so prices increased

   _____**(2)** shortage of toys so prices declined

   _____**(3)** shortage of toys so prices increased

   ANSWERS ARE ON PAGE 313.

TOTAL VALUE, SPENDING, AND INVESTMENT

> **KEY WORDS**
>
> **capital goods**–goods and services companies buy to use in producing other goods or services
>
> **consumer goods**–goods and services that people buy for their own use
>
> **gross domestic product (GDP)**–the amount of all goods and services produced within a country in one year
>
> **gross national product (GNP)**–the amount of all goods and services produced by a country in one year

The total value of all goods and services produced by a country in one year is called its gross national product (GNP). This figure includes products produced by companies with headquarters in that country that are actually made in other countries. For example, Ford Motor Company produces cars in Canada and Mexico as well as in the United States. Because it is an American company, the United States counts Ford's production in Canada and Mexico as part of the U.S. GNP. Gross domestic product (GDP) is the total of all products and services actually produced within a country. In 1993, the U.S. GNP was more than $6 trillion.

Spending by consumers makes up about 70 percent of GNP. Consumer spending, however, is not the most important force that makes the economy run. When companies buy capital goods, this has a multiplying effect. Each dollar spent on new machinery or power plants creates jobs, more investments, and eventually produces more consumer spending.

When the economy is struggling with a recession or depression, it's the result of slow spending on capital goods. Reduced production results in unemployment, which means fewer people have money to spend. Because fewer consumer goods are bought, fewer goods need to be produced and more people are laid off. A cycle of economic decline results. In our economic system, the government tries to control this cycle in order to prevent a depression or recession.

EXERCISE 4

Directions: Match each term on the left with its correct description on the right. Write the correct letter on the line.

_____ **1.** gross national product

_____ **2.** employment

_____ **3.** consumer spending

_____ **4.** machine shop tools

_____ **5.** capital goods

_____ **6.** television

_____ **7.** unemployment

_____ **8.** gross domestic product

(a) an example of a capital good

(b) the largest part of the GDP

(c) a drastic decrease in investment in capital goods would increase this

(d) the amount of all goods and services produced by a country in one year

(e) an increase in consumer spending would result in an increase in this

(f) during a recession, the government might encourage companies to invest in this

(g) an example of a consumer good

(h) the amount of all goods and services produced within a country in one year

ANSWERS ARE ON PAGE 314.

WRITING ACTIVITY 18

Describe in a few paragraphs the role consumers and companies play in helping the economy to grow. What does the government do to help the economy from sliding into a depression or a recession?

ANSWERS WILL VARY.

HOW BUSINESSES BEHAVE

factors of production—the things needed to make a product

marketing—the part of business that deals with sales

monopoly—a marketing situation in which one person or company sells all of a product or accounts for a large part of the total sales of the product

oligopoly—a market situation in which very few sellers account for a large part of the total sales of a product

productivity—the efficient use of the factors of production to produce goods

In a capitalist economy, businesses exist to make a profit. Businesses make a profit by managing the factors of production. These are the land, labor, and capital that are needed to produce goods. In a capitalist economy, all of these factors are for sale in the market.

In order to make a profit, businesses must keep the cost of buying the factors of production lower than the income received from selling the goods produced.

One way to keep the cost of the factors of production low is to increase productivity. Productivity is usually measured by how many goods are produced by an hour of labor. For example, a group of workers produces 60 cars per hour and together are paid $1,000 per hour. If production increases to 120 cars per hour, productivity has increased 100 percent. The workers, however, are still being paid the same amount of money. The owner has reduced one factor of production—the cost of labor—by paying less for the labor to produce each car.

Productivity can also be increased by improving the factors of production. Improving the training of the work force, investing in more efficient equipment, improving planning, and organizing the manufacturing process more efficiently are some ways to improve productivity.

In addition to making the product more cheaply, a company can increase profits by increasing sales. The part of business that deals with sales is called marketing. Companies invest heavily in marketing. They study their customers and create advertising that appeals to them.

COMPETITION VERSUS MONOPOLY

In a market economy, businesses must compete with other businesses. Certain parts of the economy have many businesses so there is a great deal of competition. There are lots of fast-food restaurants, for example, so competition is intense.

Other areas of the economy include only a few businesses. The aluminum industry, for example, is made up of only a few very large corporations. A market in which there are few sellers of a product is called an oligopoly. Usually, there is little price competition among the sellers. Instead, they compete by advertising and offering special customer service.

A monopoly is a market situation in which there is only one seller of a product. Actually, a pure monopoly has never existed. The word has come to mean a situation in which one seller controls most of the market. American Telephone and Telegraph (AT&T), for example, is said to have had a monopoly prior to its breakup in 1984. Although a few other companies offered telephone services, AT&T was by far the dominant company. It controlled prices and services throughout the country.

EXERCISE 5

Directions: Underline the correct word or words that complete each statement below.

1. If a company increases productivity, its profits will (increase, decrease).

2. A marketing department (plans sales campaigns, manages employee morale).

3. A monopoly exists when there is only one (buyer for a product, seller that dominates the market).

4. To increase profits, it is best to (lay off employees, lower production factors).

5. In business, you sometimes hear that "the bottom line determines everything." The bottom line means (the amount of goods produced, the total profits made).

ANSWERS ARE ON PAGE 314.

≡ PRE-GED Practice ≡
EXERCISE 6

Questions 1–3 are based on the following passage.

Giant corporations have long dominated American business. The top 500 industrial firms account for more that 80 percent of all industrial sales. The 800 largest corporations employ as many people as the remaining 14,000,000 businesses.

A new trend has emerged in recent decades: the growth of large corporations into multinational corporations with businesses located throughout the world. Ford, for example, has forty subsidiary corporations around the globe. They account for one-third of Ford's invested capital and 30 percent of its work force. The foreign growth of companies like Ford has caused direct U.S. foreign investment to grow from $11 billion in 1950 to more than $486 billion in 1992. More than 25 percent of the *assets*, or total resources, of our largest corporations are invested abroad.

This growth of foreign investment has caused a number of problems for U.S. domestic industry. Production in labor-intensive industries, like electronic assembly, has been moved out of the U.S. to areas where labor costs are lower. Much of the work has gone to Asian countries, but there has also been substantial investment in new plants and equipment in Western Europe.

The growth of multinationals has also made it more difficult for the federal government to manage the national economy. Government plans either to slow inflation or stimulate the economy can be offset by the multinationals' ability to move money around the world to escape government control.

1. Based on the passage, the growth of multinationals would

   (1) increase the power of labor unions because workers would be part of bigger corporations
   (2) reduce the power of unions because companies can use nonunion labor abroad
   (3) not have any influence on U.S. labor-management relations
   (4) increase the power of unions by reducing the number of plants in the United States
   (5) increase the labor costs of bigger corporations

2. The largest American corporations have invested what percentage of their assets in other countries?

   (1) less than 10 percent
   (2) 20 percent
   (3) more than 25 percent
   (4) more than 30 percent
   (5) 80 percent

3. How much have direct U.S. foreign investments increased in the past 40 years?

   (1) about $100 billion
   (2) less than $150 billion
   (3) less than $225 billion
   (4) about $475 billion
   (5) more than $500 billion

ANSWERS ARE ON PAGE 314.

FINANCIAL INSTITUTIONS

> ## KEY WORDS
>
> *money*—cash and all other assets that can be used to purchase goods and services or to pay debts
>
> *multiplier effect*—the growth in the value of a deposit in a bank when it is, in turn, loaned out to a succession of other banks

In economics, money is anything that is widely accepted as a means of buying goods or paying debts. It includes cash (coins and bills), but it also includes other assets, such as checks and credit cards. In fact, most money exists only as figures in bank accounts, loan statements, and other financial statements.

The most important form of money in the economy is checking accounts. This makes sense if you remember that most workers are paid by check. In addition, most money that is spent—for rent, mortgage payments, utilities, credit payments—is paid in the form of checks. All of these checks are drawn on banks and later deposited in banks.

When a bank takes in money from depositors, it loans out some of it. The loaned money is then deposited in another bank. The second bank uses the new deposit to make its loans, which are then deposited in a third bank. This pattern continues indefinitely. Each loan creates new money. The original deposit is multiplied many times. This is called the multiplier effect. It provides money to finance the growth of the economy.

To keep the economy growing, money must circulate. If everyone were paid in cash and then kept it in a shoe box under the bed, the economy would grind to a halt. As long as people and businesses save money and borrow money, the economy prospers.

EXERCISE 7

Directions: Circle *T* if the statement is true, or *F* if it is false.

T F 1. If people, businesses, and the government spent only what money was on hand rather than borrowing money, the economy would become weak.

T F 2. The multiplier effect describes the way the money supply increases when banks make loans.

T F 3. A gasoline credit card is both an asset and money.

T F 4. The most important form of money in the economy is cash.

ANSWERS ARE ON PAGE 314.

THE FEDERAL RESERVE SYSTEM

KEY WORD

monetary policy—the regulation of the nation's supply of money and credit by the Federal Reserve Board

The money supply is controlled by the Federal Reserve System, a central bank operated by the federal government. The "Fed," as it is sometimes called, controls the amount of money available. It does this in many ways. One way is by telling banks how much money they must keep on deposit in the form of cash. When the Fed increases the amount from 20 percent to 25 percent, for example, the banks have less money to use for loans. This reduces the money supply.

The Fed controls the money supply in order to control the economy. When inflation becomes too high, the Fed may require banks to keep more money on hand as cash. This is called increasing the reserve requirement. This policy reduces the supply of money that can be loaned out. Interest rates rise because more borrowers compete for a limited supply of loanable funds. As a result, inflation is reduced since there is less money in circulation.

If the economy is weak, unemployment is high, and business is slow, the Fed may reduce the amount of cash a bank must hold. More money becomes available for loans and the interest rate on the loans goes down. People and businesses borrow more and buy more, so the economy grows. The way in which the Fed controls the money in the economy is called the monetary policy.

Money is what makes the economy work. Monetary policy is the way the supply of money is controlled. The Fed uses this control carefully to keep the economy running smoothly.

EXERCISE 8

Directions: Put a check in front of the correct answer to the questions that follow.

1. If the country was in a recession and the Federal Reserve wanted to help the economy grow, it would probably

   _____(1) increase the money supply

   _____(2) reduce the money supply

   _____(3) require banks to keep more cash on deposit

   _____(4) increase interest rates

2. Monetary policy refers to

   _____(1) the policy of keeping all your money in cash

   _____(2) government spending

   _____(3) the Federal Reserve's ways of controlling the money supply

   _____(4) the process of multiplying the effect of money in the economy

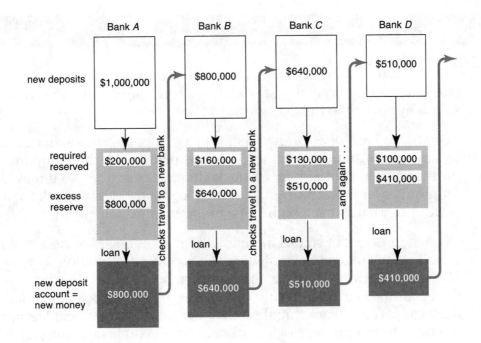

3. The diagram shown above illustrates

____**(1)** the multiplier effect

____**(2)** how economies can stop growing

____**(3)** the monetary policy

____**(4)** inflation

4. Which bank has the smallest amount of excess reserve?

____**(1)** Bank *A*

____**(2)** Bank *B*

____**(3)** Bank *C*

____**(4)** Bank *D*

ANSWERS ARE ON PAGE 314.

THE STOCK MARKET

The **stock market** is a market where stocks and bonds of corporations are bought and sold. It is a form of saving and investment, so it is important to the economy.

Stocks are shares of ownership in a company. The owner of a share receives **dividends**, which are payments made from the company's profits. The value of a share of stock changes over time, so it may be sold for more or less than it originally cost. People try to buy stocks at a low price and sell them at a high price in order to make a profit.

When prices of stocks increase, the market is said to be a bull market. Usually a bull market occurs when the economy as a whole is growing. When stock prices decrease, this signals a bear market. In a bear market, the economy is usually having difficulties. In 1929, stock prices fell drastically. This collapse marked the beginning of the Great Depression. Keeping an eye on the stock market can give you insight into the health of the economy.

Selling stock on the stock market is a way that businesses raise money for expansion. When owners or directors of the company sell stock in their business, they are selling a part of the company. The money they receive can be invested in new machinery, plants, stores, or other capital goods. This way of raising money is especially important for new companies and for utilities.

Consumers benefit from the stock market in several ways. First, when the market grows, new wealth is created so the economy improves. Second, the market is an effective way for individuals to save money. Most investors in the stock market are not banks, companies, or even mutual funds. In 1993, almost 46 percent of the investors in stocks were individuals.

EXERCISE 9

Directions: Underline the correct answer that completes each of the statements that follow.

1. If the value of stocks increased by 35 percent over a period of six months, this would be termed a (bull market, bear market).

2. If the value of stocks has steadily decreased in value for several months, this tells you that the general economy is probably in (good shape, bad shape).

3. When owners of stock are paid a share of the company's profits, they are receiving (investments, dividends).

ANSWERS ARE ON PAGE 314.

GOVERNMENT IN THE ECONOMY

Although the United States has a market economy, it does not operate entirely according to market forces. The federal and state governments manage the economy in various ways.

At the most basic level, the government sets up rules for doing business. For example, laws define business contracts and what they can and cannot include. Courts enforce these contracts.

At another level, the government provides public goods. National defense—the army and navy, war planes, tanks, and ships—are public goods. Highways and bridges, education, public health, fire protection, and air traffic control are other important government services. These are goods that private companies will not or should not provide.

The government also regulates the market. Laws prevent monopolies from controlling the market. Agencies, such as the Food and Drug Administration (FDA) and the Federal Trade Commission (FTC), control how some kinds of businesses operate and the products they sell.

Government laws also affect the costs and uses of some factors of production. Zoning ordinances and housing codes, for instance, affect the real estate market and where businesses can locate. Labor laws and minimum wage laws affect the cost of labor. The government also deals with by-products of production. Such things as industrial wastes and air pollution result from businesses in the market. The government must control these effects of the economy before they affect the quality of people's lives.

Demand management, also called fiscal policy, is another way the government influences the economy. Demand management refers to how the government budget and taxes are used to influence demand in the economy. Before the Great Depression, the government did little to control the level of demand. Since then, the government has tried to create more demand for goods and services in order to avoid another depression.

One way the government uses demand management is by increasing its own spending when spending in the private sector slows down and workers are unemployed. By increasing government spending, more money is put into the economy. For example, the government might extend unemployment benefits. This puts more money in the hands of unemployed people. When they spend it, demand is created and the economy benefits. When the economy picks up again, the government will reduce unemployment benefits or other spending in order to slow inflation.

EXERCISE 10

Directions: Circle *T* if the statement is true, or *F* if it is false.

T   F   **1.** The government provides public goods because it can make a profit.

T   F   **2.** Demand management is used by the government to keep the economy healthy.

T   F   **3.** If the economy were booming and inflation was becoming a problem, the government might reduce spending on public goods.

T   F   **4.** Privately owned businesses regulate the market.

T   F   **5.** Decreasing unemployment benefits causes inflation rates to increase.

T   F   **6.** Another term for demand management is fiscal policy.

T   F   **7.** The United States does not operate entirely according to market forces.

T   F   **8.** The passage says that fire protection and air traffic control should be provided by private companies.

T   F   **9.** Zoning ordinances and housing codes are controlled by government laws.

ANSWERS ARE ON PAGE 315.

GOVERNMENT AND FINANCES

KEY WORDS

national debt—the total amount of money owed by the federal government of the United States to its creditors

progressive tax—a tax that takes a larger portion of income as that income increases

regressive tax—a tax that takes a smaller portion of income as that income increases

transfer payments—payments that transfer income from one group of people to another through the tax system

One of the most rapidly growing government expenses is welfare programs. These include Aid to Dependent Children and other forms of public aid. Welfare payments are called transfer payments because they transfer income from one group of people to another. Taxes are used to make the transfer.

Taxation is the main source of government funding. The federal government relies on income taxes. State and local governments use income, property, and sales taxes. The federal income tax is a progressive tax. This means that as people make more money, they pay a higher percentage of their income in taxes. The opposite of a progressive tax is a regressive tax. A sales tax on food is a regressive tax. It is a tax that is the same for everyone. People have to buy a certain amount of food. The less they earn, the larger the percentage of their income goes toward food and, therefore, toward taxes on food.

Governments often finance their activities by borrowing. Savings bonds, treasury bills, and municipal bonds are examples of government borrowing. This type of borrowing has added greatly to our national debt.

There is a great debate going on about the growth of government spending. In 1900, the federal budget was $400 million. In 1990, it was $1.4 trillion. In addition, state and local governments spent an additional $976 billion. Together, this represents more than 40 percent of the gross national product. Is this too much? The question is the focus of public debate.

EXERCISE 11

Directions: Answer the questions below in the space provided.

1. Federal, state, and local government spending account for what percentage of the GNP?

   _____

2. What is the main source of government funds?

   _____

3. A city government adds a one percent tax to movie tickets. Is this a progressive or regressive tax? Why?

   _____

4. How are welfare payments funded?

   _____

5. What are transfer payments?

   _____

6. Did the amount spent by the federal, state, and local governments in 1990 add up to about $2.4 trillion or about $9.7 trillion?

   _____

7. Name three ways the government finances its borrowing.

   _____

   _____

ANSWERS ARE ON PAGE 315.

CONSUMERS IN THE ECONOMY

> **KEY WORDS**
>
> ***compound interest***—the interest that is figured for a period of time based on the total of the principal plus any interest that has been earned over a period of time
>
> ***discretionary income***—the difference in a budget between fixed costs and income
>
> ***equity***—the value in property after debt and other liabilities are paid

Consumers are the target of intense advertising and marketing efforts. In order to keep your own budget balanced, you should decide on specific economic goals. Do you want to buy a house or a car, go on a vacation, or just get by from day to day? In order to reach your goal, you need a plan and a budget.

A budget is a plan for spending your income. It involves figuring out how much money you have and how you will use it. The first step is to figure out your fixed costs. These are expenses you must pay each month. Examples include rent, food, utilities, and car payments. The difference between what you must spend and your total income is called discretionary income. This is income you can spend as you choose.

If you are not happy with the amount of your discretionary income, you can do three things: (1) increase your income, (2) decrease your fixed costs, or (3) change your goals.

When you set aside discretionary income to pay for your long-term goals, you can put it in a savings account. The bank will pay you interest in return for using your money. Savings accounts are safe and are usually insured by the federal government. You will receive compound interest on your savings. In other words, you will receive interest on the original amount you put in savings. In addition, each time interest is paid it will go into your account and interest will then be paid on that interest. In this way, the deposit will grow.

The most important economic decision most people make is to buy a home. When you buy a home, you develop equity in it. Equity is what you would get out of the property if you sold it and paid off the mortgage. You develop equity in two ways. By paying the mortgage each month, the amount you own slowly increases. Second, during times of inflation, the value of a house rises and equity increases.

There are several kinds of home mortgages. Traditionally, they are long-term (twenty-five to thirty years) and have a fixed interest rate. In other words, the amount paid remains the same over the life of the loan. Today, other types of loans are also available, some with adjustable interest rates. These mortgages give home buyers more choices in how much they want to pay. They can buy a house now, for example, knowing their income will grow in the future.

Part of your economic plan should also include insurance. Health insurance is vital because of the high costs of medical care. Homeowners insurance is necessary to protect the value of your home against burglary, fire, and other disasters. Rent insurance can protect your possessions if you rent an apartment.

≡ PRE-GED Practice ≡
EXERCISE 12

Choose the best answer to the questions that follow.

1. A home purchase is an investment that
   (1) pays compound interest
   (2) keeps up with inflation
   (3) loses equity during times of inflation
   (4) is insured by the federal government
   (5) is paid off with a fixed interest rate

2. The Garcia family has an income of $2,000 per month. Their expenses (including rent, food, car payment, insurance, clothes, and miscellaneous) total $1,550. What is the Garcias' discretionary income?
   (1) $200
   (2) $450
   (3) $800
   (4) $1,000
   (5) $1,500

3. An old fable tells about an ant who works all summer to store extra food. A grasshopper, meanwhile, sings and dances and fiddles away his time, not saving anything for the future. When winter comes, the ant has plenty to eat. The grasshopper starves. The grasshopper had
   (1) failed to budget his resources
   (2) fallen victim to inflation
   (3) too little discretionary income
   (4) not received compound interest
   (5) too little equity

4. Which of the following is NOT an example of a fixed cost?
   (1) rent
   (2) utilities
   (3) car payment
   (4) vacation
   (5) mortgage payment

ANSWERS ARE ON PAGE 315.

CREDIT AND CONSUMER FRAUD

One of the biggest threats to your budget and economic plans is credit. When you use credit, you are adding to your fixed costs. Unlike a mortgage, which is a form of credit but one that is used to make an investment, most forms of credit are not investments.

There are many kinds of credit, including credit cards, charge accounts, and automobile loans. Credit *does* have advantages. It allows you to buy things you couldn't afford if you had to make one cash payment. However, credit is expensive. Before you agree to a loan of any kind, find out how much it will cost. Look for two kinds of costs: higher prices for the things you buy and interest on the loan.

If you pay off a loan in monthly installments, interest is charged on the remaining balance. Bank credit cards are an example of this kind of credit. Interest is usually high, often much higher than you would get if you took out a loan from the bank.

Laws help protect you from excessive interest charges and other kinds of consumer fraud. For instance, the Truth-in-Lending Act requires lenders to tell the consumer what the real rate of interest is. This is the annual percentage rate (APR). Consumers must also be informed of the total dollar cost of a loan.

WRITING ACTIVITY 19

Do you have a credit card that you use frequently? Have you ever taken out a loan to purchase a car or a home, or to pay for college tuition? In a few paragraphs, either describe the advantages and disadvantages of paying for items with a credit card vs. paying in cash or by check, or explain how paying off a loan has worked for you.

ANSWERS WILL VARY.

EXERCISE 13

Directions: Based on the following passage and chart, circle *T* for each true statement, or *F* for each false statement.

Distribution of Family Income and Wealth

The chart below shows that income is actually distributed unevenly. For instance, in 1991, the top 5 percent of American families earned 17 percent of the total family income. Twenty percent of the families shared just 4.5 percent of income earned in the United States.

FAMILY INCOME 1970–1991		
Families Ranked by Income	Percentage of U.S. Total Income Before Taxes	
	1970	1991
Lowest fifth (20%)	4.8	4.5
Second fifth (20%)	12.2	10.7
Third fifth (20%)	17.6	16.6
Fourth fifth (20%)	23.8	24.1
Highest fifth (20%)	40.9	44.2
Top 5%	15.6	17.1

T F 1. In 1991, 20 percent of U.S. families earned 44.2 percent of the total income in the United States.

T F 2. The chart shows that in 1991, the top 40 percent of the population earned less than 40 percent of the total income.

T F 3. The chart shows that the percentage of total income of the poorest fifth of Americans declined from 1970 to 1991.

T F 4. The main idea of the paragraph and chart is that the income was fairly evenly divided among people in the United States in 1991.

ANSWERS ARE ON PAGE 315.

THE LABOR MARKET, INDUSTRY, AND UNIONS

The **labor market** is a term used to describe the availability of jobs. When the economy is healthy, unemployment is low and jobs are plentiful. When the economy is weak, unemployment is high and jobs are hard to find. During the last three decades, the labor market and industry have both changed radically.

During the 1970s and 1980s, manufacturing industries, such as the steel and automobile industries, suffered serious declines in sales. Many companies closed; others remained open but employed far fewer people. Some of these changes resulted from fierce, new competition from companies in other countries. The U.S. steel industry, for example, was hit especially hard. The plants and equipment were old and inefficient. The companies could no longer compete successfully with foreign steel producers. As a result, many of them closed rather than investing in modernizing the plants that would make them competitive.

Some industries left the United States altogether. Many clothing and shoe manufacturers, for instance, moved to foreign countries where labor costs were cheaper. Thousands of workers were left jobless.

Still more changes resulted from the way in which products are manufactured. Robots and computers, for example, made American industry more competitive. However, they also replaced many workers in certain industries.

While these changes cost thousands of American workers their jobs, the service industries were growing rapidly. Service industries are those businesses not involved in the production of goods. They include restaurants, hotels, retail stores, health care, office jobs, and so on. Although many unemployed workers found jobs in these new businesses, they often had to take lower paying jobs.

In the 1990s, the character of American industry began undergoing another change. International trade barriers began disappearing, first with Canada and then Mexico. Trade barriers with Europe, South America, and Asia were reduced. The immediate effect of these changes has been improved trade and more jobs in the United States. The long-term effects on U.S. industry and the U.S. labor market remain unknown.

EXERCISE 14

Directions: Put a check in front of all the following statements that accurately describe industry and the labor market during the 1970s, 1980s, and 1990s.

_____ **1.** Many industries faced strong competition from abroad.

_____ **2.** Companies that had out-dated equipment and plants often went out of business.

_____ **3.** When industrial workers lost their jobs, most found new, better-paying jobs in the service industry.

_____ **4.** Robots and computers made U.S. industry more competitive.

_____ **5.** Reducing international trade barriers cost thousands of American workers their jobs.

ANSWERS ARE ON PAGE 315.

LABOR UNIONS

Unions are associations of workers, usually in a particular occupation or at a certain workplace. The workers organize and bargain as a group for wages, benefits, and other working conditions. The process of bargaining as a group with management is called ***collective bargaining***. And since workers are acting as a group, they can have great influence. The management may represent a small business, a multinational corporation, or even a state or local government.

The goal of collective bargaining is to agree to a ***labor contract***. This is a legally binding agreement between management and labor. It states what the duties of labor and management will be for the term of the contract. It usually defines salaries, working conditions, benefits, and other terms of employment.

Often, issues dealt with by labor contract are also covered in part by federal and state laws. Racial and sexual discrimination, health and safety conditions, and rate of minimum wages are all issues that are covered in part by government regulation. However, labor contracts may go beyond these laws.

When labor and management are unable to reach an agreement, the labor union leaders may call for a ***strike***. When this happens, workers as a group stop working. The power to strike is the ultimate weapon of labor unions.

In recent decades, the power of unions has weakened. This has happened in part because the industries that unions once dominated have declining work forces. The steel, auto, and railroad industries, for example, once had powerful labor unions. As these industries have grown weaker, so have the unions. In 1992, fewer than 16 percent of American workers belonged to unions.

EXERCISE 15

Directions: Based on the passage you just read, circle *T* for each true statement, or *F* for each false statement.

T F 1. When a union cannot gain salary increases, benefits, or other working conditions that workers want, union leaders may call for a strike.

T F 2. More than 20 percent of American workers belong to unions.

T F 3. When management and union leaders discuss working issues, they are engaging in collective bargaining.

T F 4. A labor contract may include rules that prevent unfair hiring practices.

T F 5. Federal and state laws protect workers from unsafe working conditions.

T F 6. Management refers to those who head local businesses.

T F 7. Labor contracts are entered into for an unspecified period of time.

T F 8. The passage states that as work forces decline, the power of unions decreases.

ANSWERS ARE ON PAGE 316.

≡ PRE-GED·Practice ≡
ECONOMICS

Questions 1–3 are based on the chart below.

U.S. GROSS AND NET NATIONAL PRODUCTS (in billions/trillions of dollars)				
Gross National Product	1960 515.3	1970 1,015.5	1980 2,732.0	1990 5,524.5
Less Capital Consumption Allowance	−46.4	−88.8	−303.0	−594.8
Equals Net National Product	468.9	926.7	2,429.0	4,929.7

Source: *U.S. Department of Commerce*

1. By 1990, the U.S. GNP was

   (1) more than $5 1/2 trillion
   (2) less than $2 1/2 billion
   (3) less than the GNP in 1980
   (4) double the GNP in 1960
   (5) on the decline

2. To find the Net National Product, you

   (1) add the GNPs for the 30-year period
   (2) add the Capital Consumption Allowance to the GNP
   (3) subtract the Capital Consumption Allowance from the GNP
   (4) divide the GNP by the Capital Consumption Allowance
   (5) average the GNP for the 30-year period

3. If the GNP continues to grow at the same rate, by the year 2000 it will be

   (1) about $8 million
   (2) about $8 trillion
   (3) about $20 billion
   (4) more than $20 trillion
   (5) more than $11 trillion

Questions 4–8 are based on the following passage and the graph on the next page.

In 1990, the total national debt of the United States was $3 trillion, 206.3 billion. This comes to about $13,000 for every man, woman, and child in the country.

The national debt is money the U.S. government has borrowed to pay for government expenses. This is in addition to funds raised by taxation. World Wars I and II were major causes for increases in the national debt. Deep recessions in 1974–1975 and 1979–1982 reduced tax revenues and greatly increased debt. Additional tax cuts along with increased military spending added billions more to the debt during the 1980s.

The federal government borrows money by selling financial instruments such as Treasury certificates, notes, and U.S. Savings Bonds. These are sold to investors. Most of these are U.S. citizens or financial institutions. About 80 percent of the debt is owed to American citizens.

PERCENTAGE CHANGE IN U.S. NATIONAL DEBT, 1900–1990

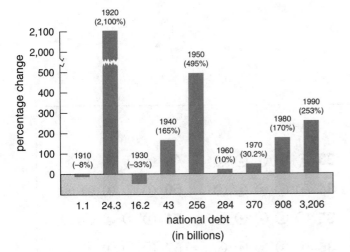

4. The greatest percentage of increase in national debt occurred during what ten-year period?

(1) 1900–1910
(2) 1910–1920
(3) 1920–1930
(4) 1940–1950
(5) 1980–1990

5. During what two ten-year periods did the total amount of the national debt decrease?

(1) 1900–1910 and 1920–1930
(2) 1910–1920 and 1940–1950
(3) 1940–1950 and 1980–1990
(4) 1960–1970 and 1970–1980
(5) 1970–1980 and 1980–1990

6. During what ten-year period did the actual amount of the national debt increase by the greatest number of dollars?

(1) 1910–1920
(2) 1940–1950
(3) 1950–1960
(4) 1970–1980
(5) 1980–1990

7. According to the passage, the greatest cause of increased national debt has been

(1) consumer spending
(2) selling financial instruments
(3) capital spending on domestic programs
(4) financing wars and military spending
(5) welfare programs during the Great Depression

8. Another severe recession, such as the one in 1979–1982, would probably

(1) raise the national debt
(2) lower the national debt
(3) not affect the national debt
(4) lower the interest on the debt
(5) lower the debt ceiling

ANSWERS ARE ON PAGE 316.

1 ① ② ③ ④ ⑤	17 ① ② ③ ④ ⑤	33 ① ② ③ ④ ⑤	49 ① ② ③ ④ ⑤
2 ① ② ③ ④ ⑤	18 ① ② ③ ④ ⑤	34 ① ② ③ ④ ⑤	50 ① ② ③ ④ ⑤
3 ① ② ③ ④ ⑤	19 ① ② ③ ④ ⑤	35 ① ② ③ ④ ⑤	51 ① ② ③ ④ ⑤
4 ① ② ③ ④ ⑤	20 ① ② ③ ④ ⑤	36 ① ② ③ ④ ⑤	52 ① ② ③ ④ ⑤
5 ① ② ③ ④ ⑤	21 ① ② ③ ④ ⑤	37 ① ② ③ ④ ⑤	53 ① ② ③ ④ ⑤
6 ① ② ③ ④ ⑤	22 ① ② ③ ④ ⑤	38 ① ② ③ ④ ⑤	54 ① ② ③ ④ ⑤
7 ① ② ③ ④ ⑤	23 ① ② ③ ④ ⑤	39 ① ② ③ ④ ⑤	55 ① ② ③ ④ ⑤
8 ① ② ③ ④ ⑤	24 ① ② ③ ④ ⑤	40 ① ② ③ ④ ⑤	56 ① ② ③ ④ ⑤
9 ① ② ③ ④ ⑤	25 ① ② ③ ④ ⑤	41 ① ② ③ ④ ⑤	57 ① ② ③ ④ ⑤
10 ① ② ③ ④ ⑤	26 ① ② ③ ④ ⑤	42 ① ② ③ ④ ⑤	58 ① ② ③ ④ ⑤
11 ① ② ③ ④ ⑤	27 ① ② ③ ④ ⑤	43 ① ② ③ ④ ⑤	59 ① ② ③ ④ ⑤
12 ① ② ③ ④ ⑤	28 ① ② ③ ④ ⑤	44 ① ② ③ ④ ⑤	60 ① ② ③ ④ ⑤
13 ① ② ③ ④ ⑤	29 ① ② ③ ④ ⑤	45 ① ② ③ ④ ⑤	61 ① ② ③ ④ ⑤
14 ① ② ③ ④ ⑤	30 ① ② ③ ④ ⑤	46 ① ② ③ ④ ⑤	62 ① ② ③ ④ ⑤
15 ① ② ③ ④ ⑤	31 ① ② ③ ④ ⑤	47 ① ② ③ ④ ⑤	63 ① ② ③ ④ ⑤
16 ① ② ③ ④ ⑤	32 ① ② ③ ④ ⑤	48 ① ② ③ ④ ⑤	64 ① ② ③ ④ ⑤

Post-Test

The Post-Test consists of 64 multiple-choice questions. It should give you a good idea of how well you have learned the skills you have studied in this book. You should take the Post-Test only after you have completed all the chapters. Work as quickly and as carefully as you can. If a question seems too difficult, make an educated guess.

Record your answers on the answer grid on page 266. Choose the best of five answer choices by filling in the corresponding circle on the answer grid.

Using the Evaluation Chart on page 295, circle the number of each question that you missed to determine which topics you might need to review before you move on to Contemporary Books' *GED Test 2: Social Studies, Preparation for the High School Equivalency Examination.*

Question 1 is based on the following information.

1. Geographers often look at the places they study in terms of regions. A region does not have distinct boundaries or an exact population. It is simply an area of land with certain characteristics.

Suppose a geographer studies precipitation patterns in the Pacific Northwest. Which of the following would best define this region?

(1) changes in altitude from the coast to the mountains
(2) a high annual rate of rainfall
(3) the state boundaries of Washington and Oregon
(4) the Pacific Northwest Railroad
(5) the greatest amount of cultivated farmland

2. Joe and Ida Williams find that every month their money just seems to disappear. They can never save for any long-term goals. The first thing they should do to correct this situation is

(1) increase their monthly income
(2) draw up a family budget
(3) buy some life insurance
(4) try a few get-rich-quick schemes
(5) apply for a credit card

Questions 3 and 4 are based on the following table.

MARRIAGES AND DIVORCES IN THE UNITED STATES
(per 1,000 people)

Year	Marriages	Divorces
1930	9.2	1.6
1940	12.1	2.0
1950	11.1	2.6
1960	8.5	2.2
1970	10.6	3.5
1980	10.6	5.2
1992	9.3	4.8

Source: *World Almanac, 1994*

3. This table tells you the

(1) number of marriages that ended in divorce
(2) percentage of the population that married or divorced
(3) number of marriages and divorces for every 1,000 people
(4) percentage of change in the marriage and divorce rate from 1930 to 1992
(5) statistical evidence of social decline

4. Based on the information in the table, you can conclude that

(1) twice as many marriages as divorces took place for each year shown
(2) between 1980 and 1992, the number of marriages and the number of divorces fell
(3) the baby boom has affected the divorce rate
(4) the divorce rate has always been at the same percentage as the marriage rate
(5) there are now more divorces than marriages

Question 5 refers to the following passage and cartoon.

Many Americans are shocked about the large number of deaths caused by guns and want strict gun control. Other Americans are equally determined to have the right to own guns. They point to the Second Amendment for constitutional support. It clearly states that "the right of the people to keep and bear arms shall not be infringed."

5. Which of the following might best sum up the cartoonist's view of the Second Amendment?

(1) favors it

(2) wants it done away with

(3) believes it no longer goes along with the Founding Fathers' intent

(4) believes it has run into disfavor with the gun lobby

(5) causes too many Americans and their pets to lose sleep

Questions 6 and 7 refer to the following graph.

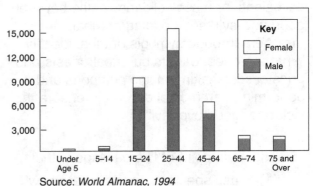

Source: *World Almanac, 1994*

6. Which of the following groups has the greatest number of deaths from firearms?

(1) males 75 and over

(2) females 65 to 74

(3) males 45 to 64

(4) males 25 to 44

(5) females 25 to 44

7. From the fact that half of all children 16 years old and under injured in a handgun accident were shot in their own home, you can infer that parents

(1) failed to store handguns properly

(2) had no control over curious children

(3) forgot to lock gun cabinets

(4) have become lax in disciplining children

(5) should tell children to play outside the home

Question 8 refers to the following paragraph.

Mass spectator sports have replaced many older tribal ceremonies. Sports provide occasions for mass solidarity, battle between good and evil, and bonding of tribal members through symbols of tribal identity. What are cheerleaders but tribal priests and priestesses shaking magic pompons and performing ceremonial dances to ensure the victory of good over evil?

8. The main point of this passage is that
   (1) mass spectator sports create new cultural needs
   (2) sports are important in building character
   (3) tribal ceremonies are not related to modern life
   (4) modern sport is mainly a business enterprise
   (5) mass spectator sports are a modern adjustment to older tribal needs

Questions 9 and 10 refer to the following passage.

Childcare facilities first appeared in U.S. cities around 1900. They were charities, run by wealthy women who raised the money and managed the staff. These women saw that some mothers were forced to work to take care of their families. They feared that without the day nurseries small children would be left home alone. Critics worried that day nurseries would encourage mothers to work instead of stay home with their children.

9. Day-care centers were started by
   (1) mothers who hired people to take care of their children while they worked
   (2) factories that hired women workers
   (3) wealthy women who thought they could make a profit
   (4) people who wanted mothers to stay home with their children
   (5) wealthy women who worried about the safety of the small children of working mothers

10. Based on the passage, you can hypothesize that the practice of giving welfare benefits to mothers of dependent children could have developed because
   (1) there were not enough jobs for working women
   (2) of the belief that children should have their mothers at home with them
   (3) working women did not have enough day-care centers for their children
   (4) day care was too expensive for most mothers
   (5) divorce was so common that many women had no husbands to support them

Questions 11–13 refer to the following definitions.

direct initiative—a process that allows citizens to draft laws and present them directly to the voters

referendum—a process by which voters in a state or community can repeal laws in a general election

recall—a process by which citizens can vote an elected government official out of office

primary election—an election held in advance of the general election allowing voters to select candidates for public office from one or more political parties

general election—the final election held on the same day throughout the United States

11. Citizens who want to write a tax reform law and present it directly to the voters would use a

(1) referendum
(2) general election
(3) direct initiative
(4) recall
(5) primary election

12. A person who wishes to become his or her political party's candidate for governor must first be selected in a

(1) referendum
(2) general election
(3) direct initiative
(4) recall
(5) primary election

13. California voters unhappy with Governor Pete Wilson's support of Proposition 187 (an initiative denying education and health care services to illegal immigrants) could remove him from office before his term expires in 1999 by a

(1) referendum
(2) general election
(3) direct initiative
(4) recall
(5) primary election

Question 14 is based on the following passage.

In the 1930s, the United States was preoccupied with the Great Depression and did not get involved in world affairs. During this time, England and France followed a policy of appeasement toward Germany, who was taking over territory that belonged to others. Germany seized all of Austria and Czechoslovakia, and threatened Poland. England and France did nothing and kept their soldiers at home. Many experts in world affairs claim that appeasing Germany led to World War II.

14. In this passage, appeasement means

(1) refusing to allow Germany to expand its territory
(2) taking in unlimited numbers of immigrants
(3) using land that belonged to someone else
(4) compromising in the face of attacks on other nations
(5) working to bring about world peace

Questions 15 and 16 refer to the following passage.

Consumer cooperatives are businesses that are owned and controlled by their members—the consumers who use them. Member-owners of co-ops vote on rules and policies and elect officers. Co-ops can often provide services at a lower cost because the member-owners run the business for their own use, not to make a profit. A co-op can be any kind of business, such as a grocery store or a gasoline station.

15. The decision-making process in consumer cooperatives is controlled by

(1) the government
(2) the co-op's officers
(3) neighborhood groups
(4) the co-op's members
(5) grocery-store chains

16. If the average cost of food is lower at a co-op than at the local supermarket, the reason might be that

(1) the co-op is trying to compete with the supermarket
(2) the co-op is receiving a subsidy from the government
(3) the members would rather have low prices than high profits
(4) those who run co-ops pay less for food than supermarket owners do
(5) the supermarket sells food of higher quality

Question 17 is based on the following passage.

In 1992, 58 percent of African Americans ages 16–19 were employed. This compared with an 82 percent employment rate for whites and 72 percent for Hispanics in that age group.

17. From this information, you could infer that African-American teenagers

(1) should return to the old values of hard work
(2) refuse to accept minimum-wage jobs
(3) have less opportunity for summer jobs than white or Hispanic youths
(4) have stopped seeking employment
(5) prefer to stay in school

Question 18 refers to the following graph.

EQUILIBRIUM PRICE FOR COMPUTERS

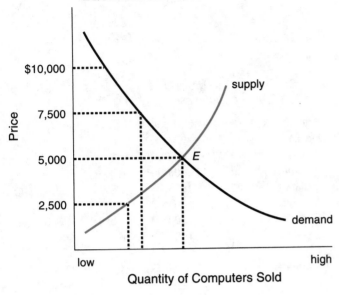

18. The equilibrium price of goods or services (E) takes place at the point where supply equals demand. According to the graph, what is the equilibrium price for computers?

(1) $2,500
(2) $5,000
(3) $7,500
(4) $10,000
(5) $15,000

Questions 19 and 20 are based on the graph and table below.

Muslims are a growing part of the U.S. population. Their religion is called Islam. It may soon become the country's second-largest religion.

U.S. MUSLIM POPULATION

Most U.S. Muslims are immigrants

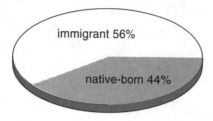

immigrant 56%

native-born 44%

States with the highest Muslim population

California	1,000,000
New York	800,000
Illinois	420,000
New Jersey	200,000
Indiana	180,000
Michigan	170,000
Virginia	150,000
Texas	140,000
Ohio	130,000
Maryland	70,000

19. Most Muslims in the United States are

  (1) native-born and live in California, New York, and Ohio

  (2) native-born and live in New Jersey, Texas, and Maryland

  (3) immigrants and live in California, New Jersey, and Illinois

  (4) immigrants and live in California, New York, and Illinois

  (5) equally immigrants and native-born

20. Based on the data, you can infer that Muslims

  (1) prefer living in rural, agricultural states

  (2) settle in populous states that have big cities

  (3) settle in equal numbers in all 50 states

  (4) prefer to settle only on the East Coast

  (5) prefer to settle only on the West Coast

Question 21 refers to the graph on the right.

In Chicago in 1990, women who worked full time earned 65.6 percent of men's wages.

21. In 1990, about how much less did full-time female workers earn than full-time male workers in Chicago?

(1) $3 thousand
(2) $5 thousand
(3) $9 thousand
(4) $11 thousand
(5) $15 thousand

PAY GAP BETWEEN MEN AND WOMEN

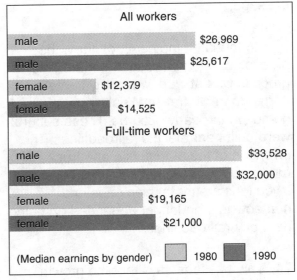

Source: *Chicago Tribune*

Questions 22 and 23 refer to the tables below.

U.S. COUNTIES: HOW THEY RANK BY AGE

Youngest Counties (Percentage under age 18)		*Oldest Counties* (Population age 65 or older)	
1. Wade Hampton, AK	45.8%	1. Llano, TX	34.1%
2. Todd, SD	45.1%	2. Charlotte, FL	33.8%
3. Shannon, SD	44.8%	3. Highlands, FL	33.5%
4. Buffalo, SD	44.7%	4. Pasco, FL	32.3%
5. San Juan, UT	43.3%	5. Sarasota, FL	32.2%

Source: *U.S. Census Bureau*

22. Based on the tables, which two counties are likely to have the largest number of retired people?

(1) Buffalo, SD, and Sarasota, FL
(2) San Juan, UT, and Shannon, SD
(3) Llano, TX, and Charlotte, FL
(4) Highlands, FL, and Pasco, FL
(5) Pasco, FL, and Todd, SD

23. In which two counties might you expect education to be an important concern?

(1) Wade Hampton, AK, and Todd, SD
(2) Llano, TX, and Charlotte, FL
(3) Buffalo, SD, and Highlands, FL
(4) San Juan, UT, and Llano, TX
(5) Wade Hampton, AK, and Llano, TX

Questions 24 and 25 refer to the following passage.

In the late nineteenth century, the process of suburbanization began. This process was at work when city centers began to decentralize. Wealthy people had homes in the early suburbs. These suburbs were built near electric railroad lines. The invention of the automobile and truck furthered the growth of suburbs. These inventions meant that factories and homeowners no longer depended on being near city railroad lines.

24. This passage says that the growth of suburbs was advanced

    (1) by the invention of the automobile
    (2) by the development of more railroad lines
    (3) when the poor moved away from the city
    (4) when industry moved to the country
    (5) as railroads became obsolete

25. From this passage, you could conclude that an important feature in shaping the physical growth of our environment is

    (1) the location of homes for wealthy people
    (2) population size
    (3) population density
    (4) transportation technology
    (5) the physical condition of the site

Questions 26 and 27 refer to the following passage.

Society makes a distinction between street crime and white-collar crime. Street crimes include theft, burglary, robbery, homicide, rape, larceny, and assault. White-collar crimes are committed by professional and business people in the course of their work activities and usually do not physically harm others. The money lost from street crime is one-fifth of the amount lost through embezzlement, fraud, and other white-collar crimes. However, white-collar criminals often get much lighter prison sentences than street criminals. Sometimes those convicted of white-collar crimes serve no time at all.

26. The passage says that the heaviest money losses from crime come from

    (1) car thefts
    (2) robbery
    (3) white-collar crime
    (4) home burglaries
    (5) gang activities

27. You could infer that street crime and white-collar crime are dealt with differently because

    (1) street crime is much more costly
    (2) street gangs have political connections
    (3) the courts go easy on street criminals
    (4) white-collar criminals have power and social status and do not usually physically harm others
    (5) white-collar crime is not committed by criminals

Questions 28 and 29 refer to the following graph.

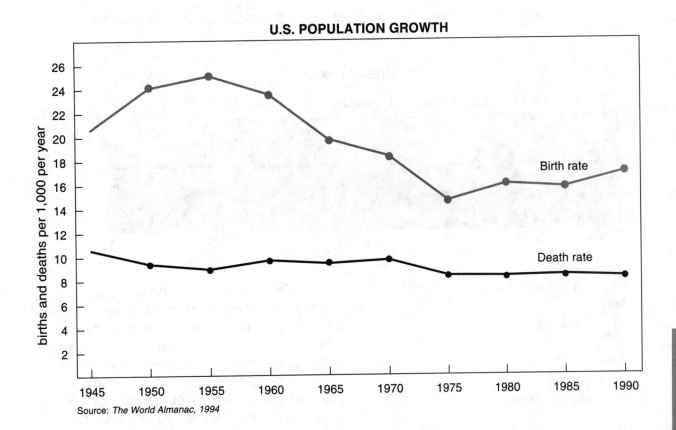

U.S. POPULATION GROWTH

Source: *The World Almanac, 1994*

28. According to the graph, in which of the following time periods did the greatest increase in birth rate take place?

(1) 1945–1955
(2) 1955–1965
(3) 1960–1970
(4) 1970–1980
(5) 1980–1990

29. The graph shows that current American population growth rates

(1) are exploding
(2) have remained very stable since 1945
(3) declined during the early 1950s
(4) have increased dramatically since 1980
(5) have declined since 1955

Questions 30 and 31 refer to the following diagram.

The cross-section view shows the five Great Lakes that separate the United States and Canada.

THE GREAT LAKES

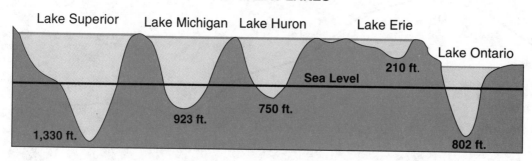

30. Which of the five Great Lakes is the deepest?
(1) Lake Ontario
(2) Lake Erie
(3) Lake Huron
(4) Lake Michigan
(5) Lake Superior

31. Which of the five Great Lakes lies above sea level?
(1) Lake Ontario
(2) Lake Erie
(3) Lake Huron
(4) Lake Michigan
(5) Lake Superior

Question 32 refers to the following two quotations:

". . . avoid the necessity of those overgrown military establishments which, under any form of government, are inauspicious [not favorable] for liberty, and which are to be regarded as particularly hostile to republican liberty."

General George Washington,
1st U.S. President,
Farewell Address, 1796

"The conjunction of an immense military establishment and a large arms industry . . . new in American experience, exercised a total influence . . . felt in every city, every state house, every office of the federal government. . . . In the councils of government, we must guard against the acquisition of unwarranted influence by the military-industrial complex."

General Dwight Eisenhower,
34th U.S. President,
Farewell Address, 1961

32. Which of the following conclusions could be drawn from both of these statements?

(1) A very large military establishment could threaten our American government.
(2) Business influence on the military has made our form of government more democratic.
(3) Only the military-industrial complex can protect our liberties.
(4) The military should be allowed more influence in government.
(5) Civilian control of the military should never be allowed.

Questions 33 and 34 refer to the following poll.

Gallup polls in 1947, 1964, and 1990 surveyed Americans on whether members of the Senate and House of Representatives should have limits on their terms in office.

CONGRESSIONAL TERM LIMITS

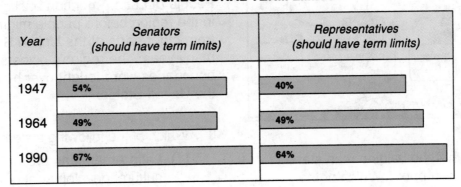

Year	Senators (should have term limits)	Representatives (should have term limits)
1947	54%	40%
1964	49%	49%
1990	67%	64%

Source: *The American Enterprise*

33. Which of the following best summarizes Americans' attitudes toward congressional term limits from 1947 to 1990?

(1) They increasingly favored term limits for senators but not for representatives.

(2) They increasingly favored term limits for both senators and for representatives.

(3) They increasingly favored term limits for representatives but not for senators.

(4) Those favoring term limits fell from 60 percent to 40 percent.

(5) By 1990, more than 75 percent of those polled favored term limits.

34. Based on the poll, which action might you expect concerning term limits?

(1) a constitutional amendment setting term limits for members of the House and Senate

(2) members of Congress leaving office voluntarily after two terms

(3) an executive order by the president setting term limits

(4) impeachment of members of Congress who refuse to leave office

(5) no action by members of Congress

Question 35 is based on the following cartoon.

35. Assume that the balding man stands for the American public. Which of the following best sums up the cartoonist's main point?

(1) Doctors and mechanics, but not lawyers and politicians, must have experience to do their jobs.

(2) The public will not allow inexperienced people to perform surgery, win a law case, or fix a car.

(3) The public accepts inexperienced politicians in Washington, but does not accept inexperienced doctors, lawyers, or mechanics.

(4) The public believes inexperienced people can become great politicians.

(5) The public is willing to let people try their hand at any job.

Question 36 is based on the following passage.

Latin Americans made rich cultural contributions to the southwestern United States long before the twentieth century. People of Latin American background lived in the region before people migrated there from other parts of the United States. For many years, the region's ownership and boundaries were fought over by Mexico and the United States.

36. Which of the following statements is true?

(1) Latin Americans prevented the cultural development of the Southwest.

(2) Mexico sold Texas to the United States to end boundary disputes.

(3) Most Mexicans left the Southwest after it became part of the United States.

(4) The United States had completely settled the Southwest before Mexico took an interest in the region.

(5) Latin American influence on regional culture in the Southwestern United States has a long, rich history.

Question 37 is based on the following cartoon.

37. The main idea of this cartoon is that American agricultural production has changed

(1) from being run by large company-owned farms

(2) as a result of government price supports

(3) from being run by small family farms

(4) in spite of high interest rates

(5) toward organic farming

Question 38 is based on the following map.

WHERE LARGE NUMBERS OF LOYALISTS LIVED DURING THE AMERICAN REVOLUTION

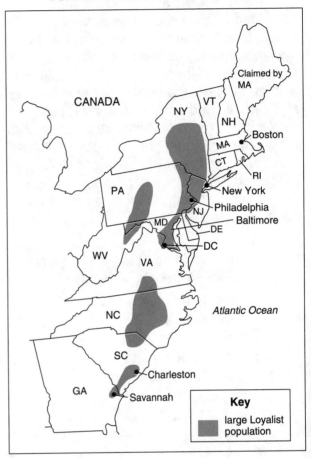

38. The Loyalists did not want the American colonies to break away from England. According to the map, which colonies had the greatest number of people opposed to the American Revolution?

(1) Georgia and New York

(2) North Carolina and New York

(3) South Carolina and North Carolina

(4) Virginia and Maryland

(5) New York and Pennsylvania

Question 39 is based on the following passage.

The U.S. Constitution guarantees American citizens protection against unreasonable search and seizure, trial by jury, the right to due process and protection against self-incrimination. The Constitution also guarantees the right to an attorney and a public trial and protection against an extremely large bail or unusual punishment. But what about the right of innocent citizens to be protected against criminals? Our judges go too easy on dangerous criminals. They often let criminals loose on the streets because of legal technicalities.

39. The author of this passage probably would like suspected criminals to be

   (1) considered innocent until proven guilty
   (2) guaranteed due process of law
   (3) kept off the streets
   (4) given lighter sentences
   (5) let out on bail

Questions 40 and 41 refer to the following passage.

Prevailing winds move nitrogen and sulfur-oxide pollution from factories and automobiles in the Midwest into the eastern parts of the United States and Canada. There these pollutants become so concentrated that they give the rain a high acid content. This acid rain is killing fish and large numbers of trees in the eastern forests. The destruction of forests, if allowed to continue, will ruin watersheds, lower water tables, and cause water shortages for eastern cities.

40. This passage states that potential water shortages in the eastern United States and Canada are

   (1) unlikely
   (2) the result of poor water management
   (3) related to industrial activity elsewhere
   (4) killing trees
   (5) killing fish

41. From this passage, you could conclude that

   (1) society can overcome nature
   (2) nature rules the development of human society
   (3) pollution affects only the region where it is created
   (4) people can affect their environment, but environmental changes also can affect people
   (5) the political effects of pollution are exaggerated

Question 42 is based on the following passage.

The Continental Divide in North America is an imaginary boundary line. In the 48 continental United States, it straddles the Rocky Mountains. The Continental Divide separates the rivers that flow east and the rivers that flow west toward the oceans. Rivers on one side, such as the Colorado, flow west. Rivers on the other side, such as the Missouri and Mississippi, flow east from the Rockies.

42. The Continental Divide in the United States separates

   (1) rivers flowing east and west
   (2) rivers flowing north and south
   (3) the Rocky Mountains and the Appalachians
   (4) Canada and the United States
   (5) North America and South America

Questions 43 and 44 refer to the following passage.

A balance sheet is a financial statement. Businesses use it to summarize their financial position at different points in time. A balance sheet has three parts: **assets** (everything the business has in its possession); **liabilities** (everything the business owes to someone else); and **net worth** (the difference between total assets and total liabilities).
The balance sheet is based on the formula: **assets − liabilities = net worth**

43. A balance sheet describes the financial position of a business

   (1) in terms of its debts
   (2) by counting its assets
   (3) at different points in time
   (4) by figuring out profit or loss
   (5) for a fiscal year

44. Jin Su's Chinese Restaurant has assets totaling $75,000 and liabilities totaling $53,000. Its net worth is

   (1) $69,700
   (2) $53,000
   (3) $30,000
   (4) $22,000
   (5) $19,400

Questions 45 and 46 refer to the following passage.

After the Civil War, the Radical Republicans were the strongest supporters of civil rights for blacks. Their most significant successes included the passage of three constitutional amendments guaranteeing basic civil rights and the establishment of the Freedmen's Bureau, an agency that helped former slaves to make the transition from slavery to citizenship.

45. The Radical Republicans supported

(1) slavery

(2) the Civil War

(3) the abolition of the Democratic Party

(4) civil rights for former slaves

(5) an end to civil rights for blacks

46. The Freedmen's Bureau

(1) helped former slaves learn to read and write

(2) helped former slaveholders to find new servants

(3) moved slaves North to safety

(4) worked for constitutional amendments on civil rights

(5) established citizenship for former slaves

Question 47 refers to the following passage and chart.

Jane Benson lives in a working-class neighborhood in a small city. She wants to open a small business in her area so that she can work near her home and be her own boss. She decided to do a market survey of the area. She made up a questionnaire listing the possible products and services she could provide. Jane went from door to door asking people to answer her questions.

JANES'S RESULTS			
business	number in favor	amount they would spend per week $20/$30/$40	total amount spent
bakery	18	12 5 1	$430
drugstore	17	5 8 4	$500
fabric store	9	5 4 0	$220
restaurant	8	4 3 1	$210

47. According to the chart, which of the four businesses would be the best investment?

(1) bakery

(2) drugstore

(3) fabric store

(4) restaurant

(5) no way to tell

Question 48 refers to the following passage.

The authors of the U.S. Constitution gave Congress the power to make laws about certain matters. In other matters, the states were given that power. However, a clause in the Constitution says that Congress may do anything "necessary and proper" to ensure the welfare of the United States and its citizens. The "implied powers" of Congress have been debated ever since. The strict interpretation of the "necessary and proper" clause is that Congress can only act in matters specifically noted in the Constitution. The broader interpretation allows Congress to further the interests of the nation in any matter.

48. The "implied powers" of Congress are
- **(1)** not defined exactly in the Constitution
- **(2)** necessary and proper to ensure the welfare of the nation
- **(3)** the authority to act on behalf of the states
- **(4)** a broad interpretation of the Constitution
- **(5)** a strict interpretation of the Constitution

Question 49 refers to the following dialogue.

Speaker A

I think people are less loyal to the major political parties today since voters tend to vote for the person rather than the party. This trend worries me. We need stability in our political system more than ever. The two-party system has worked well for us for about 200 years.

Speaker B

You're right about the trend, but I think it's great. The big parties will have to work to earn the independent vote. This way, they have to find out what people really want.

49. The two speakers
- **(1)** expect both major political parties to soon die
- **(2)** disagree on what the trend toward split-ticket voting means
- **(3)** want more than two political parties
- **(4)** disagree on whether voters are loyal to the major parties
- **(5)** are a Democrat and a Republican, respectively

Questions 50 and 51 refer to the following passage.

The term *populism* refers to a movement to organize farmers that grew out of two economic depressions and a worldwide fall in farm prices. Farmers felt that economic policy favored industry and business. They wanted reforms to help them. In particular, they asked for an increase in the amount of money in circulation in the United States, government ownership of railroads, and laws against foreigners owning land. The Populist movement was strongest in the 1890s, then declined.

50. Populism was a movement calling for

   (1) a union
   (2) economic reforms
   (3) laws against foreign immigration
   (4) political change
   (5) laws against industry and business

51. In the late nineteenth century, farmers were hurt by

   (1) the Populists
   (2) a worldwide fall in farm prices
   (3) an increase in the money supply
   (4) government ownership of railroads
   (5) industry and business

Questions 52 and 53 refer to the following passage.

The battle for women's suffrage lasted a hundred years. In 1920, the Nineteenth Amendment finally gave women the right to vote. One argument in favor of giving the vote to women was that women would bring more sensitivity, humanity, and commitment to fair dealings into politics. People opposed to this argument replied that women's spiritual purity and moral force would be undermined by political involvement.

52. Suffrage means

   (1) suffering
   (2) civil rights
   (3) fair political dealings
   (4) the right to vote
   (5) emancipation

53. According to the passage, people who opposed giving women the vote feared that women would be

   (1) less able to provide spiritual guidance
   (2) unable to do their housework
   (3) having fewer children
   (4) poor political candidates
   (5) less feminine

Questions 54 and 55 refer to the following passage.

Following World War I, many nations banded together to form the League of Nations. The league was an organization whose goal was to guarantee world peace. President Woodrow Wilson wanted the United States to take the lead in the League of Nations. However, Congress did not want the foreign policy of the United States to be tied to the articles of the league. As a result, the United States did not join the League of Nations.

54. The purpose of the League of Nations was to

(1) bring an end to World War I
(2) let the United States take the lead in world affairs
(3) bring about world peace
(4) fight communism
(5) take over world affairs from President Wilson

55. The United States did not join the League of Nations because

(1) President Wilson was a poor statesman
(2) World War I was not yet over
(3) Congress did not want the United States to take the lead
(4) the league could not guarantee peace
(5) some feared that U.S. foreign policy would be too closely connected with the league's articles

Question 56 refers to the following passage.

President Franklin D. Roosevelt and British Prime Minister Winston Churchill declared the Atlantic Charter in August 1941. One of the points of this World War II document called for all nations to join together to guarantee world peace. This charter later evolved into the United Nations.

56. From this information, you could infer that

(1) the United States was finally joining the League of Nations
(2) Congress still opposed the league
(3) the league had not guaranteed world peace
(4) Wilson's idea for a League of Nations to guarantee world peace was still alive
(5) the United States had agreed to tie its foreign policy to an international organization

Questions 57 and 58 refer to the following passage.

Many pioneers kept diaries of their incredible journeys to the American West. They wrote about their fears of hard winters, wild animals, and sickness or death. They also wrote about the loneliness of leaving behind loved ones, familiar places, and personal possessions. The pioneers described the natural beauty they came across, the friendships they established with other travelers, and the triumph of overcoming obstacles, using all the creativity they could muster.

57. Using personal diaries in historical research gives us a sense of

- **(1)** the effects of natural disasters on people
- **(2)** the daily experiences and feelings of people in the past
- **(3)** exactly what the pioneers faced
- **(4)** how the standard English language has changed
- **(5)** how the West has changed

58. The author's attitude toward the pioneers is that they

- **(1)** were very courageous
- **(2)** were afraid of bad weather
- **(3)** were foolish to leave so much behind
- **(4)** should have spent more time enjoying the natural beauty
- **(5)** made lasting friendships

Questions 59 and 60 are based on the following passage and map.

The actor John Wilkes Booth was the leader of a plot to assassinate President Abraham Lincoln and other Union leaders. On April 14, 1865, Booth shot Lincoln at Ford's Theater in Washington, D.C. Lincoln died the next day. Booth escaped on horseback into Virginia. There he was hunted down, trapped, and killed in a barn near Bowling Green on April 26.

JOHN WILKES BOOTH'S ESCAPE ROUTE

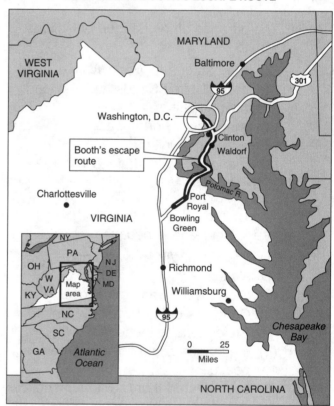

Source: *Chicago Tribune*

59. Through which states did Booth travel on his escape?

(1) West Virginia and Maryland
(2) Maryland and Virginia
(3) Maryland and North Carolina
(4) Virginia and North Carolina
(5) Virginia and West Virginia

60. Using the scale on the map, about how many miles did Booth travel from Washington, D.C., to the town of Bowling Green?

(1) 25
(2) 44
(3) 62
(4) 75
(5) 99

Question 61 is based on the following passage.

Recent scientific studies confirm that Earth's basic resources are vastly greater than what are needed to feed even the 10 billion people who are almost certain to inhabit the planet by the middle of the next century. The real threat is not that Earth will run out of land, topsoil, or water, but that nations will fail to pursue the economic, trade, and research policies that can increase the production of food, limit environmental damage, and ensure that resources reach the people who need them.

61. According to the passage, the real problem in the year 2050 is that Earth will

(1) run out of water
(2) run out of land
(3) no longer have good topsoil
(4) not follow the right economic and research policies
(5) not have the basic resources to feed 10 billion people

Question 62 is based on the following passage.

Personal computers (PCs) are no longer simple production machines. Some computer manufacturers are calling PCs the ultimate home appliance. They say that some day people will use PCs as telephones, answering machines, and stereos. Advertisers say PCs will become as much a part of daily life as the microwave oven.

62. Based on the passage, you could infer that PCs will soon be

(1) as common as radios and TVs
(2) a substitute for books
(3) only a passing fad
(4) used only by editors and writers
(5) replaced by other gadgets

Question 63 is based on the following graph.

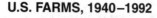
U.S. FARMS, 1940–1992

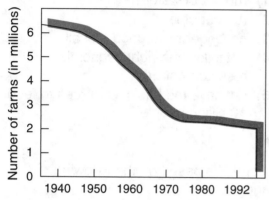

Sources: *World Almanac, 1994; U.S. Dept. of Agriculture*

63. Which of the following trends can you infer from the data shown on the graph?

   (1) More people now live and work on larger farms.
   (2) More people now live and work on smaller farms.
   (3) Fewer people now live and work on farms.
   (4) Fewer people now live and work on smaller farms.
   (5) More Americans are farmers than ever before.

Question 64 is based on the following passage.

No cure has been found for the AIDS epidemic. AIDS (acquired immunodeficiency syndrome) is a virus-caused (HIV) disease that destroys the infection-fighting blood cells. The body thus cannot fight infections or cancers, and the person dies.

In the 1870s, the French scientist Louis Pasteur discovered that the human body builds up antibodies to weak germs that enter it. This explains why Edward Jenner's smallpox vaccine and Jonas Salk's polio vaccine were successful.

64. This passage implies that, to fight AIDS, scientists must

   (1) use antibiotics to kill the germs
   (2) replace the body's blood cells by transfusions
   (3) find a vaccine that will help antibodies kill the virus
   (4) discover a vaccine that kills the antibodies
   (5) move on to other diseases because AIDS is incurable

ANSWERS ARE ON PAGE 291.

Post-Test Answer Key

1. (2) The annual rate of rainfall most closely defines the region of the geographer's study: rainfall (precipitation) patterns.

2. (2) Joe and Ida Williams need to set up a budget to have control over where their money goes. The budget will give them some guidelines. None of the other choices are sure to help them save money.

3. (3) The title and subtitle of the table give you this information.

4. (2) Only choice (2) is supported by the facts in the table. The information does not support any of the other answers.

5. (3) The man in bed says that the Second Amendment has backfired. This probably represents the cartoonist's viewpoint that the right to bear arms no longer is in keeping with the views of the men who wrote the Bill of Rights to the Constitution and who believed citizens had the right to have guns to protect themselves from the tyranny of the British government.

6. (4) The graph clearly shows that nearly 13,000 males in the 25–44 age group had the greatest number of deaths from firearms.

7. (1) From this statement, you can infer only that parents failed to keep handguns out of reach, thus contributing to accidents. While the other answers might apply to some parents, it cannot be said that they apply to all.

8. (5) The passage tells you that older tribal ceremonies served certain social purposes that are now served by sports.

9. (5) The passage tells you that day nurseries were run by wealthy women who feared that the children of working mothers would be left at home alone.

10. (2) The passage tells you that critics of day nurseries felt that mothers should stay home with their children. From this information, you can hypothesize that this concern has led to grants of aid to mothers with dependent children.

11. (3) The definition of direct initiative tells you that it is appropriate for citizens to draft and present laws themselves.

12. (5) A political party's candidate for public office, including governor, must be first selected from a list of candidates in that party in a primary election.

13. (4) Voters can remove an elected public official from office before his or her term expires through the recall process. In this case, a majority of voters in an election must approve of Governor Wilson's removal.

14. (4) Germany was able to gain territory in Europe in the 1930s. England and France were not willing to fight Germany on this issue. You can infer that England and France must have compromised in disputes over territory that Germany wanted.

15. (4) The first sentence says that consumer co-ops are controlled by their members.

16. (3) The passage tells you that co-ops sometimes have lower prices because they are not run for profit.

17. (3) Those in the 16 to 19 age range are still in school. You can infer that whites and Hispanics have more success than African Americans in finding jobs during the summer, when most schools are not in session.

18. (2) One curve is labeled supply, and the other is labeled demand. They are equal at the point of intersection (E), which represents equilibrium. The price at that point is $5,000.

19. (4) The circle graph indicates that more than half of Muslims (56 percent) are immigrants. The table lists California, New York, and Illinois as having a combined total Muslim population of 2.22 million, more than the combined total of the other states.

20. (2) The three states with the largest Muslim population also have the nation's three largest cities: New York, Los Angeles, and Chicago. None of the other answers can be verified from the data.

21. (4) Chicago's full-time female workers earned about $11,000 less than male full-time workers in 1990.

22. (3) The counties with the greatest number of people age 65 and over are likely to be where the most retired people live. These are Llano County, TX, and Charlotte County, FL.

23. (1) Both counties in choice (1) have more than 45 percent of the population under age 18, years when young people are in school.

24. (1) The passage says "The invention of the automobile and truck furthered the growth of suburbs."

25. (4) Because the passage describes the effects of new means of transportation on the growth of cities and their surrounding areas, choice (4) is the best answer.

26. (3) The passage says that losses from street crime are only one-fifth of those from embezzlement, fraud, and other white-collar crimes, so you can infer that choice (3) is the best answer.

27. (4) White-collar crime is committed by people with economic and political power—professionals, business people, and companies.

28. (1) The birth rate rose significantly from 1945 to 1955.

29. (5) The graph shows a stable death rate and a falling birthrate. Therefore, there is an overall decline in population.

30. (5) Lake Superior, at 1,330 feet, is the deepest of the Great Lakes.

31. (2) The sea level line on the cross-section passes through all the Great Lakes except Lake Erie.

32. (1) Both Washington and Eisenhower warn against allowing the military establishment to have too much influence on government. Washington says the military establishment is "hostile to republican liberty." Eisenhower says that the military-industrial complex must not be allowed to acquire too much power.

33. (2) Although the poll on senatorial term limits dropped from 54 percent in 1947 to 49 percent in 1964, the overall trend was up.

34. (1) The large number of Americans in favor of some kind of term limits for U.S. senators and representatives is likely to bring about a constitutional amendment.

35. (3) The public is willing to accept people who are not experienced politicians to represent them in Washington. But the public would not hire doctors, lawyers, or mechanics with no experience.

36. (5) Latin American influence in the Southwest took place long before the twentieth century. A history of interaction with Mexico goes back over a hundred years.

37. (3) The main idea of the cartoon is expressed in the last statement: small farmers have become as out of date as mules. The bill on the farmer's cap is labeled "small farmer."

38. (2) The map shows the heaviest concentrations of Loyalists in North Carolina and New York. Since the Loyalists wanted the colonies to remain loyal to the King of England, they opposed the American Revolution.

39. (3) The author complains that criminals are too often let back on the streets because of legal technicalities.

40. (3) The passage tells you that pollution from factories in the Midwest contributes to the acid rain problem. The killing of forests by acid rain could lead to water shortages in eastern cities.

41. (4) The passage describes a relationship in which an action of people (pollution) affects nature, creating a result that in turn, affects other people (creates water shortages).

42. (1) The passage states that the Continental Divide in the United States separates rivers flowing east and west.

43. (3) The first sentence says "A balance sheet is a financial statement. Businesses use it to summarize their financial position at different points in time."

44. (4) The passage gives you the formula: assets – liabilities = net worth. Using the formula, $75,000 – $53,000 = $22,000.

45. (4) The passage tells you that the Radical Republicans were the strongest supporters of civil rights for blacks.

46. (1) You are told that the Freedmen's Bureau was an agency that helped blacks to make the transition from slavery to citizenship. You can guess that helping them learn to read and write would serve this purpose.

47. (2) Although the bakery has the highest score in the "number in favor" column, people said they would spend more money per week at the drugstore.

48. (1) The passage tells you that the "implied powers" have been debated ever since the Constitution was written, so you can guess that they are not defined exactly.

49. (2) Speakers A and B agree that people are less loyal to the major political parties than they used to be, but they interpret the trend differently. Speaker A is worried that the result will be a lack of political stability, and Speaker B is pleased at the possibility that the major parties will become more responsive.

50. (2) The reforms the Populists wanted were economic: an increase in the amount of money in circulation, government ownership of railroads, and laws against foreigners owning land.

51. (2) The first sentence states that there was a worldwide fall in farm prices.

52. (4) This paragraph is about voting rights for women, so you can infer that suffrage means "the right to vote."

53. (1) The last sentence tells you that some people opposed women's suffrage because they thought political activity would interfere with women's spiritual purity. The other answers are not supported by the information in the passage.

54. (3) The second sentence says that the goal of the organization was to guarantee world peace.

55. (5) The passage states that "Congress did not want the foreign policy of the United States to be tied to the articles of the league."

56. (4) The Atlantic Charter's call for collective security later became the basis for the United Nations, founded at the end of World War II. The UN was modeled after the League of Nations, an indication that Wilson's idea was not dead.

57. (2) The passage describes how pioneers' use of personal diaries provide a sense of their feelings and experiences.

58. (1) Words like "incredible," "triumph," and "creativity" let you know of the author's respect for the bravery the pioneers needed for those journeys.

59. (2) The map shows clearly that Booth left Washington, D.C., passed through Maryland, and crossed the Potomac River into Virginia.

60. (4) The mileage scale shows that Booth traveled about 75 miles from Washington, D.C., to Bowling Green, Virginia.

61. (4) The passage clearly states that the real problem could be the failure of nations to pursue the necessary economic, trade, and research policies to ensure that resources reach the people who need them.

62. (1) A process of elimination leaves only choice (1), that PCs will be as common as radios and TVs. None of the other choices follow the line of thought in the passage.

63. (3) The graph shows that with the number of farms declining from 1940 to 1992, there are fewer farm families.

64. (3) The implication of the second paragraph of the passage is that a vaccine such as that discovered by Salk for polio and Jenner for smallpox must also be discovered to kill the HIV virus that causes AIDS.

Post-Test Evaluation Chart

On the following chart, circle the number of any item you got wrong. Next to each item, you will see the pages you can review for items that gave you trouble. Pay special attention to skills on which you missed half or more of the questions.

Skill Area/ Content Area	Comprehension	Application	Analysis	Evaluation
U.S. History (pages 83–147)	**28, 37**, 45, 50, 51, 54, 55, **59**	46, 58	14, 56	36, **38**, 57
Political Science (pages 149–183)	12, **33**, 52	13, 32, 49	11, **34**	**5, 35**, 39, 48, 53
Behavioral Sciences (pages 185–207)	**3, 6**, 8, 9, **19, 22**, 26	**4, 20**, 27	**7**, 64	10, **23**, 62
Geography (pages 209–233)	24, **30, 31**, 40, 42, 61	**29**	1, **60**	25, 41
Economics (pages 235–265)	15, 43	**18, 21, 47, 63**	2, 44	16, 17

Answer Key

CHAPTER 1: COMPREHENDING SOCIAL STUDIES MATERIALS

EXERCISE 1
Page 20

Analysis
1. **(1)** The passage speaks of the alarming rate of increase in teenage suicide—now third highest cause of death among youths 15 to 19 years old—while attention has been focused on drug abuse and pregnancy. These clues indicate that this is a new trend.

Evaluation
2. **(4)** The topic in answer (4) is the most logical follow-up story.

EXERCISE 2
Page 24

Analysis
1. about 550,000
2. 1955
3. 1960, 1965, 1970
4. 1990

EXERCISE 3
Page 26

Comprehension
1. T
2. F They settled in Florida and the Southwest.
3. T
4. T
5. F They came from Italy, Greece, and Russia.
6. T
7. T
8. F They came after the United States became an independent nation.
9. T
10. T

EXERCISE 4
Page 27

Comprehension
1. 1861
2. victories
3. Missouri Compromise
4. Kansas-Nebraska
5. *Dred Scott*
6. territories

PRE-GED PRACTICE
EXERCISE 5
Page 29

Comprehension
1. **(1)** The overall figures show more immigrants coming from Europe, about 63 percent.
2. **(3)** Nearly half (47%) came from Latin America and the Caribbean.
3. **(3)** The percentage of persons coming to the United States from Latin America and the Caribbean during 1981–1990 was 47 percent, a 29 percent increase over the broad period, 1820–1992.
4. **(1)** The graph on the left gives you this information.

PRE-GED PRACTICE
EXERCISE 6
Page 31

Comprehension
1. **(5)** The number of persons described as strong Democrats fell from 20 percent to 15 percent in the 1970s, but went back up to 20 percent by 1990.
2. **(3)** The number of persons defined as strong Republicans dropped to 10 percent in 1990.

Analysis
3. **(1)** The figures in the passage indicate that although the number of people who call themselves strong Democrats and strong Republicans tends to rise and fall, it does not break up the two parties. The number of people who call themselves independents rises and falls too.

EXERCISE 7
Page 33

Evaluation
1. **(3)** The word *nondenominational* in the passage refers to prayer. This kind of prayer does not refer to God in a specific way nor does it mention figures pertaining to any of the major religions. You could infer that nondenominational means not belonging to any particular religion's group.
2. **(3)** *Nomadic* peoples are defined as those who migrated back and forth from one area to another.

297

PRE-GED PRACTICE
EXERCISE 8
Page 34

Comprehension

1. (4) All the other choices either are inaccurate according to the graph or cannot be supported by the information in the graph.

2. (4) Only this answer choice covers the main idea of the graph. Choices (1), (2), and (5) make assumptions or include information not given on the graph. Choice (3), while a true statement, identifies only one piece of information, not the main idea.

Analysis

3. (2) All of the other choices cannot be supported by the graph.

4. (4) According to the graph, these two categories combined add up to 18 percent.

Comprehension

5. (3) The words "stretches over" in the passage give you the sense of a connected or continuous area. Since the megalopolis includes many cities, it would have to include suburban areas lying between the cities.

6. (3) The urban areas mentioned are New York, Philadelphia, Newark, and Baltimore. These are described as cities.

CHAPTER 2: APPLYING SOCIAL STUDIES IDEAS

EXERCISE 1
Page 38

Comprehension

1. (4) The passage states that "The most important method [of improving productivity] has been the introduction of modern technology." You can apply this idea to the information that if Japan led the United States in the area of modern technology, the Japanese economy would grow faster because of its higher level of productivity.

2. (3) In the second paragraph, the passage tells you that "the introduction of modern technology, such as computers, is leading to increased manufacturing productivity."

Analysis

3. (2) Measuring workers' output shows the amount of work per hour of labor. It does not necessarily increase productivity.

EXERCISE 2
Page 42

Analysis

1. F The key shows that more iron ore and uranium than gold are produced.

2. F Gold mines are located in the northern and southern part of the country, where there are no coal mines.

3. F None of Australia's natural resources are found in the interior of the country.

4. F The map only shows the location of natural gas in Australia.

5. F Zinc mines are also located in the northern part of Australia.

6. F The symbols on the map and key show that more uranium than bauxite is produced.

7. F Very little cobalt is produced in Australia (only one symbol is shown).

8. T

9. F All of Australia's forests are located in its outer regions.

10. T

11. F This map doesn't show Australia's imports—only its natural resources.

12. F This map doesn't compare Australia's resources with those of other countries.

EXERCISE 3
Page 46

Comprehension/Evaluation

1. China
2. United States, United Kingdom
3. Israel
4. India and Nigeria
5. Colombia, Mexico
6. 10 percent
7. United Kingdom
8. El Salvador
9. 1991

Evaluation

10. The percentage of people moving from rural areas to urban areas increased for most countries during this time period.

PRE-GED PRACTICE
EXERCISE 4
Page 48

Comprehension

1. (2) The bar graph shows lower figures for the Korean War (157,000) and Persian Gulf War (760).

2. (1) The Civil War was the most costly in the ratio of casualties to number serving—nearly one out of every three.

3. (5) Fewer than 500,000 soldiers served in the Persian Gulf War.

4. **(3)** The bar graph on the right shows that there were about 1 million, 5 thousand casualties during the Civil War and about 1 million, 110 thousand casualties during World War II.

5. **(5)** The bar graph on the left shows that about 8.7 million persons served during the Vietnam War.

6. **(3)** There were about 320 thousand casualties during World War I.

Analysis

7. **(2)** This is the only choice supported by the data on the graph. The bars for casualties are highest for the Civil War and World War II.

Comprehension

8. **(3)** The Pawnee were in the region cutting through the center of the map. The key shows that the Plains Indians lived in this region.

9. **(1)** The farthest northern parts of the map match the Eskimo and Aleut section of the key.

10. **(5)** If you check the Southwest Indians portion of the map, you will find the Hopi Indians there.

11. **(1)** The map key shows that the Cherokee were part of the Eastern Forest Indians.

12. **(4)** This answer is the only one supported by the information in the graph.

13. **(3)** The bars for Sweden, the United States, and Japan are the longest.

CHAPTER 3: ANALYZING SOCIAL STUDIES MATERIALS

EXERCISE 1
Page 54

Comprehension

Middle Ages: rich people—inner city; working classes and the poor—outer edge
Early 20th century: wealthy people—suburbs; poor people—inner cities
Recent 20th century: rich people—central part of cities; poor people—outer edges

EXERCISE 2
Page 56

Analysis

1. **(3)** The table shows that consumption of poultry products rose from 33.8 pounds in 1970 to 55.9 pounds in 1990, a rise of more than 50 percent.

2. **(2)** The table shows that Americans are eating less meat and more fruits and vegetables.

3. **(4)** The table shows that from 1980 to 1990, Americans ate more fresh fruit and more fish.

4. **(3)** Americans decreased their consumption of red meat.

PRE-GED PRACTICE
EXERCISE 3
Page 58

Comprehension

1. **(2)** The passage explains that infant mortality has dropped considerably because public health measures have reduced diseases.

Analysis

2. **(2)** More young women will survive to child-bearing age, thus further increasing population growth.

PRE-GED PRACTICE
EXERCISE 4
Page 59

Comprehension

1. **(4)** The first event in the sequence, the discovery of Soviet missile bases in Cuba, was followed by President Kennedy's naval blockade of Cuba.

2. **(1)** The United States ended the naval blockade of Cuba after the Soviet Union had not only withdrawn the missiles but had also dismantled the bases.

EXERCISE 5
Page 62

Comprehension

1. **(4)** U.S. per capita income was at its highest in 1989.

2. **(2)** The lines in graph 2 match the figures in the table.

3. **(2)** It increased by about $2,000.

4. **(1)** Only the fact that per capita income dropped in 1990 after steady upward growth in the 1980s can be inferred from the graph.

EXERCISE 6
Page 64

Comprehension

1. 1987–1989
2. 1993–1995
3. Yes, during 1993–1995
4. 1981–1985
5. increased steadily

PRE-GED PRACTICE
EXERCISE 7
Page 66

Comprehension
1. **(2)** The Catholic Church was tied closely to the Spanish government, and the Catholic religion was taught in schools. From this information, you can infer that the traditional religion of the country is Catholicism.

Analysis
2. **(2)** Because a new constitution after Franco's death did away with the special position of the Catholic Church, you can infer that the church had a special place while Franco was in power.
3. **(5)** This is the only sport mentioned that does not center on the abundance of lakes in the area.
4. **(4)** All of the other industries are mentioned in the passage except for foresting timber.

PRE-GED PRACTICE
EXERCISE 8
Page 68

Application
1. **(3)** An implication of the passage is that when you buy something that you plan to pay off a month at a time, you should be sure you will be able to pay the amount of the monthly installment.

Evaluation
2. **(3)** You conclude from the last sentence that charging an item may increase final cost because you will also be paying interest.

Analysis
3. **(2)** The passage states that the children did what they saw others do, so children who are honest are imitating people around them who are honest.
4. **(5)** All the other statements are true.
5. **(4)** This is the only statement that is clearly supported by the graph.

CHAPTER 4: EVALUATING SOCIAL STUDIES MATERIALS

EXERCISE 1
Page 72

Evaluation
1. F
2. O
3. O
4. F
5. F
6. O
7. F

EXERCISE 2
Page 74

Comprehension
1. **(2)** The passage offers two theories for the rise in crime: (1) too many rewards for the criminal and too few reasons to do honest work and (2) crime results from social and economic conditions.
2. **(2)** This answer is supported by information given in the first sentence of the second paragraph.

EXERCISE 3
Page 76

Evaluation
1. **(2)** You need to examine the writer's descriptions of the two senators. The senator from North Carolina is confident, amiable, and strides briskly (a positive description). The senator from New York darts into sight, scurries, and huddles nervously (a negative description).
2. **(3)** *Amiably* means friendly and relaxed. The other words carry negative meanings.

PRE-GED PRACTICE
EXERCISE 4
Page 78

Evaluation

1. **(5)** Sentences 1, 5, and 6 show the writer's bias.
2. **(5)** The passage states that only the Democratic and the Republican parties have ever controlled Congress and every president during the past century has belonged to one of the two parties. This shows the considerable strength and support the two parties have had and continue to have in the United States.
3. **(2)** The author's opinions in several sentences clearly indicate the author's bias toward the two-party system.
4. **(3)** The sign in the cartoon and the desolate location of the smoker show the main idea of the cartoon, that there are now far fewer areas in which people are allowed to smoke.
5. **(5)** Judging from the picture of "Uncle Sam" sitting at the loan officer's desk and the worried look on the other customers' faces, you can assume that the cartoonist believes that the Social Security system is going broke.
6. **(3)** The best of the choices is that the cartoonist has little faith in the Social Security system.

CHAPTER 5: U.S. HISTORY

EXERCISE 1
Page 84

Comprehension

1. Columbus
2. gold and silver
3. to pay for their passage from Europe
4. Indentured servants bind themselves by a contract to work for a master for a certain number of years; slaves were brought to the Americas by force, and most of them were enslaved for the rest of their lives.
5. France
6. England
7. to establish religious communities
8. between 50 and 75 percent
9. Spain

EXERCISE 2
Page 86

Comprehension

1. **(1)** The English followed the policy of mercantilism, which means that the colonies exist for the good of the mother country and should buy English manufactured goods.
2. **(3)** The passage refers to representative bodies as centers of opposition to English policies.
3. **(3)** France lost most of its North American territories to England.
4. **(2)** Seventeenth century colonists also bought manufactured goods.

EXERCISE 3
Page 89

Comprehension

1. (b)
2. (d)
3. (e)
4. (a)
5. (c)

EXERCISE 4
Page 89

Comprehension

1. **(3)** The passage states clearly that the colonists dumped the tea into Boston Harbor to protest against unfair laws such as the Sugar Act, the Stamp Act, and the Tea Act.

Analysis

2. **(2)** The only correct answer is that Spain's colonies in Latin America also rebelled.

EXERCISE 5
Page 91

Comprehension

1. English colonies, Africa, West Indies
2. Molasses was used to make rum, which in turn was traded in Africa for slaves.
3. They provided cheap labor.
4. They made voyages on which they profited by 100 percent to 1,000 percent.
5. The profits from slavery financed England's industrial growth.
6. Slavery ended after the Civil War.

EXERCISE 6
Page 92

Comprehension
1. **(3)** British control of forts on the Great Lakes and French control of the Mississippi posed the most serious problems.
2. **(2)** The last paragraph says that Americans united around national instead of regional interests after the War of 1812.

Application
3. **(1)** Governments facing a divided nation have used war against foreign enemies to temporarily unite the country.

EXERCISE 7
Page 96

Analysis
1. **(3)** The North was most opposed to the annexation of Texas.

Evaluation
2. **(1)** The Northern states were opposed to having another slave-owning Southern state in the Union.

PRE-GED PRACTICE
EXERCISE 8
Page 99

Comprehension
1. **(1)** was limited to white males

Analysis
2. **(1)** a very important part of U.S. history

EXERCISE 9
Page 99

Comprehension
1. (c)
2. (b)
3. (e)
4. (a)
5. (d)

EXERCISE 10
Page 100

Analysis
1. **(1)** The letter mentions "teams starting for several days," and that he got some information from "some distance on the prairies." You can infer that this route was well-known.

2. **(2)** The writer mentions in lines 20–21, "little or no old grass to be had as it has been eat and burned off." From this you can infer their need to bring along feed for the animals.
3. **(1)** They appear to be charging a lot for necessities. The writer mentions that some things are cheaper but "They put the screws very tight to emigrants for all small jobs and articles the emigrants are obliged to get."
4. **(4)** The first sentence of the second paragraph mentions these items that can be had "to some better advantage."

EXERCISE 11
Page 103

Comprehension
1. **T**
2. **T**
3. **F** It limited slavery to the land stretching west from the southern border of Missouri only.
4. **T**
5. **T**
6. **T**
7. **F** Brown failed in his attempt to arm the slaves for rebellion.
8. **F** Douglass was an eloquent speaker who toured the North, raising support for abolitionism.

PRE-GED PRACTICE
EXERCISE 12
Page 104

Comprehension
1. **(3)** They believed that if they did not secede, slavery would certainly be abolished when more free states were admitted to the Union.
2. **(1)** The passage states that the Emancipation Proclamation helped to undermine the South.

EXERCISE 13
Page 106

Comprehension
1. (e)
2. (d)
3. (b)
4. (a)
5. (c)

PRE-GED PRACTICE
EXERCISE 14
Page 106

Evaluation
1. **(3)** The table shows the largest percent of difference under iron and steel.
2. **(4)** The table shows that the North was clearly ahead in all areas of economic development.

EXERCISE 15
Page 107

Comprehension
1. **(4)** Despite the humorous, satiric tone, the author's main point is that he knows he was exploited in the past and has no intention of letting it happen again.

Analysis
2. **(2)** At the end of the letter Anderson says, "there was never any pay-day for the Negroes anymore than for horses or cows."

EXERCISE 16
Page 109

Comprehension
1. T

Analysis
2. T

Evaluation
3. T

PRE-GED PRACTICE
EXERCISE 17
Page 111

Comprehension
1. **(3)** The McCormick Reaper "revolutionized agriculture by mechanizing the farm."

Evaluation
2. **(5)** The last sentence of the fourth paragraph says that new immigrants often faced poverty and discrimination (an unexpected hardship).

Analysis
3. **(2)** The opposite was true. Monopolies raised prices and kept wages low.

Comprehension
4. **(4)** This is the main idea of the essay: how industrialization affected the economy, population distribution, social classes, and politics.

5. **(2)** The growth and centralization of industry hastened the growth of cities.

Evaluation
6. **(2)** This is an inference about how historical change takes place. Change in a major part of society, such as the economy, affects all other areas of society.

EXERCISE 18
Page 112

Comprehension
1. part of their crop
2. Jim Crow laws
3. poll taxes, literacy tests
4. South

EXERCISE 19
Page 114

Analysis
1. **(4)** The passage points out that the workers and farmers were organizing against the power of monopolies and that these groups supported the Populist Party.

Application
2. **(3)** The American experience showed that widespread change and social turmoil goes along with industrialization.

Comprehension
3. **(3)** The passage describes the use of police, militia, and federal troops.

Evaluation
4. **(4)** In rural areas, people protested the high cost of credit.

EXERCISE 20
Page 115

Comprehension
1. 1901–1910
2. 1821–1830

Evaluation
3. **(2)** The passage discusses urbanization in the late nineteenth and early twentieth centuries. The graph shows a high rate of immigration at the same time.

ANSWER KEY

EXERCISE 21
Page 116

Comprehension
1. (c)
2. (d)
3. (a)
4. (b)
5. (e)

EXERCISE 22
Page 118

Comprehension
1. **F** Industrialization worsened social conditions.
2. **T**
3. **F** There existed a very small class of wealthy industrialists and a large new class of poorly paid workers.
4. **T**
5. **T**
6. **F** In 1900, the United States replaced Great Britain as the leading industrial producer in the world.
7. **F** Henry Ford developed the first modern factory production line.
8. **T**
9. **T**
10. **F** Political institutions that had been suitable for farmers and small businesses could no longer deal with the problems of a large-scale industrial society.

PRE-GED PRACTICE
EXERCISE 23
Page 120

Comprehension
1. **(4)** The passage states that Theodore Roosevelt believed the Republicans had given up on reform, so he formed a third party, the Progressive (Bull Moose) Party.

Application
2. **(5)** The passage says that progressivism led to a course between private business doing as it pleased and placing large parts of the economy under government control.

Comprehension
3. **(3)** The essay points out that limited local resources at the local level caused the reformers to turn to the federal government for help.
4. **(2)** The third sentence of the third paragraph gives you this information.

EXERCISE 24
Page 121

Comprehension
1. **(2)** The speaker says, "we have no faith in man's protection. . . . Give us the ballot, and we will protect ourselves."

Evaluation
2. **(3)** Women often worked on production tasks at home. It was cheaper for many employers because working conditions and hours were not regulated.

EXERCISE 25
Page 123

Comprehension
1. Spain
2. Hawaii
3. gunboat diplomacy
4. imperialism
5. foreign trade, colonial empire
6. European colonization, interference
7. Africa, Asia
8. Spain
9. Mark Twain

EXERCISE 26
Page 124

Comprehension
1. arrows on the map and the map key
2. 1983
3. Puerto Rico, Virgin Islands, Guantánamo Bay

Analysis
4. **(2)** The number of military interventions, establishment of a military base at Guantánamo Bay in Cuba, and the building of the Panama Canal indicate great U.S. interest in the Caribbean region, as an outgrowth of the Monroe Doctrine.

PRE-GED PRACTICE
EXERCISE 27
Page 126

Comprehension
1. **(1)** The passage discusses swings between involvement and isolationism in world affairs.

Comprehension

2. (2) The United States tried to stay out of World War I, but loss of U.S. lives from increased German submarine attacks forced it to join the Allies.

EXERCISE 28
Page 127

Comprehension

1. T The passage refers to mass production and the eagerness of Americans to buy new products.

Analysis

2. T Even though President Coolidge made this remark, the passage makes it clear that consumerism, migration, etc., all fed a booming economy—a good climate for business.

Comprehension

3. F The passage states that women found jobs in the expanding economy.

Analysis

4. F African Americans left the South in large numbers and their culture influenced the country as a whole.

Comprehension

5. T The passage states that Congress passed strict immigration quotas.
6. T Many writers did become expatriates in Europe.
7. T Swing is described as a form of jazz which became popular with whites. Jazz was brought to the North by Southern blacks.

EXERCISE 29
Page 129

Analysis

1. (3) The passage states that the United States had no unemployment insurance and no Social Security, and that private relief agencies had difficulty caring for so many people. You can infer that private charitable organizations bore the brunt of public welfare when the Depression began.
2. (1) The first graph shows that unemployment rose, while the second graph shows that the gross national product declined.

Comprehension

3. (3) The passage states that the New Deal established the idea that government had a role to play in keeping people economically secure.

EXERCISE 30
Page 131

Comprehension

1. (d)   **7.** (e)
2. (a)   **8.** (k)
3. (f)   **9.** (h)
4. (b)   **10.** (i)
5. (g)   **11.** (l)
6. (c)   **12.** (j)

EXERCISE 31
Page 132

Analysis

1. (3) The description of workers' roles in the plant and families outside the plant is correct. The other choices are not shown by information in the passage.

Evaluation

2. (1) The strikers had support outside the plant.

EXERCISE 32
Page 134

Comprehension

1. F The passage states that the two countries became hostile when the war ended.
2. F They were called satellites.
3. T The passage states that the containment policy was drawn up to limit communism to areas where it was already established.
4. F NATO was the military alliance; the Marshall Plan was economic aid to help Europe rebuild after World War II.

Analysis

5. T The passage does not say directly that the Korean War was fought to contain communism, but the entire discussion is about a Cold War to contain it.

ANSWER KEY

EXERCISE 33
Page 135

Analysis
1. **(2)** The United States found containing communism of greater concern than supporting countries trying to be free of colonial powers. When the Soviet Union supported nationalism, the United States was against it.

Comprehension
2. **(3)** The passage states the many elements complicating Third World conflict in addition to nationalism. None of the other choices is correct.
3. **(4)** The last paragraph states that Fidel Castro set up a communist government in Cuba in 1959.

EXERCISE 34
Page 136

Comprehension
1. South Vietnam
2. South Vietnam
3. domino theory

Evaluation
4. at home

EXERCISE 35
Page 138

Part A
Comprehension
1. (b)
2. (e)
3. (d)
4. (c)
5. (f)
6. (a)

Part B
Comprehension
1. Nixon
2. Solidarity
3. prices, output
4. Mikhail Gorbachev

EXERCISE 36
Page 139

Evaluation
(4) The sign on the pile of bricks on the left in the cartoon says "Never Again." On the right, a new wall to keep out immigrants is being built. The cartoonist is implying that Germany has not learned its lesson from the past in facing current immigration problems.

PRE-GED PRACTICE
EXERCISE 37
Page 141

Evaluation
1. **(2)** The last sentence in the first paragraph says that his colleagues condemned his actions.
2. **(1)** The "cost in American involvement" refers both to people's lives that were lost and to the high monetary cost of the war.

EXERCISE 38
Page 143

Comprehension
1. segregation, public
2. nonviolent

Evaluation
3. successful
4. widespread

EXERCISE 39
Page 144

Analysis
1. **(2)** The figure in the chair (representing the taxpayer) cannot read the bottom line after "will cost" and so does not know the cost of Clinton's health care plan.

Evaluation
2. **(3)** The cartoonist may or may not favor Clinton's health care plan, but he is definitely concerned about its cost and implies that Clinton doesn't know how much it will cost either.

EXERCISE 40
Page 146

Comprehension
1. **(4)** The increase from 1980 to 1990 of $2,358.4 billion is larger than in any other ten-year period.

Evaluation
2. **(2)** World War II (1941-1945) accounted for the increase in the national debt from $42.9 billion in 1940 to $256.1 billion in 1950.

PRE-GED PRACTICE
U.S. HISTORY
Page 147

Comprehension
1. **(3)** Stoddart wanted the river cleaned up so that people could swim safely in it again.

Analysis
2. **(1)** Stoddart sparked the cleanup campaign, but she could not do it singlehandedly. Her solution was to build coalitions of business, labor, and the companies that caused the pollution.

Evaluation
3. **(4)** Environmental changes can be achieved in many ways, but you might infer that the more people work together and not against each another, the better chance they'll have of making changes.

CHAPTER 6: POLITICAL SCIENCE

EXERCISE 1
Page 153

Comprehension
1. (c)
2. (b)
3. (d)
4. (a)
5. (f)
6. (e)

PRE-GED PRACTICE
EXERCISE 2
Page 155

Analysis
1. **(1)** A plurality is the greatest number of votes cast when there are more than two candidates, no one of which gets a simple majority.

Application
2. **(3)** A thirty out of fifty vote constitutes a three-fifths majority.
3. **(3)** The first section discussed direct democracy in which a simple majority is normally required to reach consensus.
4. **(5)** In a representative democracy, people select delegates to represent them.

EXERCISE 3
Page 158

Evaluation
1. I
2. P
3. P
4. T
5. T
6. I
7. I
8. I

EXERCISE 4
Page 159

Evaluation
1. **(3)** The writer believes that poor people do not vote in proportion to their numbers in the population. Consequently, they have much less political influence than groups that do tend to vote in proportion to their numbers.

Analysis
2. **(1)** If lower-income people voted in significant numbers, elected officials would have to pay more attention to their interests and there might be an expansion of programs serving the poor.

ANSWER KEY

EXERCISE 5
Page 162

Comprehension
1. (c)
2. (d)
3. (e)
4. (b)
5. (a)

EXERCISE 6
Page 164

Comprehension
1. Congress
2. Bill of Rights
3. flexibility
4. three-fourths
5. seventeen
6. Eighteenth, Twenty-first
7. two-thirds majority
8. slavery

PRE-GED PRACTICE
EXERCISE 7
Page 165

Comprehension
1. **(1)** The Supreme Court has used its power to define certain rights of people who have controversial ideas. There is not a unified viewpoint about what they mean.
2. **(5)** The cases concerning obscenity and pornography are discussed in terms of the right to free speech and a free press.

EXERCISE 8
Page 168

Comprehension
1. **(3)** Executive orders issued by the president have the effect of law.
2. **(2)** The vice president succeeds the president in the event of the president's death or a severe incapacity that prevents the president from functioning in office.

Application
3. **(2)** Hamilton described the process of a presidential veto and the procedure for override.
4. **(2)** Two four-year terms constitute eight years in office.

EXERCISE 9
Page 170

Comprehension
1. T
2. T
3. F Congress does have the power to investigate the executive branch.
4. T
5. F The Speaker of the House carries out this role.

EXERCISE 10
Page 172

Comprehension
1. presidential appointment
2. is
3. nine
4. circuit courts of appeals
5. the Supreme Court
6. misconduct
7. constitutionality
8. Senate

EXERCISE 11
Page 173

Comprehension
1. **(1)** The passage points out that some Supreme Court decisions were heavily influenced by political and historical developments.
2. **(2)** The passage places the court's *Plessy* v. *Ferguson* decision in the context of white supremacist prejudice in 1896.

EXERCISE 12
Page 176

Comprehension
1. federal
2. one-house
3. within the state
4. direct initiative

PRE-GED PRACTICE
EXERCISE 13
Page 177

Comprehension
1. **(1)** Local governments are legal creations of the state.

Application
2. **(3)** The passage explains that legislation can be repealed by a referendum.
3. **(5)** The passage says that some states give their voters the right to recall unpopular elected officials.

4. (2) A city council that can overrule the mayor on key decisions describes a strong council–weak mayor form of city government.

Comprehension
5. (4) Public utilities fall within the realm of city and county governments.

Evaluation
6. (3) This is a function of state governments.

EXERCISE 14
Page 179

Comprehension
1. (d)
2. (f)
3. (e)
4. (b)
5. (c)
6. (a)

EXERCISE 15
Page 182

Comprehension
1. diplomatic, economic, and military
2. to maintain international peace and encourage friendly relations among nations
3. investigates world disagreements
4. Answers will vary. Possible answers include: to increase trade; to get help in economic development; to get a larger market for exported goods.

Analysis
5. NATO

Comprehension
6. 184
7. United Kingdom

PRE-GED PRACTICE POLITICAL SCIENCE
Page 183

Analysis
1. **(2)** Special districts have integrated specific functions on a local level.

Evaluation
2. **(3)** The author believes that this controversy has been with us for a long time and will continue.

Comprehension
3. **(4)** The passage mentions this in the first sentence of the third paragraph.

CHAPTER 7: BEHAVIORAL SCIENCES

EXERCISE 1
Page 186

Comprehension
1. anthropologist. An anthropologist would study the culture of a remote village in South America.
2. psychologist. The company would hire a psychologist to study why people behave in certain ways toward each other.
3. psychologist. A psychologist would be most able to help individual prisoners understand why they behave in certain ways.
4. sociologist. The city is trying to help a particular group of people. Sociologists specialize in studying groups.
5. anthropologist. An anthropologist would be able to look at all parts of the society and see why the people have problems setting up a good government and how they might change their society.

EXERCISE 2
Page 188

Evaluation
1. **T** The expectations that people have for us are a major factor in deciding our personalities.
2. **T** Genetic characteristics are those a person is born with. You could conclude that a child with such unusual skills at playing the violin at such an early age was born with the genetic characteristics.
3. **F** Temperament has to do with emotions. Character describes the values we have, such as honesty.
4. **T** Bad childhood experiences often affect our personalities throughout our lives.
5. **F** Character has to do with values. A sense of humor is an aspect of temperament.

EXERCISE 3
Page 190
Comprehension
1. **(2)** Each theory takes a different view of why people work and what motivates them to be productive.

Application
2. **(3)** Theory Y suggests that people are by nature creative and responsible. An efficient workplace would encourage workers to fulfill their nature by creatively trying to be more efficient.
3. **(3)** Theory Y suggests that people use creativity and curiosity to do their work.
4. **(1)** Theory X suggests that people need to be threatened, forced, or bribed to work.

EXERCISE 4
Page 191
Evaluation
1. **(2)** The graph shows that adults who had watched less violence on TV as children were less likely to be aggressive as adults.
2. **(3)** The cartoonist shows a father using physical punishment to discourage the child from using physical force. The message is confusing to the child. The cartoonist shows that he thinks parents teach their children violent behavior.
3. **(1)** Both the graph and the cartoon show how seeing and experiencing violence affects the psychological development of children. Together, they show that aggression and violence are learned behaviors.

EXERCISE 5
Page 193
Comprehension
1. stress
2. damage
3. emotional problems
4. normal
5. functional
6. self-image
7. fear
8. physical damage

EXERCISE 6
Page 195
Comprehension
1. **(3)** A primary group includes a person's closest personal relationships. Of the choices offered, only a daughter fits this definition.

Application
2. **(2)** Socialization is the process by which a person learns the behaviors and beliefs expected by society. People usually learn these from their parents.

Evaluation
3. **(3)** An institution fills the needs of society and teaches accepted behavior. A street gang does not teach accepted behavior.

EXERCISE 7
Page 196
Comprehension
1. **S** Most workers will have a formal, businesslike relationship.
2. **S** Primary groups exist within the Senate, but the relationship among most members is not close and personal.
3. **P** This is a small, intimate group in which members have close, personal relationships.
4. **P** The family is a basic primary group.
5. **S** Most members of this group will not have close personal friendships with other union members.
6. **S** Most members of this voluntary organization will not be close, personal friends.
7. **S** This is a group of strangers who are brought together by a shared interest in the game.
8. **P** This is a small, local group of firefighters who live and work together and probably know each other very well. However, it could be a secondary group if a certain level of personal intimacy has not developed.
9. **S** This is a large group. Close personal relations would not exist among all the members.
10. **P** Members of this small group are close friends who see each other daily.

EXERCISE 8
Page 198
Evaluation
1. **(2)** Linda learns new ideas about sex roles in the women's group. This directly causes her to change her own and Joe's view of sex roles.
2. **(1)** Gangs are peer groups. If the police are to change their behavior, they must understand how peer groups operate.
3. **(2)** Unions are secondary groups. Joe might develop close friendships with some members. However, he would only have a businesslike relation with most of them.
4. **(3)** Joe's family is limited to Linda, himself, and their children—a nuclear family.
5. **(2)** Joe probably makes a good income but certainly not enough to move him into the upper class.
6. **(3)** Linda joined the group to help out. She can easily leave.

7. (3) Members of Joe's church and school would be part of his peer group and socialization group, but not part of his extended family.

8. (1) Close personal friends are part of Joe's primary group.

EXERCISE 9
Page 200
Comprehension

1. aggravated assault
2. simple assault
3. personal larceny
4. 1,000
5. about 13 per 1,000

EXERCISE 10
Page 202
Comprehension

1. cultural. Margaret Mead studied the effects of culture on people.
2. physical. Don Johanson studies physical, biological changes in human beings.

EXERCISE 11
Page 203
Evaluation

1. **T** Mores are patterns of behavior that society strongly enforces, sometimes by laws.
2. **F** Ethnocentrism is a form of prejudice, which is not a value in our society.
3. **F** Folkways are behaviors that society favors. Mores are behaviors that society enforces.
4. **T** Because a society has certain values, patterns of behavior develop that reflect those values.
5. **T** An anthropologist looks at culture as a whole. A psychologist looks at individual behavior within a culture.
6. **T** Institutionalization is the process that society uses to turn its values into social behavior.

EXERCISE 12
Page 205
Comprehension

1. **(1)** Most societies borrow most of their inventions rather than developing them.

Application

2. **(2)** The spreading of a custom from one culture to another is an example of cultural diffusion.

Analysis

3. **(2)** Transportation and communications have spread new ideas and inventions very rapidly throughout the world. New inventions cause societies to change.

Comprehension

4. **(1)** The first few sentences in the first paragraph give you this information.

PRE-GED PRACTICE
BEHAVIORAL SCIENCES
Page 206
Comprehension

1. **(4)** There are several clues. Nacirema spelled backward is American. Notgnihsaw spelled backward is Washington. The description of the house shrines (bathrooms) and the holy-mouth-person (dentist) are other clues.
2. **(3)** The passage directly states that the people's basic belief is the evil of the body.
3. **(5)** Once you know the Nacirema are Americans, you know the shrine must be in an American home.

Evaluation

4. **(1)** By describing our culture so it sounds unfamiliar and odd, the author is helping us to see how our society might be viewed by people from other cultures.
5. **(2)** The Inuit owned little property and borrowed freely. There was little opportunity for stealing and other crimes against property.
6. **(1)** If one man could steal another's wife, it's clear that women had little power and were treated as property.
7. **(1)** While the Inuit had an informal legal system, they did not have a formal government.

CHAPTER 8: GEOGRAPHY

EXERCISE 1
Page 211
Comprehension

1. equator
2. prime meridian
3. hemispheres
4. North Pole
5. equator, prime meridian

EXERCISE 2
Page 217
Comprehension

1. Belize. The map key confirms this.
2. toward the center. The mountains run like a spine down the center of Central America; coastal lowlands border the Pacific Ocean and the Caribbean Sea.
3. east. Panama City lies almost due east of San Jose.
4. Nicaragua. Lake Nicaragua is in the southern part of the country.

EXERCISE 3
Page 218
Comprehension
1. **(4)** The key uses a solid color to represent a range from 0 to 1,000 feet, which covers most of Mongolia.
2. **(1)** The vertical lines indicate the highest elevation. The only place these lines appear is in the western part of China.

Analysis
3. **(4)** The map shows that Russia touches China on the north. None of the other statements is supported by information on the map.
4. **(1)** While India is labeled on the map, it is clearly not part of East Asia. You can tell this by the lack of elevations in India and the fact that only a part of India is shown on the map.

Comprehension
5. **(3)** The star next to Beijing indicates that it is the capital city of China.

EXERCISE 4
Page 222
Evaluation
1. **T**
2. **F** The mortality rate measures deaths.
3. **F** The fertility rate measures the birth rate.
4. **T**
5. **F** A change in one part of the ecological system often has an effect on other parts of the system.
6. **T**

EXERCISE 5
Page 223
Comprehension
1. eastern. The map clearly indicates that most blacks lived in eastern Texas.
2. larger. The map and the map key show that South Carolina had more counties with black residents than Texas did.
3. Maryland. The graph and the key show that Maryland had a greater number of free blacks than Virginia had.
4. South Carolina. The map labels the four South Carolina counties by name.

Analysis
5. Mississippi. The graph shows that there were more black slaves living in Mississippi than in Alabama in 1860.

Comprehension
6. Georgia. The solid black bar on the graph key shows that there were no free blacks living in Georgia
7. Florida. The map shows that very few blacks lived in Florida.

EXERCISE 6
Page 224
Comprehension
1. **T**
2. **T**
3. **F** War also caused people to flee their homes. As refugees, they were a burden on countries that already had severe food shortages.
4. **T**
5. **F** Egypt and Saudi Arabia are not a part of the region described in the passage. Djibouti and Ethiopia are missing in the statement.
6. **F** The United States intervened in Somalia to end mass starvation. When the United States got involved in political strife in Somalia, the troops were pulled out.
7. **F** The first sentence of the paragraph above the map says that the Horn of Africa is west of the Arabian Peninsula. The map shows this also.
8. **T**

EXERCISE 7
Page 227
Comprehension
1. Washington, D.C.
2. rural areas (or the countryside)
3. Phoenix, Arizona
4. suburbs
5. transportation

PRE-GED PRACTICE
EXERCISE 8
Page 228
Evaluation
1. **(2)** The passage describes how the altitude of Denver combines with the exhaust from automobiles to create air pollution.

Analysis
2. **(4)** Denver has an abundance of automobiles. Better public transportation would decrease the number of cars and thus ease pollution problems.

Comprehension
3. **(2)** This fact is stated in the second paragraph.
4. **(2)** This information is also given in the second paragraph.
5. **(1)** The second sentence in the last paragraph gives you this information.
6. **(5)** The last sentence of the first paragraph describes Denver as having become "one of America's most polluted cities."
7. **(3)** The last sentence of the passage says that people with respiratory problems have moved to the suburbs at lower altitudes.

PRE-GED PRACTICE
GEOGRAPHY
Page 230
Comprehension

1. (2) The key and the pail symbols show that the three states that have the largest yearly allotment in million acre-feet of water are Arizona (2.8), California (4.4), and Colorado (3.8).

Analysis

2. (5) California. The table above the map shows that normal rainfall is 22.1 inches but the actual rainfall was 14.6 inches, or 7.5 inches below normal. This is more than any other state in the Colorado River Basin.

Comprehension

3. (4) The pie charts show that Utah uses 93.5 percent and Arizona 88.6 percent of the water allotment for agriculture.

4. (1) The boundary of the map shows that all three cities are in the Lower Basin.

Evaluation

5. (2) In years of lower rainfall, the river might not be able to handle the increased population, so strict cutbacks may have to be put into effect.

Analysis

6. (3) Wyoming has the least increase in total population, or 185,000. While New Mexico has a lower water allotment (0.8 percent) than Wyoming (1.0 percent), New Mexico also has a projected increase in population of 700,000, or 515,000 more than Wyoming by the year 2020.

Evaluation

7. (2) The first sentence of the last paragraph says that computers have been developed for predicting when El Niño will take place. It notes that computer models have begun to detect weather events twelve to eighteen months ahead of their arrival.

Comprehension

8. (4) The first paragraph states that warming in the Pacific develops every four to seven years.

9. (1) The first paragraph notes that "the Pacific's hot and cold spells send ripples spreading through the world's atmosphere, altering weather around much of the globe."

10. (3) Paragraph two states that the El Niño of 1982–1983 was the biggest of the century and was caused by record warmth in the equatorial Pacific.

Analysis

11. (2) If El Niño occurs every four to seven years, then it will occur between 1997 and 2000.

Comprehension

12. (2) The last part of the first paragraph gives you this information.

13. (4) The last sentence of the second paragraph says that the El Niño of 1982 and 1983 caused more than $13 billion in damages.

CHAPTER 9: ECONOMICS
EXERCISE 1
Page 236
Comprehension

1. (3) The economy is the organized way in which goods and services are produced, distributed, sold, and used.

Application

2. (1) Economists would make predictions about how increased trade with Mexico would affect U.S. jobs, taxes, and other matters.

3. (2) Economists analyze the economics of different decisions. Choice (3) is incorrect because it involves day-to-day business rather than analysis and forecasting.

EXERCISE 2
Page 239
Comprehension

1. F Under capitalism, labor, like other commodities, is controlled by the market.

2. F Historically, economic systems have continuously changed. It's likely that change will continue. This statement is also false because the United States does not now have a pure capitalist economy.

3. T In the past, political systems were influenced by economic systems. This trend will probably continue in the future.

4. F In a socialist economy, business is controlled by the government. Business is not owned privately.

5. T In a market economy, workers are not tied to anyone or any place. They can sell their services to the highest bidder.

EXERCISE 3
Page 242
Analysis

1. (1) Graph 1 is the correct choice. It shows demand increasing as prices decrease. Graph 2 is incorrect because it shows demand increasing as prices increase. Graph 3 is incorrect because it shows price increasing at first then decreasing as demand increases.

2. (3) The events show that demand was high but the supply was low. A "seller's market" resulted because some people were willing to pay much higher prices for the toy.

EXERCISE 4
Page 244

Comprehension
1. (d)
2. (e)
3. (b)
4. (a)
5. (f)
6. (g)
7. (c)
8. (h)

EXERCISE 5
Page 246

Comprehension
1. increase. An increase in productivity means the business is operating more efficiently. That is, it's producing more goods with the same amount of labor or other costs. As a result, profits increase.
2. plans sales campaigns. They also work to increase sales.
3. seller that dominates the market. This happens with a monopoly.
4. lower production factors. This means that the employer pays less for materials, labor, or the other commodities needed to produce a product, so profits will increase. Laying off employees causes poor morale and can adversely affect productivity.
5. the total profits made. Making a profit is the purpose of business in a capitalist economy.

PRE-GED PRACTICE
EXERCISE 6
Page 247

Comprehension
1. (2) Multinationals can move production abroad where labor costs are low.
2. (3) According to the essay, more than 25 percent of the assets of the largest corporations are invested abroad.
3. (4) The second paragraph says that direct U.S. foreign investments grew from $11 billion in 1950 to more than $486 billion in 1992 (an increase of $475 billion).

EXERCISE 7
Page 249

Comprehension
1. **T** Credit and borrowing money are a source of economic growth. The multiplying effect helps expand the economy. Without it, the economy would not grow.
2. **T** When a deposit is made, a bank loans the money, which is then deposited in another bank, which can then loan money, which is then deposited again, and so on.
3. **T** Money is an asset that can be used to buy something. An asset is something a person has that has financial value.
4. **F** The most important form of money is checks, because they set up the multiplying effect.

EXERCISE 8
Page 250

Application
1. (1) By increasing the money supply, the Fed would encourage people and businesses to borrow and spend more money. The result would be increased business activity and a growing economy.

Comprehension
2. (3) This is how the Federal Reserve controls money.

Analysis
3. (1) The diagram shows the multiplier effect—that successive loans by banks increases the money supply.

Comprehension
4. (4) Bank *D* has the least amount of excess reserve ($410,000).

EXERCISE 9
Page 252

Comprehension
1. bull market. This happens when the value of stocks increases rapidly or by a large amount over a period of time.
2. bad shape. When the stock market does poorly, it usually indicates that the economy as a whole is not growing.
3. dividends. These are the profits paid by a company to investors who own stock, or shares, of the company.

EXERCISE 10
Page 254

Analysis
1. **F** The government provides public goods because they are needed by the public and either will not or should not be produced by private companies.
2. **T** Demand management is used to boost or limit economic growth.
3. **T** By removing money from the economy, the government can reduce the rate of economic growth, thereby controlling inflation.
4. **F** This is one of the functions of the government.
5. **F** No. When unemployment benefits are reduced, this slows down inflation.
6. **T** The second to last paragraph says that demand management is also called fiscal policy and that it's another way the government influences the economy.
7. **T** The first sentence of the passage says that although the United States has a market economy, it does not operate entirely according to market forces. The state and federal governments manage the economy in various ways.
8. **F** The third paragraph says that fire protection and air traffic control are important government services that private companies will not or should not provide.
9. **T** The fifth paragraph says that these are two factors of production that are controlled by government laws.

EXERCISE 11
Page 256

Comprehension
1. more than 40 percent
2. taxes
3. This is a regressive tax because it is the same for everyone.
4. through taxes
5. They transfer income from one group of people to another.
6. about 2.4 trillion ($1.4 trillion by the federal government and $976 billion by state and local governments)
7. through savings bonds, treasury bills, and municipal bonds

Comprehension
1. **(2)** The value of a house usually increases during times of inflation.

Application
2. **(2)** Discretionary income is the difference between fixed, or necessary, costs and total income ($2,000 – $1,550 = $450).
3. **(1)** The grasshopper had eaten up his discretionary income in immediate consumption and failed to budget for the long term.
4. **(4)** Fixed costs are expenses that you must pay on a regular basis. Money for vacations is likely to come out of discretionary income.

EXERCISE 13
Page 260

Comprehension
1. **T** About 44.2 percent of U.S. income is earned by the top 20 percent (highest fifth) of the population.
2. **F** The chart shows that in 1991, the top 40 percent of the population earned about 68.3 percent of total income.
3. **T** The poorest fifth of the population earned 4.8 percent of the total income in 1970 but only 4.5 percent in 1991.
4. **F** The main idea of the paragraph and chart is that the United States has a society made up of different economic classes. The facts demonstrate that income is not evenly distributed in the United States.

EXERCISE 14
Page 262

Comprehension
Choices (1), (2), and (4) are correct. Choice (3) is incorrect because many industrial workers lost their jobs, and many did find new jobs in the service industry. However, jobs in the service industry rarely paid as much as jobs in manufacturing. Choice (5) is incorrect because the immediate effect of reduced international trade barriers has been an increase in the number of jobs in the United States.

EXERCISE 15

Page 263

Comprehension

1. **T** Strikes are the most powerful tool unions have.
2. **F** Fewer than 16 percent of American workers belong to unions.
3. **T** Collective bargaining is the negotiating, or bargaining, process that takes place between unions and management.
4. **T** Hiring practices are often included in labor agreements.
5. **T** Many federal and state laws and agencies oversee the health and safety of American workers.
6. **F** Management may represent a small business, a multinational corporation, or even a state or local government.
7. **F** A labor contract is a legally binding agreement about the duties of labor and management that lasts for the term of the contract.
8. **T** As once powerful industries decline, so do their unions.

PRE-GED PRACTICE
ECONOMICS

Page 264

1. **(1)** The chart indicates that by 1990, the GNP was $5,524,500,000,000, or more than $5 1/2 trillion.
2. **(3)** The Net National Product is less than the GNP, and the column on the left shows that the GNP less the Capital Consumption Allowance equals the Net National Product.
3. **(5)** Since 1960, the GNP has approximately doubled every 10 years. If it doubles again, it will equal more than $11 trillion in the year 2000.
4. **(2)** From 1910 to 1920, the national debt increased by 2,100 percent.
5. **(1)** The chart shows that during 1900–1910 the national debt increased by –8 percent and from 1920–1930 the national debt increased by –33 percent.
6. **(5)** The national debt grew by more than $2 trillion from 1980–1990.
7. **(4)** World Wars I and II were major causes of the debt. Military spending during the 1980s added billions more to the debt.
8. **(1)** Since past recessions added to the debt, it is likely another will also increase the national debt.

Glossary

A

abnormal behavior: behavior that is not normal and that deviates from the average

abolitionist: member of an antislavery movement before the Civil War

absolute monarchy: a type of government in which the king or queen's word is the law

analyze: to break something down into its basic parts to better understand the meaning of the whole

annexation: taking over of lands not originally part of a country

anthropology: the study of the origin and development of the physical, social, and cultural aspects of human beings

apply: to use information from one situation to explain or understand information in another

armistice: a stopping of fighting between countries

arms race: a continuous buildup of large amounts of weapons and of a huge military force by one country in order to gain an advantage over another country

assets: total resources of a person or a business

B

bar graph: a graph that compares quantities by using bars of different lengths

behavioral sciences: the study of how people behave

bicameral: composed of two houses or legislative parts

Bill of Rights: the first ten amendments to the U.S. Constitution that state the freedoms and rights of individuals

Brown v. Board of Education: the unanimous Supreme Court decision in 1954 that struck down racial segregation in public schools

C

capital goods: goods and services companies buy to use in producing other goods and services

capitalism: an economic system based on private ownership of property

cause and effect: the process of showing how one event causes another event to happen

character: the personal values that make a person decide how to behave

checks and balances: a system among the branches of the federal government that prevents any one branch from dominating the other two

circle graph: a graph that shows how a total amount of something is divided into parts

Cold War: the period of conflict between the superpowers of the United States and the former Soviet Union and their allies after World War II

collective bargaining: a meeting between labor representatives and employers to settle disputes about hours, wages, and working conditions

commodities: goods and services for which ownership can be traded or exchanged

communism: a system practiced in the former Soviet Union in which private ownership of property and the means of production was not permissible

C

comparison: the process of examining similarities

compass rose (direction arrow): a drawing on a map that uses abbreviations to show directions

compound interest: the interest that is figured for a period of time based on the total of the principal plus any interest that has been earned over a period of time

comprehend: to understand what something means

constitutional monarchy: a limited monarchy that has constitutional checks upon the ruler

consumer goods: goods and services that people buy for their own use

containment: U.S. foreign policy to block further expansion of communism after World War II

context: the words surrounding an unknown word that help define the word

continent: a large continuous landmass that makes up part of Earth's surface

contour map: shows changes in elevation of a land surface by a series of lines representing different heights

contrast: the process of looking at differences between people, things, or ideas

cultural anthropology: the study of the social and cultural differences among humans

cultural diffusion: the spreading of ideas, values, beliefs, and other parts of a culture to other societies

cultural geography: the study of race, religion, and population

cultural relativity: the act of respecting the values of other societies without judging them

culture: all the beliefs, values, ideas, customs, knowledge, and traditions of a society

D

demand: the desire and ability of consumers to buy a product or service

demand management: government actions to influence how much demand there is in the economy; also called fiscal policy

demography: the statistical study of the size, growth, movement, and distribution of human population

deténte: a policy that called for more peaceful cooperation between the United States and the former Soviet Union

dictatorship: a form of government in which a dictator or ruler has complete control

diplomatic recognition: a government's formal recognition of another country's government, including the exchange of ambassadors

direct democracy: a democracy in which the people have a direct voice and vote in the government

direct initiative: the process that allows citizens to draft laws by obtaining enough signatures on a petition to present the law directly to the voters

discretionary income: the difference in a budget between fixed costs and income

dividends: payments made from a company's profits

domino theory: the argument noted by President Eisenhower that if one nation faces great danger, so will its neighbor and then the next country until a whole region falls

drawing conclusions: predicting the outcome of events or determining the relationship of facts in a passage

***Dred Scott* case:** the controversial 1857 Supreme Court decision ruling that slaves were not citizens and that slaves were the property of their masters

E

ecological system: the relationships between living things and their environment

economics: the study of how people produce, distribute, and consume goods and services

economy: the organized way in which a society produces, distributes, and consumes goods and services

editorial (political) cartoons: drawings that express an opinion and bring attention to a social or political problem

electoral college: a special group of voters from each state that elects the president and vice president

equator: 0° of latitude that divides Earth into Northern and Southern Hemispheres

equilibrium: the price at which supply equals demand

equity: the value in property after debt and other liabilities are paid

ethnic background: the racial or cultural origins of people

ethnocentrism: the act of judging another society by one's own standards

evaluate: judge the value or logic of an idea

evaluation of logic: a judgment of the way writers present and use their ideas

F

fact: a statement that can be proved

factors of production: the things needed to make a product

fascism: a political system that always puts the state above the individual, and which usually has a dictator to carry out its social and economic policies

federal system: the sharing of power between the states and the central government

fertility rate: the rate of births in a particular time and place

G

geography: the study of Earth; namely, its physical description and the places on it

globe: a round model of Earth's surface

government: the body or institution that makes and administers society's laws

gross domestic product (GDP): the amount of all goods and services produced within a country in one year

gross national product (GNP): the amount of all goods and services produced by a country in one year

guerrilla: a person who carries out acts of sabotage, strike-and-run military action, or terror against the enemy

gunboat diplomacy: U.S. practice of sending troops into countries of the Western Hemisphere to protect U.S. interests

H

history: the study of important events that happened in the past

home rule laws: state laws that provide local governments with a great deal of self-government

I

impeachment: the process of charging a public officeholder with a crime or misconduct in office so that the person can be removed from office

imperialism: a policy by which a nation extends its control over other lands

indentured servant: one who worked for a specific period of time in the American colonies as payment of a debt

industrialization: the development of large-scale industries and mass-production techniques

I

industrial unionism: organizing of unskilled and semiskilled factory workers chiefly by the CIO

inference: going beyond the directly stated information and finding a meaning that is only suggested; reading between the lines

information map (or thematic map): a map that gives information on a specific subject

institution: a system that society uses to fill the needs of its people and to teach patterns of behavior

interest group: a group of people who organize for a specific reason

isolationism: national policy or attitude that a nation will do better if it pays more attention to domestic matters rather than to international matters

J

Jacksonian Democracy: an age of reform that roughly paralleled President Andrew Jackson's term in office

Jim Crow laws: racial segregation laws passed in the South during the late nineteenth and early twentieth centuries

judicial review: the power of the Supreme Court to rule on the constitutionality of laws

K

key (or legend): a list that explains the symbols used on a map

L

labor contract: an agreement between management and labor that establishes salaries, terms of employment, working conditions, benefits, duties, responsibilities, and the rights of labor and management

labor market: a term used to describe the availability of jobs

latitude: line that measures distance north and south of the equator

line graph: graph that shows how one or more items of information have changed over time by using a series of connected points

literal understanding: understanding information that is stated directly

location: the exact point on Earth where a place is; can be expressed in degrees of latitude and longitude

logical consistency: the writer's use of sound reasoning in developing an idea

longitude: line that measures distance east and west of the prime meridian

M

main idea: a statement that tells what a whole selection is about

Manifest Destiny: American belief that it was the country's destiny to take over the entire North American continent

map: a representation of some part of Earth and its features on flat paper

market economy: another name for free enterprise where buyers and sellers, not the government, determine prices and output

marketing: the part of business that deals with sales

material culture: the level of tools and technology in a given society

McCarthyism: careless and groundless attacks on people suspected of being communists; associated with Senator McCarthy's anti-communist tactics

mercantilism: seventeenth-century practice in which the colonies supplied the mother country with raw materials and became a market for manufactured goods

migration: the movement of people from one country or location to another

mixed economies: an economic system that combines capitalism and socialism

monetary policy: the regulation of the nation's supply of money and credit by the Federal Reserve Board

money: cash and all other assets that can be used to purchase goods and services or to pay debts

monopoly: a market situation in which one person or company sells all of a product or accounts for a large part of the total sales of the product

mortality rate: the rate of deaths in a particular time and place

motivation: reasons why a person starts, stops, or continues an activity

muckrakers: writers who exposed corruption in business and politics during the early twentieth century

multiplier effect: the growth in the value of a deposit in a bank when it is, in turn, loaned out to a succession of other banks

N

national debt: the total amount of money owed by the federal government of the United States to its creditors

neurosis: a personality disorder in which a person is unusually anxious in dealing with others

norms: the normal accepted behavior society expects of a person

O

oligarchy: a type of government in which a small group of people rule

oligopoly: a market situation in which very few sellers account for a large part of the total sales of a product

opinion: a personal belief or feeling that cannot be proved

organization: a group formed for a specific purpose or goal

P

peer group: a group of people who share some common characteristic, such as working together or being on the same team

personality: the special qualities that make a person an individual

phobia: an irrational fear

physical anthropology: the study of the physical characteristics of humans

physical map: a map that shows different geographic features such as mountains, deserts, lakes, and rivers

pictograph: a graph that uses a series of symbols to show an amount or a quantity

plurality: the greatest number of votes in an election

pocket veto: an automatic veto of a bill not signed by the president within ten days of a congressional adjournment

political geography: the study of the relationships among people and nations

political science: the study of the institutions of government and how they work

political system: an institution that organizes power relationships in a society

primary group: a group of people who know each other well and have much personal, face-to-face contact

primary motives: biological reasons (such as thirst and pain) for behavior

prime meridian: 0° of longitude that divides Earth into Eastern and Western Hemispheres

productivity: the efficient use of the factors of production to produce goods

Progressive Era: a period of many social and political reforms largely backed by Presidents Theodore Roosevelt, Taft, and Wilson

progressive tax: a tax that takes a larger portion of income as that income increases

P

psychology: the study of individual behavior

psychosis: a mental or personality disorder that prevents a person from doing normal, everyday things

public goods: goods and services the government provides for its citizens

R

recall: a procedure that permits voters to remove an elected official from office before his or her term is over

referendum: the process by which voters can approve or reject legislation

region: an area of land having characteristics that make it different from another area of land

regressive tax: a tax that takes a smaller portion of income as that income increases

representative: one who stands or acts for another through delegated authority

representative democracy: a democracy in which people select delegates or substitutes to represent them

role: expected pattern of behavior in a group or in society

S

scale: a line on a map that shows the relationship between the distance on the map and the actual distance on land

scanning: the practice of rapidly looking over a passage or graphic to find a specific detail

secession: the act of a state seceding (leaving) a country to which it belongs

secondary group: a group of people who know each other in a formal, businesslike way

secondary motives: reasons a person learns for behaving in certain ways

sectionalism: the economic, political, and social differences among the regions of the United States

sequence-of-events: an approach that organizes a series of events in the order in which they happened

sharecropper: a tenant farmer who pays a portion of the crop as rent for the land

simple majority: 50 percent of the votes plus a minimum of one vote

social class: a group of people who share a common economic position in society

Social Darwinism: the theory that the development of society is based on the survival of the fittest

socialism: an economic system that is based on government control of the market

socialization: the way in which a person learns the normal behavior, habits, and beliefs of a society

social status: a person's standing in society based on his or her income, occupation, education, and ethnic background

social stratification: the division of society into classes

society: a group of people with shared values and organized patterns of behavior

sociology: the study of the behavior of groups of people

special-purpose map: a map that uses different colors, patterns, and symbols to give information

stock market: a market where stocks and bonds of corporations are bought and sold

stocks: shares of ownership in a company

strike: a work stoppage by members of a union to force an employer to agree to demands for salaries, terms of employment, or benefits

subpoena: a written order requiring someone to appear in court

suburb: a settlement that lies outside a city but within commuting distance to it

supply: the quantity of goods and services available for sale at all possible prices

supporting details: details that expand on the main idea or make it clearer

T

table: a list of numbers placed in columns and rows to make it easier to make comparisons

temperament: the emotions that affect how a person acts

theory: a belief that explains an event or a behavior

third party: any U.S. political party that is independent of the two major parties

Third World: developing nations of Asia, Africa, and Latin America, many of which gained their independence after World War II, and were not allied with either superpower

tone: a writer's own bias or opinion about a subject expressed in a piece of writing

topography: the physical features of a land surface, including mountain ranges, plateaus, and lowlands

totalitarianism: an extreme type of dictatorship that controls the political, economic, and social life of a country

trade deficit: an excess of the value of imports over the value of exports; also called unfavorable balance of trade

transfer payments: payments that transfer income from one group of people to another through the tax system

treaties: formal agreements among nations

tyranny: a government in which all power is in the hands of a single ruler

U

unstated main idea: an idea that is only suggested and not stated directly

urbanization: the growth of large cities, with a population shift away from rural areas

V

values: standards of behavior or beliefs set by a society

veto: the presidential power to refuse to sign into law a bill that has been approved by Congress; can be overridden by Congress

W

women's suffrage: the right of women to vote

Index